THE COLLECTED PAPERS OF ROBERT EZRA PARK

VOLUME II

EDITED BY

Everett Cherrington Hughes

Charles S. Johnson

Jitsuichi Masuoka

Robert Redfield

Louis Wirth

Robert Ezra Park

HUMAN COMMUNITIES

THE CITY
AND HUMAN ECOLOGY

The Free Press, Glencoe, Illinois

COPYRIGHT:

1952 by The Free Press

PRINTING:

By American Book–Stratford Press, Inc., New York. This book was set on the linotype in Janson type and printed on Antique Wove paper supplied by Perkins and Squier Paper Co.

DESIGN:

By Sidney Solomon

Library of Congress Catalog Card Number: 52–8155

MANUFACTURED IN THE U.S.A.

PREFACE

"THERE remains the studies of the city, of urban and rural communities, what R. D. McKenzie and I call, quite properly I believe, 'human ecology.'

"While I was a newspaper reporter, I used to do a good deal of writing for the Sunday papers. In those days the daily papers wrote their own Sunday papers and did not depend to the extent they do now upon syndicated articles.

"I found that the Sunday paper was willing to publish anything so long as it concerned the local community and was interesting. I wrote about all sorts of things and became in this way intimately acquainted with many different aspects of city life. I expect that I have actually covered more ground, tramping about in cities in different parts of the world, than any other living man. Out of all this I gained, among other things, a conception of the city, the community, and the region, not as geographical phenomenon merely, but as a kind of social organism."

In these words Robert E. Park accounts, in retrospect, for his interest in the city and in human ecology. What he wrote on these subjects appears in this, the second volume of his articles, prefaces and reviews.

About the time he came to the University of Chicago, Park wrote and published a long article entitled, "The City: Some Sug-

---

"An Autobiographical Note," *Race and Culture*, p. viii.

gestions for the Study of Human Behavior in the Urban Environment." The proposals in it became the research program of Park himself, of his students, and of many colleagues in other fields as well as in sociology; a program realized in part in *The Hobo, The Gold Coast and the Slum, The Ghetto, The Gang* and other studies of city types and city areas. The suggestions have not been exhausted in some thirty-five years of active work by an ever-increasing army of students of cities and city life.

While these studies of the more colorful and lively aspects of city life were progressing, Park was seeking some more abstract, systematic and less dramatic way of describing cities. He found it in his own adaptation of the system of concepts developed by ecologists to describe the processes by which plant and animal communities develop and change. As this new scheme developed, Park made his students into enthusiastically collaborating colleagues. Parole officers, settlement workers, reformers and ministers began to spot saints and sinners, philanthropists and paupers, fortune tellers and stock brokers, the noted and the notorious in appropriate colors on maps of Chicago and other cities. Missionaries and defenders of the under-dog races came to preach and remained to draw maps of the movements of goods, ships, flags, pirates and Bibles over the surface of the earth. The late Roderick D. McKenzie became his special collaborator in the ecological studies (Park had a way of laying upon each of his students a special problem to work upon for the rest of his life). McKenzie published a number of papers applying ecological concepts to the world community, and a book entitled *The Metropolitan Community* (McGraw-Hill, 1933). The reader of Park's papers on human ecology should be aware of this collaboration and of the fact that it was cut short by McKenzie's early death.

But if Park turned the characters of the urban and of the world drama into types and the drama itself into spots on a map and into measured gradients, he was never content until he had turned them back again. The reader will see that the ecological order is always used to the end of understanding the moral order better. His real passion was man, the struggler—and, unlike many of those who have drawn—as he did—a sharp contrast between the city and those communities where life appears to run in safer, smoother channels, Park's choice lay with the city, where—as he put it—every man is on his own.

In a third and final volume will appear those of Park's papers which, following his own terminology, may appropriately appear under the title, "Collective Behavior and the Moral Order."

Thanks are again due the several associates of Professor Park who have helped in the assembling of the papers. Among them let me mention especially Professor Amos H. Hawley of the University of Michigan. Out of his intimate knowledge of both Park's and McKenzie's work, he gave valuable advice on the selection and arrangement of the items.

EVERETT CHERRINGTON HUGHES

CONTENTS

Preface by Everett C. Hughes   5

PART I: THE CITY

    1. The City: Suggestions for the Investigation of Human Behavior in the Urban Environment   13

    2. Community Organization and Juvenile Delinquency   52

    3. Community Organization and the Romantic Temper   64

    4. The City as a Social Laboratory   73

    5. Local Communities in the Metropolis   88

    6. The Mind of the Hobo: Reflections Upon the Relation Between Mentality and Locomotion   91

    7. The Habitat of the Gang   96

    8. The Ghetto   99

    9. Magic, Mentality and City Life   102

    10. The City as a Natural Phenomenon   118

    11. The City and Civilization   128

Contents

PART II: HUMAN ECOLOGY

12. Human Ecology   *145*

13. Dominance: The Concepts, Its Origin and
    Natural History   *159*

14. The Urban Community as a Spatial Pattern
    and Moral Order   *165*

15. Sociology, Community and Society   *178*

16. Newspaper Circulation and Metropolitan
    Regions   *210*

17. Succession, An Ecological Concept   *223*

18. Hawaii and the Natural History of World
    Economy   *233*

19. Symbiosis and Socialization: A Frame of
    Reference for the Study of Society   *240*

INDEX OF NAMES   *263*

SUBJECT INDEX   *267*

PART ONE: *The City*

CHAPTER I

THE CITY: SUGGESTIONS FOR THE INVESTIGATION OF HUMAN BEHAVIOR IN THE URBAN ENVIRONMENT

THE city, from the point of view of this paper, is something more than a congeries of individual men and of social conveniences—streets, buildings, electric lights, tramways, and telephones, etc.; something more, also, than a mere constellation of institutions and administrative devices—courts, hospitals, schools, police, and civil functionaries of various sorts. The city is, rather, a state of mind, a body of customs and traditions, and of the organized attitudes and sentiments that inhere in these customs and are transmitted with this tradition. The city is not, in other words, merely a physical mechanism and an artificial construction. It is involved in the vital processes of the people who compose it; it is a product of nature, and particularly of human nature.

The city has, as Oswald Spengler has recently pointed out, its own culture: "What his house is to the peasant, the city is to civilized man. As the house has its household gods, so has the city its protecting Deity, its local saint. The city also, like the peasant's hut, has its roots in the soil." [1]

Reprinted by permission of the publisher from the *American Journal of Sociology*, XX (March, 1916), pp. 577-612. This was later reprinted in R. E. Park, E. W. Burgess and R. D. McKenzie, *The City* (Chicago: University of Chicago Press, 1925), pp. 1-46.

[1] Oswald Spengler, *Der Untergang des Abendlandes*, IV (München, 1922), 105.

The city has been studied, in recent times, from the point of view of its geography, and still more recently from the point of view of its ecology. There are forces at work within the limits of the urban community—within the limits of any natural area of human habitation, in fact—which tend to bring about an orderly and typical grouping of its population and institutions. The science which seeks to isolate these factors and to describe the typical constellations of persons and institutions which the co-operation of these forces produces, is what we call human, as distinguished from plant and animal, ecology.

Transportation and communication, tramways and telephones, newspapers and advertising, steel construction and elevators—all things, in fact, which tend to bring about at once a greater mobility and a greater concentration of the urban populations—are primary factors in the ecological organization of the city.

The city is not, however, merely a geographical and ecological unit; it is at the same time an economic unit. The economic organization of the city is based on the division of labor. The multiplication of occupations and professions within the limits of the urban population is one of the most striking and least understood aspects of modern city life. From this point of view, we may, if we choose, think of the city, that is to say, the place and the people, with all the machinery and administrative devices that go with them, as organically related; a kind of psychophysical mechanism in and through which private and political interests find not merely a collective but a corporate expression.

Much of what we ordinarily regard as the city—its charters, formal organization, buildings, street railways, and so forth—is, or seems to be, mere artifact. But these things in themselves are utilities, adventitious devices which become part of the living city only when, and in so far as, through use and wont they connect themselves, like a tool in the hand of man, with the vital forces resident in individuals and in the community.

The city is, finally, the natural habitat of civilized man. It is for that reason a cultural area characterized by its own peculiar cultural type:

"It is a quite certain, but never fully recognized, fact," says Spengler, "that all great cultures are city-born. The outstanding man of the second generation is a city-building animal. This is the actual criterion of world-history, as distinguished from the history of mankind: world-history is the history of city men. Nations, governments, politics, and religions—all rest on the basic phenomenon of human existence, the city." [2]

Anthropology, the science of man, has been mainly concerned up to the present with the study of primitive peoples. But civilized man is quite as interesting an object of investigation, and at the same time his life is more open to observation and study. Urban life and culture are more varied, subtle, and complicated, but the fundamental motives are in both instances the same. The same patient methods of observation which anthropologists like Boas and Lowie have expended on the study of the life and manners of the North American Indian might be even more fruitfully employed in the investigation of the customs, beliefs, social practices, and general conceptions of life prevalent in Little Italy on the lower North Side in Chicago, or in recording the more sophisticated folkways of the inhabitants of Greenwich Village and the neighborhood of Washington Square, New York.

We are mainly indebted to writers of fiction for our more intimate knowledge of contemporary urban life. But the life of our cities demands a more searching and disinterested study than even Émile Zola has given us in his "experimental" novels and the annals of the Rougon-Macquart family.

We need such studies, if for no other reason than to enable us to read the newspapers intelligently. The reason that the daily chronicle of the newspaper is so shocking, and at the same time so fascinating, to the average reader is because the average reader knows so little about the life of which the newspaper is the record.

The observations which follow are intended to define a point of view and to indicate a program for the study of urban life: its physical organization, its occupations, and its culture.

I. THE CITY PLAN AND LOCAL ORGANIZATION

Physical organization

The city, particularly the modern American city, strikes one at first blush as so little a product of the artless processes of nature and growth, that it is difficult to recognize it as a living entity. The ground plan of most American cities, for example, is a checkerboard. The unit of distance is the block. This geometrical form suggests that the city is a purely artificial construction which might conceiv-

---

[2] Oswald Spengler, *Untergang des Abendlandes*, IV, 106.

ably be taken apart and put together again, like a house of blocks.

The fact is, however, that the city is rooted in the habits and customs of the people who inhabit it. The consequence is that the city possesses a moral as well as a physical organization, and these two mutually interact in characteristic ways to mold and modify one another. It is the structure of the city which first impresses us by its visible vastness and complexity. But this structure has its basis, nevertheless, in human nature, of which it is an expression. On the other hand, this vast organization which has arisen in response to the needs of its inhabitants, once formed, imposes itself upon them as a crude external fact, and forms them, in turn, in accordance with the design and interests which it incorporates. Structure and tradition are but different aspects of a single cultural complex which determines what is characteristic and peculiar to city, as distinguished from village, life and the life of the open fields.

The city plan.—It is because the city has a life quite its own that there is a limit to the arbitrary modifications which it is possible to make (1) in its physical structure and (2) in its moral order.

The city plan, for example, establishes metes and bounds, fixes in a general way the location and character of the city's constructions, and imposes an orderly arrangement, within the city area, upon the buildings which are erected by private initiative as well as by public authority. Within the limitations prescribed, however, the inevitable processes of human nature proceed to give these regions and these buildings a character which it is less easy to control. Under our system of individual ownership, for instance, it is not possible to determine in advance the extent of concentration of population which is likely to occur in any given area. The city cannot fix land values, and we leave to private enterprise, for the most part, the task of determining the city's limits and the location of its residential and industrial districts. Personal tastes and convenience, vocational and economic interests, infallibly tend to segregate and thus to classify the populations of great cities. In this way the city acquires an organization and distribution of population which is neither designed nor controlled.

The Bell Telephone Company is now making, particularly in New York and Chicago, elaborate investigations, the purpose of which is to determine, in advance of its actual changes, the probable growth and distribution of the urban population within the metropolitan areas. The Sage Foundation, in the course of its city-planning studies, sought to find mathematical formulae that would enable them to predict future expansion and limits of population in New York City. The recent development of chain stores has made the problem of location a matter of concern to different chain-store corporations. The result has been the rise of a new profession.

There is now a class of experts whose sole occupation is to discover and locate, with something like scientific accuracy, taking account of the changes which present tendencies seem likely to bring about, restaurants, cigar stores, drug-stores, and other smaller retail business units whose success depends largely on location. Real-estate men are not infrequently willing to finance a local business of this sort in locations which they believe will be profitable, accepting as their rent a percentage of the profits.

Physical geography, natural advantages and disadvantages, including means of transportation, determine in advance the general outlines of the urban plan. As the city increases in population, the subtler influences of sympathy, rivalry, and economic necessity tend to control the distribution of population. Business and industry seek advantageous locations and draw around them certain portions of the population. There spring up fashionable residence quarters from which the poorer classes are excluded because of the increased value of the land. Then there grow up slums which are inhabited by great numbers of the poorer classes who are unable to defend themselves from association with the derelict and vicious.

In the course of time every section and quarter of the city takes on something of the character and qualities of its inhabitants. Each separate part of the city is inevitably stained with the peculiar sentiments of its population. The effect of this is to convert what was at first a mere geographical expression into a neighborhood, that is to say, a locality with sentiments, traditions, and a history of its own. Within this neighborhood the continuity of the historical processes is somehow maintained. The past imposes itself upon the present, and the life of every locality moves on with a certain momentum of its own, more or less independent of the larger circle of life and interests about it.

The organization of the city, the character of the urban environment and of the discipline which it imposes is finally determined by the size of the population, its concentration and distribution within the city area. For this reason it is important to study the growth of cities, to compare the idiosyncrasies in the distribution of city populations. Some of the first things we want to know about the city, therefore are:

What are the sources of the city's population?

What part of its population growth is normal, i.e., due to excess of births over deaths?

What part is due to migration (*a*) of native stocks? (*b*) foreign stocks?

What are the outstanding "natural" areas, i.e., areas of population segregation?

How is distribution of population within the city area affected by (*a*) economic interest, i.e., land values? (*b*) by sentimental interest, race? vocation, etc.?

Where within the city is the population declining? Where is it expanding?

Where are population growth and the size of families within the different natural areas of the city correlated with births and deaths, with marriages and divorces, with house rents and standards of living?

The neighborhood.—Proximity and neighborly contact are the basis for the simplest and most elementary form of association with which we have to do in the organization of city life. Local interests and associations breed local sentiment, and, under a system which makes residence the basis for participation in the government, the neighborhood becomes the basis of political control. In the social and political organization of the city it is the smallest local unit.

It is surely one of the most remarkable of all social facts that, coming down from untold ages, there should be this instinctive understanding that the man who establishes his home beside yours begins to have a claim upon your sense of comradeship. . . . . The neighborhood is a social unit which, by its clear definition of outline, its inner organic completeness, its hair-trigger reactions, may be fairly considered as functioning like a social mind. . . . . The local boss, however autocratic he may be in the larger sphere of the city with the power he gets from the neighborhood, must always be in and of the people; and he is very careful not to try to deceive the local people so far as their local interests are concerned. It is hard to fool a neighborhood about its own affairs.[3]

The neighborhood exists without formal organization. The local improvement society is a structure erected on the basis of the spontaneous neighborhood organization and exists for the purpose of giving expression to the local sentiment in regard to matters of local interest.

[3] Robert A. Woods, "The Neighborhood in Social Reconstruction," *Papers and Proceedings of the Eighth Annual Meeting of the American Sociological Society, 1913.*

Under the complex influences of the city life, what may be called the normal neighborhood sentiment has undergone many curious and interesting changes, and produced many unusual types of local communities. More than that, there are nascent neighborhoods and neighborhoods in process of dissolution. Consider, for example, Fifth Avenue, New York, which probably never had an improvement association, and compare with it 135th Street in the Bronx (where the Negro population is probably more concentrated than in any other single spot in the world), which is rapidly becoming a very intimate and highly organized community.

In the history of New York the significance of the name Harlem has changed from Dutch to Irish to Jewish to Negro. Of these changes the last has come most swiftly. Throughout colored America, from Massachusetts to Mississippi and across the continent to Los Angeles and Seattle, its name, which as late as fifteen years ago had scarcely been heard, now stands for the Negro metropolis. Harlem is, indeed, the great Mecca for the sight-seer, the pleasure-seeker, the curious, the adventurous, the enterprising, the ambitious, and the talented of the Negro world; for the lure of it has reached down to every island of the Carib Sea and has penetrated even into Africa.[4]

It is important to know what are the forces which tend to break up the tensions, interests, and sentiments which give neighborhoods their individual character. In general these may be said to be anything and everything that tends to render the population unstable, to divide and concentrate attentions upon widely separated objects of interest.

What part of the population is floating?
Of what elements, i.e., races, classes, etc., is this population composed?
How many people live in hotels, apartments, and tenements?
How many people own their own homes?
What proportion of the population consists of nomads, hobos, gypsies?

On the other hand, certain urban neighborhoods suffer from isolation. Efforts have been made at different times to reconstruct and quicken the life of city neighborhoods and to bring them in touch with the larger interests of the community. Such is, in part, the purpose of the social settlements. These organizations and others which are attempting to reconstruct city life have developed certain methods and a technique for stimulating and controlling local communi-

---

[4] James Weldon Johnson, "The Making of Harlem," *Survey Graphic*, March 1, 1925.

ties. We should study, in connection with the investigation of these agencies, these methods and this technique, since it is just the method by which objects are practically controlled that reveals their essential nature, that is to say, their predictable character (*Gesetzmässigkeit.*)[5]

In many of the European cities, and to some extent in this country, reconstruction of city life has gone to the length of building garden suburbs, or replacing unhealthful and run-down tenements with model buildings owned and controlled by the municipality.

In American cities the attempt has been made to renovate evil neighborhoods by the construction of playgrounds and the introduction of supervised sports of various kinds, including municipal dances in municipal dance halls. These and other devices which are intended primarily to elevate the moral tone of the segregated populations of great cities should be studied in connection with the investigation of the neighborhood in general. They should be studied, in short, not merely for their own sake, but for what they can reveal to us of human behavior and human nature generally.

Colonies and segregated areas.—In the city environment the neighborhood tends to lose much of the significance which it possessed in simpler and more primitive forms of society. The easy means of communication and of transportation, which enable individuals to distribute their attention and to live at the same time in several different worlds, tend to destroy the permanency and intimacy of the neighborhood. On the other hand, the isolation of the immigrant and racial colonies of the so-called ghettos and areas of population segregation tend to preserve and, where there is racial prejudice, to intensify the intimacies and solidarity of the local and neighborhood groups. Where individuals of the same race or of the same vocation live together in segregated groups, neighborhood sentiment tends to fuse together with racial antagonisms and class interests.

---

[5] "Wenn wir daher das Wort [Natur] als einen logischen Terminus in der Wissenschaftslehre gabrauchen wollen, so werden wir sagen dürfen, dass Natur die Wirklichkeit ist mit Rücksicht auf ihren gesetzmässigen Zusammenhang. Diese Bedeutung finden wir z. B. in dem Worte Naturgesetz. Dann aber können wir die Natur der Dinge auch das nennen was in die Begriffe eingeht, oder am kürzesten uns dahin ausdrücken: die Natur ist die Wirklichkeit mit Rücksicht auf das Allgemeine. So gewinnt dann das Wort erst eine logische Bedeutung" (H. Rickert, *Die Grenzen der naturwissenschaftlichen Begriffsbildung*, p. 212).

Physical and sentimental distances reinforce each other, and the influences of local distribution of the population participate with the influences of class and race in the evolution of the social organization. Every great city has its racial colonies, like the Chinatowns of San Francisco and New York, the Little Sicily of Chicago, and various other less pronounced types. In addition to these, most cities have their segregated vice districts, like that which until recently existed in Chicago, their rendezvous for criminals of various sorts. Every large city has its occupational suburbs, like the Stockyards in Chicago, and its residential enclaves, like Brookline in Boston, the so-called "Gold Coast" in Chicago, Greenwich Village in New York, each of which has the size and character of a complete separate town, village, or city, except that its population is a selected one. Undoubtedly the most remarkable of these cities within cities, of which the most interesting characteristic is that they are composed of persons of the same race, or of persons of different races but of the same social class, is East London, with a population of 2,000,000 laborers.

The people of the original East London have now overflowed and crossed the Lea, and spread themselves over the marshes and meadows beyond. This population has created new towns which were formerly rural villages. West Ham, with a population of nearly 300,000; East Ham, with 90,000; Stratford, with its "daughters," 150,000; and other "hamlets" similarly overgrown. Including these new populations, we have an aggregate of nearly two millions of people. The population is greater than that of Berlin or Vienna, or St. Petersburg, or Philadelphia.

It is a city full of churches and places of worship, yet there are no cathedrals, either Anglican or Roman; it has a sufficient supply of elementary schools, but it has no public or high school, and it has no colleges for the higher education and no university; the people all read newspapers, yet there is no East London paper except of the smaller and local kind. . . . In the streets there are never seen any private carriages; there is no fashionable quarter . . . one meets no ladies in the principal thoroughfares. People, shops, houses, conveyances—all together are stamped with the unmistakable seal of the working class.

Perhaps the strangest thing of all is this: in a city of two millions of people there are no hotels! That means, of course, that there are no visitors.[6]

In the older cities of Europe, where the processes of segregation have gone farther, neighborhood distinctions are likely to be more marked than they are in America. East London is a city of a single

<hr>

[6] Walter Besant, *East London*, pp. 7-9.

class, but within the limits of that city the population is segregated again and again by racial, cultural, and vocational interests. Neighborhood sentiment, deeply rooted in local tradition and in local custom, exercises a decisive selective influence upon the populations of the older European cities and shows itself ultimately in a marked way in the characteristics of the inhabitants.

What we want to know of these neighborhoods, racial communities, and segregated city areas, existing within or on the outer rims of great cities, is what we want to know of all other social groups:

What are the elements of which they are composed?
To what extent are they the product of a selective process?
How do people get in and out of the group thus formed?
What are the relative permanence and stability of their populations?
What about the age, sex, and social condition of the people?
What about the children? How many of them are born, and how many of them remain?

What is the history of the neighborhood? What is there in the subconsciousness—in the forgotten or dimly remembered experiences—of this neighborhood which determines its sentiments and attitudes?

What is there in clear consciousness, i.e., what are its avowed sentiments, doctrines, etc.?

What does it regard as matter of fact? What is news? What is the general run of attention? What models does it imitate and are these within or without the group?

What is the social ritual, i.e., what things must one do in the neighborhood in order to escape being regarded with suspicion or looked upon as peculiar?

Who are the leaders? What interests of the neighborhood do they incorporate in themselves and what is the technique by which they exercise control?

II. INDUSTRIAL ORGANIZATION AND THE MORAL ORDER

The ancient city was primarily a fortress, a place of refuge in time of war. The modern city, on the contrary, is primarily a convenience of commerce, and owes its existence to the market place around which it sprang up. Industrial competition and the division of labor, which have probably done most to develop the latent powers of mankind, are possible only upon condition of the existence of markets, of money, and other devices for the facilitation of trade and commerce.

An old German adage declares that "city air makes men free" (*Stadt Luft macht frei*). This is doubtless a reference to the days when the free cities of Germany enjoyed the patronage of the emperor, and laws made the fugitive serf a free man if he succeeded for a year and a day in breathing city air. Law, of itself, could not, however, have made the craftsman free. An open market in which he might sell the products of his labor was a necessary incident of his freedom, and it was the application of the money economy to the relations of master and man that completed the emancipation of the serf.

Vocational classes and vocational types.—The old adage which describes the city as the natural environment of the free man still holds so far as the individual man finds in the chances, the diversity of interests and tasks, and in the vast unconscious co-operation of city life the opportunity to choose his own vocation and develop his peculiar individual talents. The city offers a market for the special talents of individual men. Personal competition tends to select for each special task the individual who is best suited to perform it.

The difference of natural talents in different men is, in reality, much less than we are aware of; and the very different genius which appears to distinguish men of different professions, when grown up to maturity, is not upon many occasions so much the cause, as the effect of the division of labour. The difference between the most dissimilar characters, between a philosopher and a common street porter, for example, seems to arise not so much from nature, as from habit, custom, and education. When they came into the world, and for the first six or eight years of their existence, they were perhaps very much alike, and neither their parents nor playfellows could perceive any remarkable difference. About that age, or soon after, they come to be employed in different occupations. The difference of talents comes then to be taken notice of, and widens by degrees, till at last the vanity of the philosopher is willing to acknowledge scarce any resemblance. But without the disposition to truck, barter, and exchange, every man must have procured to himself every necessary and conveniency of life which he wanted. All must have had the same duties to perform, and the same work to do, and there could have been no such difference of employment as could alone give occasion to any great difference of talent. . . .
As it is the power of exchanging that gives occasion to the division of labour, so the extent of this division must always be limited by the extent of that power, or, in other words, by the extent of the market. . . . . There are some sorts of industry, even of the lowest kind, which can be carried on nowhere but in a great town.[7]

Success, under conditions of personal competition, depends upon concentration upon some single task, and this concentration stimu-

---

[7] Adam Smith, *The Wealth of Nations*, pp. 28-29.

lates the demand for rational methods, technical devices, and exceptional skill. Exceptional skill, while based on natural talent, requires special preparation, and it has called into existence the trade and professional schools, and finally bureaus for vocational guidance. All of these, either directly or indirectly, serve at once to select and emphasize individual differences.

Every device which facilitates trade and industry prepares the way for a further division of labor and so tends further to specialize the tasks in which men find their vocations.

The outcome of this process is to break down or modify the older social and economic organization of society, which was based on family ties, local associations, on culture, caste, and status, and to substitute for it an organization based on occupation and vocational interests.

In the city every vocation, even that of a beggar, tends to assume the character of a profession and the discipline which success in any vocation imposes, together with the associations that it enforces, emphasizes this tendency—the tendency, namely, not merely to specialize, but to rationalize one's occupation and to develop a specific and conscious technique for carrying it on.

The effect of the vocations and the division of labor is to produce, in the first instance, not social groups, but vocational types: the actor, the plumber, and the lumber-jack. The organizations, like the trade and labor unions which men of the same trade or profession form, are based on common interests. In this respect they differ from forms of association like the neighborhood, which are based on contiguity, personal association, and the common ties of humanity. The different trades and professions seem disposed to group themselves in classes, that is to say, the artisan, business, and professional classes. But in the modern democratic state the classes have as yet attained no effective organization. Socialism, founded on an effort to create an organization based on "class consciousness," has never succeeded, except, perhaps, in Russia, in creating more than a political party.

The effects of the division of labor as a discipline, i.e., as means of molding character, may therefore be best studied in the vocational types it has produced. Among the types which it would be interesting to study are: the shopgirl, the policeman, the peddler, the cabman, the nightwatchman, the clairvoyant, the vaudeville performer, the quack doctor, the bartender, the ward boss, the strikebreaker, the labor agitator, the school teacher, the reporter, the stockbroker, the pawnbroker; all of these are characteristic products of the conditions of city life; each, with its special experience, insight, and point of view determines for each vocational group and for the city as a whole its individuality.

To what extent is the grade of intelligence represented in the different trades and professions dependent upon natural ability?

To what extent is intelligence determined by the character of the occupation and the conditions under which it is practiced?

To what extent is success in the occupations dependent upon sound judgment and common-sense; to what extent upon technical ability?

Does native ability or special training determine success in the different vocations?

What prestige and what prejudices attach to different trades and professions and why?

Is the choice of the occupation determined by temperamental, by economic, or by sentimental considerations?

In what occupations do men, in what occupations do women, succeed better, and why?

How far is occupation, rather than association, responsible for the mental attitude and moral predilections? Do men in the same profession or trade, but representing different nationalities and different cultural groups, hold characteristic and identical opinions?

To what extent is the social or political creed, that is, socialism, anarchism, syndicalism, etc., determined by occupation? by temperament?

To what extent have social doctrine and social idealism superseded and taken the place of religious faith in the different occupations, and why?

Do social classes tend to assume the character of cultural groups? That is to say, do the classes tend to acquire the exclusiveness and independence of a caste or nationality; or is each class always dependent upon the existence of a corresponding class?

To what extent do children follow the vocations of their parents and why?

To what extent do individuals move from one class to another, and how does this fact modify the character of class relationships?

News and the mobility of the social group.—The division of labor, in making individual success dependent upon concentration upon a special task, has had the effect of increasing the interdependence of the different vocations. A social organization is thus created in which the individual becomes increasingly dependent upon the community of which he is an integral part. The effect, under conditions of personal competition, of this increasing interdependence of the parts is to create in the industrial organization as a whole a certain sort of social solidarity, but a solidarity based, not on sentiment and habit, but on community of interests.

In the sense in which the terms are here used, sentiment is the more concrete, interest the more abstract, term. We may cherish a sentiment for a person, a place, or any object whatsoever. It may be a sentiment of aversion, or a sentiment of possession. But to possess or to be possessed by a sentiment for, or in regard to, anything means that we are incapable of acting toward it in a thoroughly rational way. It means that the object of our sentiment corresponds in some special way to some inherited or acquired disposition. Such a disposition is the affection of a mother for her child, which is instinctive. Or even the feeling she may have for the child's empty cradle, which is acquired.

The existence of a sentimental attitude indicates that there are motives for action of which the individual who is moved by them is not wholly conscious; motives over which he has only a partial control. Every sentiment has a history, either in the experience of the individual, or in the experience of the race, but the person who acts on that sentiment may not be aware of the history.

Interests are directed less toward specific objects than toward the ends which this or that particular object at one time or another embodies. Interests imply, therefore, the existence of means and a consciousness of the distinction between means and ends. Our sentiments are related to our prejudices, and prejudices may attach to anything—persons, races, as well as inanimate things. Prejudices are related also to taboos, and so tend to maintain "social distances" and the existing social organization. Sentiment and prejudice are elementary forms of conservatism. Our interests are rational and mobile, and make for change.

Money is the cardinal device by which values have become rationalized and sentiments have been replaced by interests. It is just because we feel no personal and no sentimental attitude toward our money, such as we do toward, for example, our home, that money becomes a valuable means of exchange. We will be interested in acquiring a certain amount of money in order to achieve a certain purpose, but provided that purpose may be achieved in any other way we are likely to be just as well satisfied. It is only the miser who becomes sentimental about money, and in that case he is likely to prefer one sort of money, say gold, to another, irrespective of its value. In this case the value of gold is determined by personal sentiment rather than by reason.

An organization which is composed of competing individuals and of competing groups of individuals is in a state of unstable equilibrium, and this equilibrium can be maintained only by a process of continuous readjustment. This aspect of social life and this type of social organization are best represented in the world of business which is the special object of investigation of political economy.

The extension of industrial organization, which is based on the impersonal relations defined by money, has gone forward hand in hand with an increasing mobility of the population. The laboring man and the artisan fitted to perform a specific task are compelled, under the conditions created by city life, to move from one region to another in search of the particular kind of employment which they are fitted to perform. The tide of immigration which moves back and forth between Europe and America is to some extent a measure of this same mobility.[8]

On the other hand, the tradesman, the manufacturer, the professional man, the specialist in every vocation, seeks his clients as the difficulties of travel and communication decrease over an ever widening area of territory. This is another way in which the mobility of the population may be measured. However, mobility in an individual or in a population is measured, not merely by change of location, but rather by the number and variety of the stimulations to which the individual or the population responds. Mobility depends, not merely upon transportation, but upon communication. Education and the ability to read, the extension of the money economy to an ever increasing number of the interests of life, in so far as it has tended to depersonalize social relations, has at the same time vastly increased the mobility of modern peoples.

The term "mobility," like its correlative, "isolation," covers a wide range of phenomena. It may represent at the same time a character and a condition. As isolation may be due to the existence of purely physical barriers to communication, or to a peculiarity of temperament and a lack of education, so mobility may be a consequence of the natural means of communication or of an agreeable manner and a college education.

It is now clearly recognized that what we ordinarily call a lack of

---

[8] Walter Bagehot, *The Postulates of Political Economy* (London, 1885), pp. 7-8.

intelligence in individuals, races, and communities is frequently a result of isolation. On the other hand, the mobility of a population is unquestionably a very large factor in its intellectual development.

There is an intimate connection between the immobility of the primitive man and his so-called inability to use abstract ideas. The knowledge which a peasant ordinarily possesses, from the very nature of his occupation, is concrete and personal. He knows individually and personally every member of the flock he tends. He becomes in the course of years so attached to the land he tills that the mere transposition from the strip of soil on which he has grown up to another with which he is less intimately acquainted is felt by him as a personal loss. For such a man the neighboring valley, or even the strip of land at the other end of the village is in a certain sense alien territory. A large part of the peasant's efficiency as an agricultural laborer depends upon this intimate and personal acquaintance with the idiosyncrasies of a single plot of land to the care of which he has been bred. It is apparent that, under conditions like these, very little of the peasant's practical knowledge will take the abstract form of scientific generalization. He thinks in concrete terms because he knows and needs no other.

On the other hand, the intellectual characteristics of the Jew and his generally recognized interest in abstract and radical ideas are unquestionably connected with the fact that the Jews are, before all else, a city folk. The "Wandering Jew" acquires abstract terms with which to describe the various scenes which he visits. His knowledge of the world is based upon identities and differences, that is to say, on analysis and classification. Reared in intimate association with the bustle and business of the market place, constantly intent on the shrewd and fascinating game of buying and selling, in which he employs that most interesting of abstractions, money, he has neither opportunity nor inclination to cultivate that intimate attachment to places and persons which is characteristic of the immobile person.[8a]

Concentration of populations in cities, the wider markets, the division of labor, the concentration of individuals and groups on special tasks, have continually changed the material conditions of life, and in doing this have made readjustments to novel conditions increasingly necessary. Out of this necessity there have grown up a number of special organizations which exist for the special purpose of facilitating these readjustments. The market which brought the modern city into existence is one of these devices. More interesting, however, are the exchanges, particularly the stock exchange and the board of trade, where prices are constantly being made in response to changes, or rather the reports of changes, in economic conditions all over the world.

[8a] Cf. W. I. Thomas, *Source Book of Social Origins*, p. 169.

These reports, so far as they are calculated to cause readjustments, have the character of what we call news. It is the existence of a critical situation which converts what were otherwise mere information into news. Where there is an issue at stake, where, in short, there is crisis, there information which might affect the outcome one way or another becomes "live matter," as the newspaper men say. Live matter is news; dead matter is mere information.

What is the relation of mobility to suggestion, imitation, etc.?

What are the practical devices by which suggestibility and mobility are increased in a community or in an individual?

Are there pathological conditions in communities corresponding to hysteria in individuals? If so, how are they produced and how controlled?

To what extent is fashion an indication of mobility?

What is the difference in the manner in which fashions and customs are transmitted?

What is social unrest, and what are the conditions under which it manifests itself?

What are the characteristics of a progressive, what the characteristics of a static, community in respect to its resistance to novel suggestions?

What mental characteristics of the gypsy, of the hobo, and of the nomad generally can be traced to these nomadic habits?

The stock exchanges and the mob.—The exchanges, upon which we may watch the fluctuation of prices in response to the news of economic conditions in different parts of the world, are typical. Similar readjustments are taking place in every department of social life, where, however, the devices for making these readjustments are not so complete and perfect. For example, the professional and trade papers, which keep the professions and the trades informed in regard to new methods, experiences, and devices, serve to keep the members of these trades and professions abreast of the times, which means that they facilitate readjustments to changing conditions.

There is, however, this important distinction to be made: Competition in the exchanges is more intense; changes are more rapid and, as far as the individuals directly concerned, more momentous. In contrast with such a constellation of forces as we find on the exchanges, where competing dealers meet to buy and sell, so mobile a form of social organization as the crowd and the mob exhibits a relative stability.

It is a commonplace that decisive factors in the movements of crowds, as in the fluctuations of markets, are psychologic. This means that among the individuals who make up the crowd, or who compose the public which participates in the movements reflected in the market, a condition of instability exists which corresponds to what has been defined elsewhere as crisis. It is true of the exchanges, as it is of crowds, that the situation they represent is always critical, that is to say, the tensions are such that a slight cause may precipitate an enormous effect. The current euphemism, "the psychological moment," defines such a critical condition.

Psychological moments may arise in any social situation, but they occur more frequently in a society which has acquired a high state of mobility. They occur more frequently in a society where education is general, where railways, telegraph, and the printing press have become an indispensable part of the social economy. They occur more frequently in cities than in smaller communities. In the crowd and the public every moment may be said to be "psychological."

Crisis may be said to be the normal condition on the exchanges. What are called financial crises are merely an extension of this critical condition to the larger business community. Financial panics which sometimes follow upon financial crises are a precipitate of this critical condition.

The fascinating thing about the study of crises, as of crowds, is that in so far as they are in fact due to psychological causes, that is, in so far as they are the result of the mobility of the communities in which they occur, they can be controlled. The evidence for this is the fact that they can be manipulated, and there is abundant evidence of manipulation in the transactions of the stock market. The evidence for the manipulation of crowds is less accessible. Labor organizations have, however, known how to develop a pretty definite technique for the instigation and control of strikes. The Salvation Army has worked out a book of tactics which is very largely devoted to the handling of street crowds; and professional revivalists, like Billy Sunday, have an elaborate technique for conducting their revivals.

Under the title of collective psychology much has been written in recent years in regard to crowds and kindred phenomena of social life. Most that has been written thus far has been based upon general observation and almost no systematic methods exist for the study of this type of social organization. The practical methods which practical men like the political boss, the labor agitator, the stock-exchange speculator, and others have worked out for the control and manipulation of the public and the crowd furnish a body of materials from which it is possible to make a more detailed, a more intimate study of what may be called, in order to distinguish it from that of more highly organized groups, collective behavior.

The city, and particularly the great city, in which more than elsewhere human relations are likely to be impersonal and rational, defined in terms of interest and in terms of cash, is in a very real sense a laboratory for the investigation of collective behavior. Strikes and minor revolutionary movements are endemic in the urban environment. Cities, and particularly the great cities, are in unstable equilibrium. The result is that the vast casual and mobile aggregations which constitute our urban populations are in a state of perpetual agitation, swept by every new wind of doctrine, subject to constant alarms, and in consequence the community is in a chronic condition of crisis.

What has been said suggests first of all the importance of a more detailed and fundamental study of collective behavior. The questions which follow will perhaps suggest lines of investigation that could be followed profitably by students of urban life.

What is the psychology of crisis? What is the cycle of events involved in the evolution of a crisis, political or economic?

To what extent may the parliamentary system, including the electoral system, be regarded as an attempt to regularize revolution and to meet and control crises?

To what extent are mob violence, strikes, and radical political movements the results of the same general conditions that provoke financial panics, real estate booms, and mass movements in the population generally?

To what extent are the existing unstable equilibrium and social ferment due to the extent and speed of economic changes as reflected in the stock exchange?

What are the effects of the extension of communication and of news upon fluctuations in the stock market and economic changes generally?

Does the scale of stocks on the exchanges tend to exaggerate the fluctuations in the market, or to stabilize them?

Do the reports in the newspapers, so far as they represent the facts, tend to speed up social changes, or to stabilize a movement already in progress?

What is the effect of propaganda and rumor in cases where the sources of accurate information are cut off?

To what extent can fluctuations of the stock market be controlled by formal regulation?

To what extent can social changes, strikes, and revolutionary movements be controlled by the censorship?

To what extent can the scientific forecasting of economic and social
changes exercise a useful control over the trend of prices and of events?

To what extent can the prices recorded by the stock exchange be
compared with public opinion as recorded by the newspaper?

To what extent can the city, which responds more quickly and more
decisively to changing events, be regarded as a nerve center of the social
organism?

III. SECONDARY RELATIONS AND SOCIAL CONTROL

Modern methods of urban transportation and communication—
the electric railway, the automobile, the telephone, and the radio—
have silently and rapidly changed in recent years the social and
industrial organization of the modern city. They have been the
means of concentrating traffic in the business districts, have changed
the whole character of retail trade, multiplying the residence suburbs and making the department store possible. These changes in
the industrial organization and in the distribution of population
have been accompanied by corresponding changes in the habits,
sentiments, and character of the urban population.

The general nature of these changes is indicated by the fact
that the growth of cities has been accompanied by the substitution
of indirect, "secondary," for direct, face-to-face, "primary" relations in the associations of individuals in the community.

By primary groups I mean those characterized by intimate face-to-
face association and co-operation. They are primary in several senses, but
chiefly in that they are fundamental in forming the social nature and
ideals of the individual. The result of intimate association, psychologi-
cally, is a certain fusion of individualities in a common whole, so that
one's very self, for many purposes at least, is the common life and purpose of the group. Perhaps the simplest way of describing this whole-
ness is by saying that it is a "we"; it involves the sort of sympathy and
mutual identification for which "we" is the natural expression. One lives
in the feeling of the whole and finds the chief aims of his will in that
feeling. . . . .[9]

Touch and sight, physical contact, are the basis for the first and
most elementary human relationships. Mother and child, husband
and wife, father and son, master and servant, kinsman and neighbor, minister, physician, and teacher—these are the most intimate

---

[9] Charles Horton Cooley, *Social Organization*, p. 15.

and real relationships of life, and in the small community they are practically inclusive.

The interactions which take place among the members of a community so constituted are immediate and unreflecting. Intercourse is carried on largely within the region of instinct and feeling. Social control arises, for the most part spontaneously, in direct response to personal influences and public sentiment. It is the result of a personal accommodation, rather than the formulation of a rational and abstract principle.

The church, the school, and the family.—In a great city, where the population is unstable, where parents and children are employed out of the house and often in distant parts of the city, where thousands of people live side by side for years without so much as a bowing acquaintance, these intimate relationships of the primary group are weakened and the moral order which rested upon them is gradually dissolved.

Under the disintegrating influences of city life most of our traditional institutions, the church, the school, and the family, have been greatly modified. The school, for example, has taken over some of the functions of the family. It is around the public school and its solicitude for the moral and physical welfare of the children that something like a new neighborhood and community spirit tends to get itself organized.

The church, on the other hand, which has lost much of its influence since the printed page has so largely taken the place of the pulpit in the interpretation of life, seems at present to be in process of readjustment to the new conditions.

It is important that the church, the school, and the family should be studied from the point of view of this readjustment to the conditions of city life.

What changes have taken place in recent years in the family sentiments? in the attitudes of husbands toward wives? of wives toward husbands? of children toward parents, etc.?

What do the records of the juvenile and morals courts indicate in regard to this matter?

In what regions of social life have the mores on the subject of the family life changed most?

To what extent have these changes taken place in response to the influences of the city environment?

Similarly, investigations might be carried on with reference to the school and the church. Here, too, there is a changed attitude and changed policy in response to a changed environment. This is important because it is, in the last analysis, upon these institutions in which the immediate and vital interests of life find a corporate expression that social organizations ultimately rests.

It is probably the breaking down of local attachments and the weakening of the restraints and inhibitions of the primary group, under the influence of the urban environment, which are largely responsible for the increase of vice and crime in great cities. It would be interesting in this connection to determine by investigation how far the increase in crime keeps pace with the increasing mobility of the population and to what extent this mobility is a function of the growth of population. It is from this point of view that we should seek to interpret all those statistics which register the disintegration of the moral order, for example, the statistics of divorce, of truancy, and of crime.

What is the effect of ownership of property, particularly of the home, on truancy, on divorce, and on crime?

In what regions and classes are certain kinds of crime endemic?

In what classes does divorce occur most frequently? What is the difference in this respect between farmers and, say, actors?

To what extent in any given racial group, for example, the Italians in New York or the Poles in Chicago, do parents and children live in the same world, speak the same language, and share the same ideas, and how far do the conditions found account for juvenile delinquency in that particular group?

How far are the home mores responsible for criminal manifestations of an immigrant group?

Crisis and the courts.—It is characteristic of city life that all sorts of people meet and mingle together who never fully comprehend one another. The anarchist and the club man, the priest and the Levite, the actor and the missionary who touch elbows on the street still live in totally different worlds. So complete is the segregation of vocational classes that it is possible within the limits of the city to live in an isolation almost as complete as that of some remote rural community.

Walter Besant tells the following anecdote of his experience as editor of the *People's Palace Journal:*

In that capacity I endeavored to encourage literary effort, in the hope of lighting upon some unknown and latent genius. The readers of the *Journal* were the members of the various classes connected with the educational side of the place. They were young clerks chiefly—some of them very good fellows. They had a debating society which I attended from time to time. Alas! They carried on their debates in an ignorance the most profound, the most unconscious, and the most satisfied. I endeavored to persuade them that it was desirable at least to master the facts of the case before they spoke. In vain. Then I proposed subjects for essays, and offered prizes for verses. I discovered, to my amazement, that among all the thousands of these young people, lads and girls, there was not discoverable the least rudimentary indication of any literary power whatever. In all other towns there are young people who nourish literary ambitions, with some measure of literary ability. How should there be any in this town, where there were no books, no papers, no journals, and, at that time, no free libraries? [10]

In the immigrant colonies which are now well established in every large city, foreign populations live in an isolation which is different from that of the population of East London, but in some respects more complete.

The difference is that each one of these little colonies has a more or less independent political and social organization of its own, and is the center of a more or less vigorous nationalist propaganda. For example, each one of these groups has one or more papers printed in its own language. In New York City there were, a few years ago, 270 publications, most of them supported by the local population, printed in 23 different languages. In Chicago there were 19 daily papers published in 7 foreign languages with a combined daily circulation of 368,000 papers.

Under these conditions the social ritual and the moral order which these immigrants brought with them from their native countries have succeeded in maintaining themselves for a considerable time under the influences of the American environment. Social control, based on the home mores, breaks down, however, in the second generation.

We may express the relation of the city to this fact in general terms by saying that the effect of the urban environment is to intensify all effects of crisis.

The term "crisis" is not to be understood in a violent sense. It is involved in any disturbance of habit. There is a crisis in the boy's life when he leaves home. The emancipation of the Negro and the immigration of the European peasant are group crises. Any strain of crisis involves three possible changes: greater fitness, reduced efficiency, or death. In biological terms, "survival" means successful adjustment to crisis, accompanied

---

[10] Walter Besant, *East London*, p. 13.

typically by a modification of structure. In man it means mental stimulation and greater intelligence, or mental depression, in case of failure.[11]

Under the conditions imposed by city life in which individuals and groups of individuals, widely removed in sympathy and understanding, live together under conditions of interdependence, if not of intimacy, the conditions of social control are greatly altered and the difficulties increased.

The problem thus created is usually characterized as one of "assimilation." It is assumed that the reason for rapid increase of crime in our large cities is due to the fact that the foreign element in our population has not succeeded in assimilating American culture and does not conform to the American mores. This would be interesting, if true, but the facts seem to suggest that perhaps the truth must be sought in the opposite direction.

One of the most important facts established by the investigation concerns the American-born children of immigrants—the "second generation." The records of convictions in the New York Court of General Sessions during the period from October 1, 1908, to June 30, 1909, and of all commitments to Massachusetts penal institutions, except those to the state farm, during the year ending September 30, 1909, form the basis of this analysis of the criminal tendencies of the second generation.

From these records it appears that a clear tendency exists on the part of the second generation to differ from the first or immigrant generation in the character of its criminality. It also appears that this difference is much more frequently in the direction of the criminality of the American-born of non-immigrant parentage than it is in the opposite direction. This means that the movement of the second-generation crime is away from the crimes peculiar to immigrants and toward those of the American of native parentage. Sometimes this movement has carried second-generation criminality even beyond that of the native-born of native parentage. Of the second-generation groups submitted to this comparison, one maintains a constant adherence to the general rule above referred to, while all the others at some point fail to follow it. This unique group is the Irish second generation.[12]

What we do observe, as a result of the crisis, is that control that was formerly based on mores was replaced by control based on positive law. This change runs parallel to the movement by which sec-

[11] William I. Thomas, "Race Psychology: Standpoint and Questionnaire with Particular Reference to the Immigrant and Negro," *American Journal of Sociology*, XVII (May, 1912), 736.

[12] *Reports of the United States Immigration Commission*, VI, 14-16.

ondary relationships have taken the place of primary relationships in the association of individuals in the city environment.

It is characteristic of the United States that great political changes should be effected experimentally under the pressure of agitation or upon the initiative of small but militant minorities. There is probably no other country in the world in which so many "reforms" are in progress as at the present time in the United States. Reform has, in fact, become a kind of popular "indoor sport." The reforms thus effected, almost without exception, involve some sort of restriction or governmental control over activities that were formerly "free" or controlled only by the mores and public opinion.

The effect of this extension of what is called the police power has been to produce a change, not merely in the fundamental policy of the law, but in the character and standing of the courts.

The juvenile and morals courts illustrate a change which is perhaps taking place elsewhere. In these courts the judges have assumed something of the functions of administrative officers, their duties consisting less in the interpretation of law than in prescribing remedies and administering advice intended to restore delinquents brought before them to their normal place in society.

A similar tendency to give judges a wide discretion and to impose upon them a further responsibility is manifest in those courts which have to deal with the technical affairs of the business world, and in the growth in popularity of commissions in which judicial and administrative functions are combined, for example, the Interstate Commerce Commission.

In order to interpret in a fundamental way the facts in regard to social control it is important to start with a clear conception of the nature of corporate action.

Corporate action begins when there is some sort of communication between individuals who constitute a group. Communication may take place at different levels; that is, suggestions may be given and responded to on the instinctive, senso-motor, or ideo-motor levels. The mechanism of communication is very subtle, so subtle, in fact, that it is often difficult to conceive how suggestions are conveyed from one mind to another. This does not imply that there is any special form of consciousness, any special sense of kinship or consciousness of kind, necessary to explain corporate action.

In fact, it has recently been shown that in the case of certain highly organized and static societies, like that of the well-known ant, probably nothing that we would call communication takes place.

It is a well-known fact that if an ant be removed from a nest and afterward put back it will not be attacked, while almost invariably an ant belonging to another nest will be attacked. It has been customary to use the words memory, enmity, friendship, in describing this fact. Now Bethe made the following experiment. An ant was placed in the liquids (blood and lymph) squeezed out from the bodies of nest companions and was then put back into its nest; it was not attacked. It was then put in the juice taken from the inmates of a "hostile" nest, and was at once attacked and killed.[13]

A further instance of the manner in which ants communicate will illustrate how simple and automatic communication may become on the instinctive level.

An ant, when taking a new direction from the nest for the first time, always returns by the same path. This shows that some trace must be left behind which serves as a guide back to the nest. If an ant returning by this path bears no spoils, Bethe found that no other ants try this direction. But if it bring back honey or sugar, other ants are sure to try the path. Hence something of the substances carried over this path by the ants must remain on the path. These substances must be strong enough to affect the ants chemically.[14]

The important fact is that by means of this comparatively simple device corporate action is made possible.

Individuals not only react upon one another in this reflex way, but they inevitably communicate their sentiments, attitudes, and organic excitements, and in doing so they necessarily react, not merely to what each individual actually does, but to what he intends, desires, or hopes to do. The fact that individuals often betray sentiments and attitudes to others of which they are themselves only dimly conscious makes it possible for individual A, for example, to act upon motives and tensions in B as soon, or even before, B is able to do so. Furthermore, A may act upon the suggestions that emanate from B without himself being clearly conscious of the source from which his motives spring. So subtle and intimate may the reactions be which control individuals who are bound together in a social-psychological process.

It is upon the basis of this sort of instinctive and spontaneous

13 Jacques Loeb, *Comparative Physiology of the Brain*, pp. 220-21.
14 *Ibid.*, p. 221.

control that every more formal sort of control must be based in order to be effective.

Changes in the form of social control may for the purposes of investigation be grouped under the general heads:

1. The substitution of positive law for custom, and the extension of municipal control to activities that were formerly left to individual initiative and discretion.

2. The disposition of judges in municipal and criminal courts to assume administrative function so that the administration of the criminal law ceases to be a mere application of the social ritual and becomes an application of rational and technical methods, requiring expert knowledge or advice, in order to restore the individual to society and repair the injury that his delinquency has caused.

3. Changes and divergencies in the mores among the different isolated and segregated groups in the city. What are the mores, for example, of the shop-girl? the immigrant? the politician? and the labor agitator?

It should be the aim of these investigations to distinguish not merely the causes of these changes, the direction in which they are moving, but also the forces that are likely to minimize and neutralize them. For example, it is important to know whether the motives which are at present multiplying the positive restrictions on the individual will necessarily go as far in this country as they have already done in Germany. Will they eventually bring about a condition approaching socialism?

Commercialized vice and the liquor traffic.—Social control, under the conditions of city life, can, perhaps, be best studied in its attempts to stamp out vice and control the liquor traffic.

The saloon and the vice establishments have come into existence as a means of exploiting appetites and instincts fundamental to human nature. This makes the efforts that have been made to regulate and suppress these forms of exploitation and traffic interesting and important as subjects of investigation.

Such an investigation should be based upon thorough study: (1) of the human nature upon which the commerce has been erected, (2) of the social conditions which tend to convert normal appetites into social vices, (3) of the practical effects of the efforts to limit, control, and stamp out the vice traffic and to do away with the use and sale of liquor.

Among the things that we should desire to know are:

To what extent is the appetite for alcoholic stimulus a prenatal disposition?

To what extent may such an appetite be transferred from one form of stimulation to another; that is, e.g., from whiskey to cocaine, etc.?

To what extent is it possible to substitute normal and healthful for pathological and vicious stimulations?

What are the social and moral effects of secret drinking?

Where a taboo is established early in life, does it have the effect of idealizing the delights of indulgence? Does it do this in some cases and not in others? If so, what are the contributing circumstances? Do men suddenly lose the taste for liquor and other stimulants? What are the conditions under which this happens?

Many of these questions can be answered only by a study of individual experiences. Vices undoubtedly have their natural history, like certain forms of disease. They may therefore be regarded as independent entities which find their habitat in human environment, are stimulated by certain conditions, inhibited by others, but invariably exhibit through all changes a character that is typical.

In the early days the temperance movement had something of the character of a religious revival, and the effects were highly picturesque. In recent years the leaders have displayed a more deliberate strategy, but the struggle against the liquor traffic still has all the characteristics of a big popular movement, a movement which, having first conquered the rural districts, is now seeking to enforce itself in the cities.

On the other hand, the vice crusade started with the cities, where, in fact, commercialized vice is indigenous. The mere discussion of this subject in public has meant an enormous change in the sex mores. The fact that this movement is everywhere coincident with the entrance of women into a greater freedom, into industry, the professions, and party politics, is significant.

There are conditions peculiar to the life of great cities (referred to under the heading "Mobility of the Population of Great Cities") which make the control of vice especially difficult. For example, crusades and religious movements generally do not have the same success in the city environment that they do in the smaller and less heterogeneous communities. What are the conditions which make this true?

Perhaps the facts most worth studying in connection with the movement for suppression of vice are those which indicate the changes which have taken place in fifty years in sex mores, particularly with reference to what is regarded as modest and immodest in the dress and behavior, and with reference to the freedom with which sexual matters are now discussed by young men and young women.

It seems, in fact, as if we were in the presence of two epoch-making changes, the one which seems destined finally to put intoxicating liquors in the category of poisonous drugs, and the other to lift the taboo which, particularly among Anglo-Saxon peoples, has effectually prevented up to the present time the frank discussion of the facts of sex.

Party politics and publicity.—There is everywhere at present a disposition to increase the power of the executive branch of the government at the expense of the legislative. The influence of state legislatures and of city councils has been diminished in some instances by the introduction of the referendum and the recall. In others they have been largely superseded by the commission form of government. The ostensible reason for these changes is that they offer a means for overthrowing the power of the professional politicians. The real ground seems to me the recognition of the fact that the form of government which had its origin in the town meeting and was well suited to the needs of a small community based on primary relations is not suitable to the government of the changing and heterogeneous populations of cities of three or four millions.

Much, of course, depends upon the character and size of the population. Where it is of American stock, and the number of voting citizens is not too great for thorough and calm discussion, no better school of politics can be imagined nor any method of managing affairs more certain to prevent jobbery and waste, to stimulate vigilance and breed contentment. When, however, the town meeting has grown to exceed seven or eight hundred persons, and, still more, when any considerable section are strangers, such as Irish or French Canadians, who have latterly poured into New England, the institution works less perfectly because the multitude is too large for debate, factions are likely to spring up, and the immigrants, untrained in self-government, become the prey of wire pullers or petty demagogues.[15]

For one thing, the problems of city government have become, with the growth and organization of city life, so complicated that it is no longer desirable to leave them to the control of men whose only qualification for handling them consists in the fact that they have succeeded in gaining office through the ordinary machinery of ward politics.

Another circumstance which has made the selection of city officials by popular vote impractical under the conditions of city life is the fact that, except in special cases, the voter knows little or

---

[15] James Bryce, *The American Commonwealth*, I, 566.

nothing about the officials he is voting for; knows little or nothing about the functions of the office to which that official is to be elected; and, besides all the rest, is too busy elsewhere to inform himself about conditions and needs of the city as a whole.

At a recent election in Chicago, for example, voters were called upon to select candidates from a ballot containing 250 names, most of them unknown to the voters. Under these circumstances the citizen who wishes to vote intelligently relies on some more or less interested organization or some more or less interested advisor to tell him how to vote.

To meet this emergency, created primarily by conditions imposed by city life, two types of organization have come into existence for controlling those artificial crises that we call elections. One of these is the organization represented by the political boss and the political machine. The other is that represented by the independent voters' leagues, taxpayers' associations, and organizations like the bureaus of municipal research.

It is an indication of the rather primitive conditions in which our political parties were formed that they sought to govern the country on the principle that the remedy for all sorts of administrative evils was to "turn the rascals out," as the popular phrase expressed it, a change of government. The political machine and the political boss have come into existence in the interest of party politics. The parties were necessarily organized to capture elections. The political machine is merely a technical device invented for the purpose of achieving this end. The boss is the expert who runs the machine. He is as necessary to the winning of an election as a professional coach is necessary to success at football.

It is characteristic of the two types of organization which have grown up for the purpose of controlling the popular vote that the first, the political machine, is based, on the whole, on local, personal, that is to say, primary, relationships. The second, the good-government organizations, make their appeal to the public, and the public, as we ordinarily understand that expression, is a group based on secondary relationships. Members of a public are not as a rule personally acquainted.

The political machine is, in fact, an attempt to maintain, inside the formal administrative organization of the city, the control of a primary group. The organizations thus built up, of which Tammany Hall is the classic illustration, appear to be thoroughly feudal in their character. The relations between the boss and his ward captain seem to be precisely that, of personal loyalty on one side and personal protection on the other, which the feudal relation implies. The virtues which such an organization calls out are the old tribal ones of fidelity, loyalty, and devotion to the interests of the chief and the clan. The people within the organization, their friends and supporters, constitute a "we" group, while the rest of the city is merely the outer world, which is not quite alive and not quite human in the sense in which the members of the "we" group are. We have here something approaching the conditions of primitive society.

The conception of "primitive society" which we ought to form is that of small groups scattered over a territory. The size of the groups is determined by the conditions of the struggle for existence. The internal organization of each group corresponds to its size. A group of groups may have some relation to each other (kin, neighborhood, alliance, *connubium*, and *commercium*) which draws them together and differentiates them from others. Thus a differentiation arises between ourselves, the we-group or in-group, and everybody else or the others-groups, outgroups. The insiders in a we-group are in a relation of peace, order, law, government, and industry, to each other. Their relation to all outsiders, or others-groups, is one of war and plunder, except so far as agreements have modified it.

The relation of comradeship and peace in the we-group and that of hostility and war toward others-groups are correlative to each other. The exigencies of war with outsiders are what make peace inside, lest internal discord should weaken the we-group for war. These exigencies also make government and law in the in-group, in order to prevent quarrels and enforce discipline.[16]

The politics of most great cities offer abundant materials for the study of the type represented by the political boss, as well as the social mechanisms created by and embodied in the political machine. It is necessary, however, that we study them disinterestedly. Some of the questions we should seek to answer are:

What, as a matter of fact, is the political organization at any point within the city? What are the sentiments and attitudes and interests which find expression through it?

What are the practical devices it employs for mobilizing its forces and putting them into action?

What is the character of the party appeal in the different moral regions of which the city is made up?

---

[16] Sumner, *Folkways*, p. 12.

How much of the interest in politics is practical and how much is mere sport?

What part of the cost of elections is advertising? How much of it can be classed as "educational publicity," and how much is pure graft?

To what extent, under existing conditions, particularly as we find them in great cities, can elections be practically controlled by purely technical devices, card catalogues, torch-light processions, spellbinders —machinery?

What effect will the introduction of the referendum and recall have upon present methods of conducting elections in cities?

Advertising and social control.—In contrast with the political machine, which has founded its organized action on the local, personal, and immediate interests represented by the different neighborhoods and localities, the good-government organizations, the bureaus of municipal research, and the like have sought to represent the interests of the city as a whole and have appealed to a sentiment and opinion neither local nor personal. These agencies have sought to secure efficiency and good government by the education of the voter, that is to say, by investigating and publishing the facts regarding the government.

In this way publicity has come to be a recognized form of social control, and advertising—"social advertising"—has become a profession with an elaborate technique supported by a body of special knowledge.

It is one of the characteristic phenomena of city life and of society founded on secondary relationships that advertising should have come to occupy so important a place in its economy.

In recent years every individual and organization which has had to deal with the public, that is to say the public outside the smaller and more intimate communities of the village and small town, has come to have its press agent, who is often less an advertising man than a diplomatic man accredited to the newspapers, and through them to the world at large. Institutions like the Russell Sage Foundation and, to a less extent, the General Education Board have sought to influence public opinion directly through the medium of publicity. The Carnegie Report upon Medical Education, the Pittsburgh Survey, the Russell Sage Foundation Report on Comparative Costs of Public-School Education in the several states, are something more than scientific reports. They are rather a high form of journalism, dealing with existing conditions critically, and seeking through the agency of publicity to bring about radical reforms.

The work of the Bureau of Municipal Research in New York has had a similar practical purpose. To these must be added the work accomplished by the child-welfare exhibits, by the social surveys undertaken in different parts of the country, and by similar propaganda in favor of public health.

As a source of social control public opinion becomes important in societies founded on secondary relationships, of which great cities are a type. In the city every social group tends to create its own milieu and, as these conditions become fixed, the mores tend to accommodate themselves to the conditions thus created. In secondary groups and in the city fashion tends to take the place of custom, and public opinion, rather than the mores, becomes the dominant force in social control.

In any attempt to understand the nature of public opinion and its relation to social control it is important to investigate first of all the agencies and devices which have come into practical use in the effort to control, enlighten, and exploit it.

The first and the most important of these is the press, that is, the daily newspaper and other forms of current literature, including books classed as current.[17]

After the newspaper, the bureaus of research which are now springing up in all the large cities are the most interesting and the most promising devices for using publicity as a means of control.

The fruits of these investigations do not reach the public directly, but are disseminated through the medium of the press, the pulpit, and other sources of popular enlightenment.

In addition to these there are the educational campaigns in the interest of better health conditions, the child-welfare exhibits, and the numerous "social advertising" devices which are now employed, sometimes upon the initiative of private societies, sometimes upon that of popular magazines or newspapers, in order to educate the public and enlist the masses of the people in the movement for the improvement of conditions of community life.

The newspaper is the great medium of communication within the city, and it is on the basis of the information which it supplies that public opinion rests. The first function which a newspaper supplies is that which formerly was performed by the village gossip.

In spite, however, of the industry with which newspapers pursue

---

[17] Cf. Bryce, *The American Commonwealth*, p. 267.

facts of personal intelligence and human interest, they cannot compete with the village gossips as a means of social control. For one thing, the newspaper maintains some reservations not recognized by gossip, in the matters of personal intelligence. For example, until they run for office or commit some other overt act that brings them before the public conspicuously, the private life of individual men or women is a subject that is, for the newspaper, taboo. It is not so with gossip, partly because in a small community no individual is so obscure that his private affairs escape observation and discussion; partly because the field is smaller. In small communities there is a perfectly amazing amount of personal information afloat among the individuals who compose them.

The absence of this in the city is what, in large part, makes the city what it is.

Some of the questions that arise in regard to the nature and function of the newspaper and of publicity generally are:

What is news?

What are the methods and motives of the newspaper man? Are they those of an artist? a historian? or merely those of a merchant?

To what extent does the newspaper control and to what extent is it controlled by public sentiment?

What is a "fake" and why?

What is yellow journalism and why is it yellow?

What would be the effect of making the newspaper a municipal monopoly?

What is the difference between advertising and news?

IV. TEMPERAMENT AND THE URBAN ENVIRONMENT

Great cities have always been the melting-pots of races and of cultures. Out of the vivid and subtle interactions of which they have been the centers, there have come the newer breeds and the newer social types. The great cities of the United States, for example, have drawn from the isolation of their native villages great masses of the rural populations of Europe and America. Under the shock of the new contacts the latent energies of these primitive peoples have been released, and the subtler processes of interaction have brought into existence not merely vocational, but temperamental, types.

Mobilization of the individual man.—Transportation and communication have effected, among many other silent but far-reaching changes, what I have called the "mobilization of the individual man." They have multiplied the opportunities of the individual man for contact and for association with his fellows, but they have made these contacts and associations more transitory and less stable. A very large part of the populations of great cities, including those who make their homes in tenements and apartment houses, live much as people do in some great hotel, meeting but not knowing one another. The effect of this is to substitute fortuitous and casual relationship for the more intimate and permanent associations of the smaller community.

no —
extend,
not
substitute

Under these circumstances the individual's status is determined to a considerable degree by conventional signs—by fashion and "front"—and the art of life is largely reduced to skating on thin surfaces and a scrupulous study of style and manners.

Not only transportation and communication, but the segregation of the urban population tends to facilitate the mobility of the individual man. The processes of segregation establish moral distances which make the city a mosaic of little worlds which touch but do not interpenetrate. This makes it possible for individuals to pass quickly and easily from one moral milieu to another, and encourages the fascinating but dangerous experiment of living at the same time in several different contiguous, but otherwise widely separated, worlds. All this tends to give to city life a superficial and adventitious character; it tends to complicate social relationships and to produce new and divergent individual types. It introduces, at the same time, an element of chance and adventure which adds to the stimulus of city life and gives it, for young and fresh nerves, a peculiar attractiveness. The lure of great cities is perhaps a consequence of stimulations which act directly upon the reflexes. As a type of human behavior it may be explained, like the attraction of the flame for the moth, as a sort of tropism.

quote

The attraction of the metropolis is due in part, however, to the fact that in the long run every individual finds somewhere among the varied manifestations of city life the sort of environment in which he expands and feels at ease; finds, in short, the moral climate in which his peculiar nature obtains the stimulations that bring his innate dispositions to full and free expression. It is, I suspect, motives of this kind which have their basis, not in interest nor even in sentiment, but in something more fundamental and primitive which draw many, if not most, of the young men and young women from the security of their homes in the country into the big, booming confusion and excitement of city life. In a small community it is the normal man, the man without eccentricity or genius, who seems most likely to succeed. The small community often tolerates eccentricity. The city, on the contrary, rewards it. Neither the criminal, the defective, nor the genius has the same opportunity to develop his innate disposition in a small town that he invariably finds in a great city.

Fifty years ago every village had one or two eccentric characters who were treated ordinarily with a benevolent toleration, but who were regarded meanwhile as impracticable and queer. These exceptional individuals lived an isolated existence, cut off by their very eccentricities, whether of genius or of defect, from genuinely intimate intercourse with their fellows. If they had the making of criminals, the restraints and inhibitions of the small community rendered them harmless. If they had the stuff of genius in them, they remained sterile for lack of appreciation or opportunity. Mark Twain's story of *Pudd'n Head Wilson* is a description of one such obscure and unappreciated genius. It is not so true as it was that

> Full many a flower is born to blush unseen
> And waste its fragrance on the desert air.

Gray wrote the "Elegy in a Country Churchyard" before the rise of the modern metropolis.

In the city many of these divergent types now find a milieu in which, for good or for ill, their dispositions and talents parturiate and bear fruit.

In the investigation of those exceptional and temperamental types which the city has produced we should seek to distinguish, as far as possible, between those abstract mental qualities upon which technical excellence is based and those more fundamental native characteristics which find expression in temperament. We may therefore ask:

To what extent are the moral qualities of individuals based on native character? To what extent are they conventionalized habits imposed upon by them or taken over by them from the group?

What are the native qualities and characteristics upon which the moral or immoral character accepted and conventionalized by the group are based?

What connection or what divorce appears to exist between mental and moral qualities in the groups and in the individuals composing them?

Are criminals as a rule of a lower order of intelligence than noncriminals? If so, what types of intelligence are associated with different types of crime? For example, do professional burglars and professional confidence men represent different mental types?

What are the effects upon these different types of isolation and of mobility, of stimulus and of repression?

To what extent can playgrounds and other forms of recreation supply the stimulation which is otherwise sought for in vicious pleasures?

To what extent can vocational guidance assist individuals in finding vocations in which they will be able to obtain a free expression of their temperamental qualities?

The moral region.—It is inevitable that individuals who seek the same forms of excitement, whether that excitement be furnished by a horse race or by grand opera, should find themselves from time to time in the same places. The result of this is that in the organization which city life spontaneously assumes the population tends to segregate itself, not merely in accordance with its interests, but in accordance with its tastes or its temperaments. The resulting distribution of the population is likely to be quite different from that brought about by occupational interests or economic conditions.

Every neighborhood, under the influences which tend to distribute and segregate city populations, may assume the character of a "moral region." Such, for example, are the vice districts, which are found in most cities. A moral region is not necessarily a place of abode. It may be a mere rendezvous, a place of resort.

In order to understand the forces which in every large city tend to develop these detached milieus in which vagrant and suppressed impulses, passions, and ideals emancipate themselves from the dominant moral order, it is necessary to refer to the fact or theory of latent impulses of men.

The fact seems to be that men are brought into the world with all the passions, instincts, and appetites, uncontrolled and undisciplined. Civilization, in the interests of the common welfare, demands the suppression sometimes, and the control always, of the these wild, natural dispositions. In the process of imposing its discipline upon the individual, in making over the individual in accordance with the accepted community model, much is suppressed altogether, and much more finds a vicarious expression in forms that are socially valuable, or at least innocuous. It is at this point that sport, play, and art function. They permit the individual to purge himself by means of symbolic expression of these wild and suppressed impulses. This is the catharsis of which Aristotle wrote in his *Poetic,* and which has been given new and more positive significance by the investigations of Sigmund Freud and the psychoanalysts.

No doubt many other social phenomena such as strikes, wars, popular elections, and religious revivals perform a similar function in releasing the subconscious tensions. But within smaller communities, where social relations are more intimate and inhibitions more imperative, there are many exceptional individuals who find within the limits of the communal activity no normal and healthful expression of their individual aptitudes and temperaments.

The causes which give rise to what are here described as "moral regions" are due in part to the restrictions which urban life imposes; in part to the license which these same conditions offer. We have, until very recently, given much consideration to the temptations of city life, but we have not given the same consideration to the effects of inhibitions and suppressions of natural impulses and instincts under the changed conditions of metropolitan life. For one thing, children, which in the country are counted as an asset, become in the city a liability. Aside from this fact it is very much more difficult to rear a family in the city than on the farm. Marriage takes place later in the city, and sometimes it doesn't take place at all. These facts have consequences the significance of which we are as yet wholly unable to estimate.

Investigation of the problems involved might well begin by a study and comparison of the characteristic types of social organization which exist in the regions referred to.

What are the external facts in regard to the life in Bohemia, the half-world, the red-light district, and other "moral regions" less pronounced in character?

What is the nature of the vocations which connect themselves with the ordinary life of these regions? What are the characteristic mental types which are attracted by the freedom which they offer?

How do individuals find their way into these regions? How do they escape from them?

To what extent are the regions referred to the product of the license; to what extent are they due to the restrictions imposed by city life on the natural man?

Temperament and social contagion.—What lends special importance to the segregation of the poor, the vicious, the criminal, and exceptional persons generally, which is so characteristic a feature of city life, is the fact that social contagion tends to stimulate in divergent types the common temperamental differences, and to suppress characters which unite them with the normal types about them. Association with others of their own ilk provides also not merely a stimulus, but a moral support for the traits they have in common which they would not find in a less select society. In the great city the poor, the vicious, and the delinquent, crushed together in an unhealthful and contagious intimacy, breed in and in, soul and body, so that it has often occurred to me that those long genealogies of the Jukes and the tribes of Ishmael would not show such a persistent and distressing uniformity of vice, crime, and poverty unless they were peculiarly fit for the environment in which they are condemned to exist.

We must then accept these "moral regions" and the more or less eccentric and exceptional people who inhabit them, in a sense, at least, as part of the natural, if not the normal, life of a city.

It is not necessary to understand by the expression "moral region" a place or a society that is either necessarily criminal or abnormal. It is intended rather to apply to regions in which a divergent moral code prevails, because it is a region in which the people who inhabit it are dominated, as people are ordinarily not dominated, by a taste or by a passion or by some interest which has its roots directly in the original nature of the individual. It may be an art, like music, or a sport, like horse-racing. Such a region would differ from other social groups by the fact that its interests are more immediate and more fundamental. For this reason its differences are likely to be due to moral, rather than intellectual, isolation.

Because of the opportunity it offers, particularly to the exceptional and abnormal types of man, a great city tends to spread out and lay bare to the public view in a massive manner all the human characters and traits which are ordinarily obscured and suppressed in smaller communities. The city, in short, shows the good and evil in human nature in excess. It is this fact, perhaps, more than any other, which justifies the view that would make of the city a laboratory or clinic in which human nature and social processes may be conveniently and profitably studied.

CHAPTER 2

Community Organization and Juvenile Delinquency

I. THE "NATURAL DEPRAVITY" OF MANKIND

IN VIEW of the fact that man is so manifestly—as Aristotle described him—a political animal, predestined to live in association with, and dependence upon, his fellows, it is strange and interesting to discover, as we are compelled to do, now and again, how utterly unfitted by nature man is for life in society.

It is true, no doubt, that man is the most gregarious of animals, but it is nevertheless true that the thing of which he still knows the least is the business of carrying on an associated existence. Here, as elsewhere, it is those who have given the subject the closest study—the educator, the criminologist, and the social worker—who are most aware of the incalculable elements in every social situation and feel most keenly their inability to control human behavior.

In his recent study, *The Unadjusted Girl*, Dr. W. I. Thomas, referring to this matter, calls attention to the fact that "The whole criminal procedure is based on punishment, and yet we do not even know that punishment deters from crime. Or, rather, we know that it sometimes deters, and sometimes stimulates to further crime, but

Reprinted by permission of the publisher from R. E. Park, E. W. Burgess and R. D. McKenzie, *The City* (Chicago: University of Chicago Press, 1925), pp. 99-112.

we do not know the conditions under which it acts in one way or another." [1]

So ill-adapted is the natural, undomesticated man to the social order into which he is born, so out of harmony are all the native impulses of the ordinary healthy human with the demands which society imposes, that it is hardly an exaggeration to say that if his childhood is spent mainly in learning what he must not do, his youth will be devoted mainly to rebellion. As to the remainder of his life, his recreations will very likely turn out to be some sort of vacation and escape from this same social order to which he has finally learned to accommodate, but not wholly reconcile, himself.

So far is this description true that our ancestors, living under a sterner discipline and in a moral order less flexible and accommodating than our own, were so impressed with the innate cantankerousness of ordinary mankind that they were driven to the assumption that there was something fundamentally diabolical in human nature, a view which found expression in the well-known doctrine of the "natural depravity of man."

One reason why human beings, in contrast with the lower animals, seem to be so ill-adapted to the world in which they are born is that the environment in which human beings live is so largely made up of the experience and memories and the acquired habits of the people who have preceded them.

This experience and these memories—crystallized and embodied in tradition, in custom, and in folkways—constitute the social, as distinguished from the biological, environment; for man is not merely an individual with certain native and inherited biological traits, but he is at the same time a person with manners, sentiments, attitudes, and ambitions.

It is the social environment to which the person, as distinguished from the individual, responds; and it is these responses of the person to his environment that eventually define his personality and give to the individual a character which can be described in moral terms.

II. SOCIETY AND THE SOCIAL MILIEU

This social environment in which mankind has acquired nearly if not all the traits that we regard as characteristically human is

---

[1] William I. Thomas, *The Unadjusted Girl—with Cases and Standpoint for Behavior Analysis, Criminal Science*, Monograph No. 4, Boston, 1923.

what we call society, society in the large; what Comte called "humanity."

When, however, we attempt to consider a little more in detail this society which ideally includes all mankind, we discover that it is composed of a number of smaller groups, little societies, each of which represents some single aspect or division of this all-enveloping social milieu in which we live and of which we are at the same time a part.

The first and most intimate portion of man's social environment, strange as the statement may at first seem, is his own body. After that, his clothing, tools, and property, which are in some sense a part of his personality, may, under certain circumstances, be regarded as a part of his environment. They become part of his social environment as soon as he becomes conscious of them; as soon as he becomes self-conscious.

Most of us have known, at some time in our lives, that "sickening sense of inferiority" that comes over one when in competition with his fellows, he realizes for the first time, perhaps, the inadequacy of his personal resources—physical, mental, and moral—to achieve his personal ambitions. But we who are presumably normal have very little understanding of the struggles of the physically or mentally handicapped to accommodate themselves to a world to which they are constitutionally not adapted.

So important to the development of personality is this interest which, with the advent of self-consciousness, the individual discovers in himself, that it has been made the basis of one of the numerous schools of psychiatry in Europe. Dr. Alfred Adler's theory of "psychic compensation" is based on the observation that an individual who is conscious of his inferiority inevitably seeks to compensate himself for this lowered self-esteem by greater concentration and effort. Eventually he may, in this way, succeed in overcoming his constitutional handicap; or he may find compensation for failure in one field by success in another and different one. Adler points out that there are numerous instances in which individuals have made striking successes in fields in which they were least fitted, constitutionally, to succeed. The classic illustration is that of Demosthenes, who, according to the anecdote that has come down to us, was a stutterer, but, by putting pebbles in his mouth and talking to the waves on the seashore, overcame his handicap and became the greatest of Athenian orators.

When this sense of inferiority is acute because of some physical deformity, or in consequence of any other constitutional inferiority, so that the person is peculiarly sensitive about himself, the result is frequently what Adler describes as "psychic overcompensation," which manifests itself in certain definite neurotic and socially pathological tendencies, usually described as "egocentrism."

In such cases, according to Adler, "the neurotic shows a series of sharply emphasized traits of character which exceed the normal standard. The marked sensitiveness, the irritable debility, the suggestibility, the egotism, the penchant for the fantastic, the estrangement from reality, but also more special traits such as tyranny, malevolence, a self-sacrificing virtue, coquetry, anxiety, and absent-mindedness are met with in the majority of case histories."

As soon as we become conscious of ourselves, self-control—which is not fundamentally different from the control we exercise over external volume—tends to become one of our most difficult and absorbing problems. Man has many advantages over the lower animals. On the other hand, the lower animals are not subject to what Frazer describes as "the perils of the soul"; they do not have the problem of managing themselves. This was evidently what Walt Whitman meant when he wrote:

> I think I could turn and live with animals, they are so placid and
>   self-contained, ...
> They do not sweat and whine about their condition,
> They do not lie awake in the dark and weep for their sins,
> They do not make me sick discussing their duty to God,
> No one is dissatisfied—not one is demented with the mania of
>   owning things,
> Not one kneels to another, nor to his kind that lived thousands
>   of years ago,
> Not one is respectable or industrious over the whole earth.

III. THE FAMILY AS A CORPORATE PERSON

After the individual's own person, the most intimate environment to which the person responds is the family. The family is, or was, under earlier and simpler conditions of life, a sort of larger corporate person. Among the Polish peasants, for example, where the family completely dominates the individual, "husband and wife," we are told, "are not individuals more or less closely connected according to their personal sentiments, but group members, controlled by both the united families." [2] It is on this basis that we can understand completely the letters written by immigrant boys to their parents asking them to send them wives:

DEAREST PARENTS:
Please do not be angry with me for what I shall write. I write you that it is hard to live alone, so please find some girl for me, but an orderly [honest] one, for in America there is not even one single orderly [Polish] girl. . . . . [December 21, 1902.] I thank you kindly for your letter, for it was happy. As to the girl, although I don't know her, my companion, who knows her, says that she is stately and pretty, and I believe him, as well as you, my parents. . . . . Please inform me which one (of the sisters) is to come, the older or the younger one, whether Aledsandra or Stanislawa.[3]

Of such a family it may almost be said that the unrebellious and completely accommodated individuals who compose it have ceased to exist as persons. They have no independent social status and no personal responsibilities except as members of the family group.

The family, as it exists under modern conditions, has fallen from the high estimation in which it was held by an earlier generation. I once heard a distinguished psychologist say that he had been forced to the conclusion, after much patient study, that the family was probably the worst possible place in which to bring up a child. In general, I should say the psychiatrists seem to have a very poor opinion of the modern family as an environment for children. This opinion, if it is not justified, is at least supported by studies of juvenile delinquency made some years ago, in which it appeared that 50 per cent of the delinquencies studied were from broken homes.

The "one-child family" is now generally recognized as one of the characteristic social situations in which egocentric behavior is likely to manifest itself. It is certain that parents, just because of their solicitude for the welfare of their offspring, are not always safe companions for them. However that may be today, it is certain that in the past it was within the limits of the family group that most of the traits which we may describe as human were originally developed.

Outside the circle of the family and the neighborhood, within which intimate and the so-called "primary relations" are maintained, there is the larger circle of influences we call the community; the

---

[2] Thomas and Znaniecki, *The Polish Peasant*, I, 87-97.
[3] *Ibid.*, II, 259.

local community, and then the larger, organized community, represented by the city and the nation. And out beyond the limits of these there are beginning to emerge the vast and vague outlines of that larger world-community which Graham Wallas has described under the title, *The Great Society*.

The community, then, is the name that we give to this larger and most inclusive social milieu, outside of ourselves, our family, and our immediate neighborhood, in which the individual maintains not merely his existence as an individual, but his life as a person.

The community, including the family, with its wider interests, its larger purposes, and its more deliberate aims, surrounds us, incloses us, and compels us to conform; not by mere pressure from without, not by the fear of censure merely, but by the sense of our interest in, and responsibility to, certain interests not our own.

The sources of our actions are, no doubt, in the organic impulses of the individual man; but actual conduct is determined more or less by public opinion, by custom, and by a code which exists outside of us in the family, in the neighborhood, and in the community. This community, however, with its less immediate purposes and its more deliberate aims, is always more or less outside of, and alien to, us; much more so than the family, for example, or any other congenial group. This is to such an extent true that certain sociological writers have conceived society as having an existence quite independent of the individuals who compose it at any given time. Under these circumstances the natural condition of the individual in society is one of conflict; conflict with other individuals, to be sure, but particularly conflict with the convention and regulations of the social group of which he is a member. Personal freedom—self-expression, as we have learned to call it in recent years—is, therefore, if not a fruitless, still a never ending, quest.

Only gradually, as he succeeds in accommodating himself to the life of the larger group, incorporating into the specific purposes and ambitions of his own life the larger and calmer purposes of the society in which he lives, does the individual man find himself quite at home in the community of which he is a part.

If this is true of mankind as a whole, it is still more true of the younger person. The natural impulses of the child are inevitably so far from conforming to the social situation in which he finds himself that his relations to the community seem to be almost completely defined in a series of "don'ts." Under these circumstances juvenile delinquency is, within certain age-limits at least, not merely something to be expected; it may almost be said to be normal.

It is in the community, rather than in the family, that our moral codes first get explicit and formal definition and assume the external and coercive character of municipal law.

IV. SOCIAL CHANGE AND SOCIAL DISORGANIZATION

In the family and in the neighborhood such organization as exists is based upon custom and tradition, and is fixed in what Sumner calls the folkways and the mores. At this stage, society is a purely natural product; a product of the spontaneous and unreflective responses of individuals living together in intimate, personal, and face-to-face relations. Under such circumstances conscious efforts to discipline the individual and enforce the social code are directed merely by intuition and common sense.

In the larger social unit, the community, where social relations are more formal and less intimate, the situation is different. It is in the community, rather than in the family or the neighborhood, that formal organizations like the church, the school, and the courts come into existence and get their separate functions defined. With the advent of these institutions, and through their mediation, the community is able to supplement, and to some extent supplant, the family and the neighborhood as a means for the discipline and control of the individual. However, neither the orphan asylum nor any other agency has thus far succeeded in providing a wholly satisfactory substitute for the home. The evidence of this is that they have no alumni association. They create no memories and traditions that those who graduate from them are disposed to cherish and keep alive.

It is in this community with its various organizations and its rational, rather than traditional, schemes of control, and not elsewhere, that we have delinquency. Delinquency is, in fact, in some sense the measure of the failure of our community organizations to function.

Historically, the background of American life has been the village community. Until a few years ago the typical American was, and perhaps still is, an inhabitant of a middle western village; such a village, perhaps, as Sinclair Lewis describes in *Main Street*. And still, today, the most characteristic trait of Homo Americanus is an inveterate individualism which may, to be sure, have been temperamental, but in that case temperament has certainly been considerably reinforced by the conditions of life on the frontier.

But with the growth of great cities, with the vast division of labor which has come in with machine industry, and with movement and change that have come about with the multiplication of the means of transportation and communication, the old forms of social control represented by the family, the neighborhood, and the local community have been undermined and their influence greatly diminished.

This process by which the authority and influence of an earlier culture and system of social control is undermined and eventually destroyed is described by Thomas—looking at it from the side of the individual—as a process of "individualization." But looking at it from the point of view of society and the community it is social disorganization.

We are living in such a period of individualization and social disorganization. Everything is in a state of agitation—everything seems to be undergoing a change. Society is, apparently, not much more than a congeries and constellation of social atoms. Habits can be formed only in a relatively stable environment, even if that stability consists merely—as, in fact, it invariably does, since there is nothing in the universe that is absolutely static—in a relatively constant form of change. Any form of change that brings any measurable alteration in the routine of social life tends to break up habits; and in breaking up the habits upon which the existing social organization rests, destroys that organization itself. Every new device that affects social life and the social routine is to that extent a disorganizing influence. Every new discovery, every new invention, every new idea, is disturbing. Even news has become at times so dangerous that governments have felt it wise to suppress its publication.

It is probable that the most deadly and the most demoralizing single instrumentality of present-day civilization is the automobile. The automobile bandit, operating in our great cities, is much more successful and more dangerous than the romantic stage robber of fifty years ago. The connection of the automobile with vice is notorious. "The automobile is connected with more seductions than happen otherwise in cities altogether." [4]

---

[4] W. I. Thomas, *The Unadjusted Girl*, p. 71.

The newspaper and the motion picture show, while not so deadly, are almost as demoralizing. If I were to attempt to enumerate all the social forces that have contributed to the disorganization of modern society I should probably be compelled to make a catalogue of everything that has introduced any new and striking change into the otherwise dull routine of our daily life. Apparently anything that makes life interesting is dangerous to the existing order.

The mere movement of the population from one part of the country to another—the present migration of the Negroes northward, for example—is a disturbing influence. Such a movement may assume, from the point of view of the migrants themselves, the character of an emancipation, opening to them new economic and cultural opportunities, but it is none the less disorganizing to the communities they have left behind and to the communities into which they are now moving. It is at the same time demoralizing to the migrating people themselves, and particularly, I might add, to the younger generation.

The enormous amount of delinquency, juvenile and adult, that exists today in the Negro communities in northern cities is due in part, though not entirely, to the fact that migrants are not able to accommodate themselves at once to a new and relatively strange environment. The same thing may be said of the immigrants from Europe, or of the younger generation of women who are just now entering in such large numbers into the newer occupations and the freer life which the great cities offer them.

"Progress," as I once heard William James remark, "is a terrible thing." It is a terrible thing in so far as it breaks up the routine upon which an existing social order rests, and thus destroys the cultural and the economic values, i.e., the habits of thrift, of skill, of industry, as well as the personal hopes, ambitions, and life-programs which are the content of that social order.

Our great cities, as those who have studied them have learned, are full of junk, much of it human, i.e., men and women who, for some reason or other, have fallen out of line in the march of industrial progress and have been scrapped by the industrial organization of which they were once a part.

A recent study by Nels Anderson of what he calls "Hobohemia," an area in Chicago just outside the "Loop," that is to say, the downtown business area, which is almost wholly inhabited by homeless men, is a study of such a human junk heap. In fact, the slum areas that invariably grow up just on the edge of the business areas of great cities, areas of deteriorated houses, of poverty, vice, and crime, are areas of social junk.

I might add, because of its immediate connection with the problems and interests of this association, that recent studies made in Chicago of boys' gangs seem to show that there are no playgrounds in the city in which a boy can find so much adventure, no place where he can find so much that may be called "real sport," as in these areas of general deterioration which we call the slums.

In order to meet and deal with the problems that have been created by the rapid changes of modern life, new organizations and agencies have sprung into existence. The older social agencies, the church, the school, and the courts, have not always been able to meet the problems which new conditions of life have created. The school, the church, and the courts have come down to us with their aims and methods defined under the influence of an older tradition. New agencies have been necessary to meet the new conditions. Among these new agencies are the juvenile courts, juvenile protective associations, parent-teachers' associations, Boy Scouts, Young Men's Christian Associations settlements, boys' clubs of various sorts, and I presume, playgrounds and playground associations. These agencies have taken over to some extent the work which neither the home, the neighborhood, nor the other older communal institutions were able to carry on adequately.

These new institutions, perhaps because they are not to the same extent hampered by our earlier traditions, are frankly experimental and are trying to work out a rational technique for dealing with social problems, based not on sentiment and tradition, but on science.

Largely on the basis of the experiments which these new agencies are making, a new social science is coming into existence. Under the impetus which the social agencies have given to social investigation and social research, sociology is ceasing to be a mere philosophy and is assuming more and more the character of an empirical, if not an exact, science.

As to the present condition of our science and of the devices that we have invented for controlling conduct and social life, I can only repeat what I said at the very outset of our paper: "The thing of which we still know least is the business of carrying on an associated existence."

V. THE GANG AND THE LOCAL COMMUNITY

I have sought, in what has been said, to indicate what seems to me to be the relation of the work of the playground association and other social agencies to the more general problem of community organization and juvenile delinquency. But I have a feeling that this paper lacks a moral, and I know that every paper on a social topic should have a moral. If I were asked to state in a few words what seems to me to be suggested by our discussion so far I should say:

1. That the problem of juvenile delinquency seems to have its sources in conditions over which, with our present knowledge, we have very little control; that the whole matter needs, therefore, a more searching investigation than we have yet been able to give it.

2. That the encouraging factor in the situation is: (1) that our social agencies are definitely experimenting with the problem; (2) that there is growing up in the universities and elsewhere a body of knowledge about human nature and society which will presently enable us to interpret these experiments, redefine the problem, and eventually gain a deeper insight into the social conditions and the social processes under which not merely juvenile delinquency but other forms of personal and social disorganization occur.

3. That what we already know about the intimate relations between the individual and the community makes it clear that delinquency is not primarily a problem of the individual, but of the group. Any effort to re-educate and reform the delinquent individual will consist very largely in finding for him an environment, a group in which he can live, and live not merely in the physical or biological sense of the word, but live in the social and in the sociological sense. That means finding a place where he can have not only free expression of his energies and native impulses, but a place where he can find a vocation and be free to formulate a plan of life which will enable him to realize in some adequate way all the fundamental wishes that, in some form or other, every individual seeks to realize, and must realize, in order to have a wholesome and reasonably happy existence.

4. This suggests to me that the playground should be something more than a place for working off steam and keeping children out of mischief. It should be a place where children form permanent associations. The play group is certainly one of the most important factors in the defining of the wishes and the forming of the charac-

ter of the average individual. Under conditions of urban life, where the home tends to become little more than a sleeping-place, a dormitory, the play group is assuming an increasing importance. Mr. Frederic M. Thrasher has recently been studying the boys' gangs in Chicago. He has located one thousand gangs, and it is interesting to notice where these gangs are located. They are for the most part in the slums. The gangs he has located and studied are by no means all the gangs in Chicago. They are, rather, the gangs that have attracted attention because they have been troublesome, because they are connected directly or indirectly with juvenile delinquency and adolescent crime.

If I ventured to state my opinion in regard to the matter, I should say that these gangs have exercised a considerably greater influence in forming the character of the boys who compose them than has the church, the school, or any other communal agency outside of the families and the homes in which the members of the gangs are reared. And it is quite possible that the influence of these homes have not been always and altogether wholesome.

5. Finally, playgrounds should, as far as possible, be associated with character-forming agencies like the school, the church, and other local institutions. For however much the older generation may have been detached by migration and movement from their local associations, the younger generation, who live closer to the ground than we do, are irresistibly attached to the localities in which they live. Their associates are the persons who live next to them. In a great city, children are the real neighbors; their habitat is the local community; and when they are allowed to prowl and explore they learn to know the neighborhood as no older person who was not himself born and reared in the neighborhood is ever likely to know it.

This is one thing that makes the gang, a little later on, when perhaps it has become an athletic club, important politically. Our political system is based upon the theory that the people who live in the same locality know one another and have the same political and social interests. The gang is not infrequently a vocational school for ward politicans.

CHAPTER 3

COMMUNITY ORGANIZATION AND THE ROMANTIC TEMPER

I. THE PROBLEM STATED

RECENT local studies in Chicago seem to show that the number of competent persons in the community is frequently no real measure of the competency—if one may use that expression in this connection—of the community itself. A high communal intelligence quotient does not always, it seems, insure communal efficiency.

The explanation that at once suggests itself is that competent persons presumably are specialists deeply concerned in the little area of human experience in which they have chosen to operate, but profoundly indifferent to the interests of the particular geographical area in which they may happen to reside.

It is the incompetent persons, apparently, who still maintain an interest that could in any sense be called lively in the local communities of our great cities. Women, particularly women without professional training, and immigrants who are locally segregated and immured within the invisible walls of an alien language, are bound

Reprinted by permission of the publisher from *Social Forces* 3 (May, 1925), pp. 675-677. Later reprinted in R. E. Park, E. W. Burgess and R. D. McKenzie, *The City* (Chicago: University of Chicago Press, 1925), pp. 113-121.

to have some sort of interest in their neighbors. Children in great cities, who necessarily live close to the ground, however, are the real neighbors. Boys' gangs are neighborhood institutions. Politicians are professional neighbors. When the boys' gangs are graduated, as they frequently are, into local politics, the local political boss assumes toward them the rôle of patron, and they assume toward him the rôle of clients.

The competent people—that is to say, the professional people—are, on the other hand, either physically or in imagination, abroad most of the time. They live in the city—in their offices and in their clubs. They go home to sleep. Most of our residential suburbs tend to assume, as far as the professional classes are concerned, the character of dormitories. It is seldom that anyone who is sufficiently eminent or sufficiently competent to find a place in *Who's Who* has time for anything more than a benevolent interest in his local community.

On the other hand, the competent people are keenly alive to the interests of their professions, and if we could organize our politics, as the Russians have sought to organize theirs, on the basis of occupations, that is, in soviets, it might be possible to awaken in our intelligensia a more than dilettante and sporting interest in local politics and the problems of the local community. But the actual situation is different.

Our political system is founded on the presumption that the local community is the local political unit. If the local community is organized, knows its own local interests, and has a mind of its own, democracy prospers. It is said that 50 per cent of the qualified voters in this country do not exercise the franchise. So far as this is an index of their indifference to local community interests, it is at the same time a measure of the efficiency or inefficiency of the local community.

The National Community Center Association represents one of many efforts in recent years to alter the situation of which non-voting is perhaps one evidence. Community organizations aim, for one thing, to discover, to organize, and to make available for the local community the local community's resources, particularly its human resources. The extent to which it succeeds is the measure of its efficiency. How to assess these resources, how to use them: these are problems.

II. THE COMMUNITY DEFINED

But what is a community and what is community organization? Before assessing the communal efficiency one should at least be able to describe a community. The simplest possible description of a community is this: a collection of people occupying a more or less clearly defined area. But a community is more than that. A community is not only a collection of people, but it is a collection of institutions. Not people, but institutions, are final and decisive in distinguishing the community from other social constellations.

Among the institutions of the community there will always be homes and something more: churches, schools, playgrounds, a communal hall, a local theater, perhaps, and, of course, business and industrial enterprises of some sort. Communities might well be classified by the number and variety of the institutions—cultural, political, and occupational—which they possess. This would indicate the extent to which they were autonomous or, conversely, the extent to which their communal functions were mediatized, so to speak, and incorporated into the larger community.

There is always a larger community. Every single community is always a part of some larger and more inclusive one. There are no longer any communities wholly detached and isolated; all are interdependent economically and politically upon one another. The ultimate community is the wide world.

a) The ecological organization.—Within the limits of any community the communal institutions—economic, political, and cultural—will tend to assume a more or less clearly defined and characteristic distribution. For example, the community will always have a center and a circumference, defining the position of each single community to every other. Within the area so defined the local populations and the local institutions will tend to group themselves in some characteristic pattern, dependent upon geography, lines of communication, and land values. This distribution of population and institutions we may call the ecological organization of the community.

Town-planning is an attempt to direct and control the ecological organization. Town-planning is probably not so simple as it seems. Cities, even those like the city of Washington, D.C., that have been most elaborately planned, are always getting out of hand. The actual plan of a city is never a mere artifact, it is always quite as much a product of nature as of design. But a plan is one factor in communal efficiency.

b) The economic organization.—Within the limits of the ecological organization, so far as a free exchange of goods and services exists, there inevitably grows up another type of community organization based on the division of labor. This is what we may call the occupational organization of the community.

The occupational organization, like the ecological, is a product of competition. Eventually every individual member of the community is driven, as a result of competition with every other, to do the thing he *can do* rather than the thing he *would like to do*. Our secret ambitions are seldom realized in our actual occupations. The struggle to live determines finally not only where we shall live within the limits of the community, but what we shall do.

The number and variety of professions and occupations carried on within the limits of a community would seem to be one measure of its competency, since in the wider division of labor and the greater specialization—in the diversities of interests and tasks—and in the vast unconscious co-operation of city life, the individual man has not only the opportunity, but the necessity, to choose his vocation and develop his individual talents.

Nevertheless, in the struggle to find his place in a changing world there are enormous wastes. Vocational training is one attempt to meet the situation; the proposed national organization of employment is another. But until a more rational organization of industry has somehow been achieved, little progress may be expected or hoped for.

c) The cultural and political organization.—Competition is never unlimited in human society. Always there is custom and law which sets some bounds and imposes some restraints upon the wild and wilful impulses of the individual man. The cultural and political organization of the community rests upon the occupational organization, just as the latter, in turn, grows up in, and rests upon, the ecological organization.

It is this final division or segment of the communal organization with which community-center associations are mainly concerned. Politics, religion, and community welfare, like golf, bridge, and other forms of recreation, are leisure-time activities, and it is the leisure time of the community that we are seeking to organize.

Aristotle, who described man as a political animal, lived a long time ago, and his description was more true of man then than it is today. Aristotle lived in a world in which art, religion, and politics were the main concerns of life, and public life was the natural vocation of every citizen.

Under modern conditions of life, where the division of labor has gone so far that—to cite a notorious instance—it takes 150 separate operations to make a suit of clothes, the situation is totally different. Most of us now, during the major portion of our waking hours, are so busy on some minute detail of the common task that we frequently lose sight altogether of the community in which we live.

On the other hand, our leisure is now mainly a restless search for excitement. It is the romantic impulse, the desire to escape the dull routine of life at home and in the local community, that drives us abroad in search of adventure. This romantic quest, which finds its most outrageous expression in the dance halls and jazz parlors, is characteristic of almost every other expression of modern life. Political revolution and social reform are themselves often merely expressions of this same romantic impulse. Millennialism in religion, the missionary enterprises, particularly those that are limited to "regions beyond," are manifestations of this same wish to escape reality.

We are everywhere hunting the bluebird of romance, and we are hunting it with automobiles and flying machines. The new devices of locomotion have permitted millions of people to realize, in actual life, flights of which they had only dreamed previously. But this physical mobility is but the reflection of a corresponding mental instability.

This restlessness and thirst for adventure is, for the most part, barren and illusory, because it is uncreative. We are seeking to escape from a dull world instead of turning back upon it to transform it.

Art, religion, and politics are still the means through which we participate in the common life, but they have ceased to be our chief concern. As leisure-time activities they must now compete for attention with livelier forms of recreation. It is in the improvident use of our leisure, I suspect, that the greatest wastes in American life occur.

III. THE MEASUREMENT OF COMMUNAL EFFICIENCY

This, then, is our community. How are we to measure its efficiency? Here, I am bound to confess, we have still much to learn.

The simplest and most elementary way of estimating the competency and efficiency of a community, as something different from the competency and efficiency of the individual men and women who compose it, is by a comparative study of that community's social statistics. Poverty, disease, and delinquency have frequently been called social diseases. They may be said to measure the extent to which the community has been able to provide an environment in which the individuals which compose it are able to live, or, to state it from the opposite point of view, they measure the extent to which the individuals who compose the community have been able to adapt themselves to the environment which the community provided.

The immigrant community manifestly exists to enable the immigrant to live. By life, however, we mean something more than mere physical existence. Man is a creature such that when he lives at all he lives in society, lives in his hopes, in his dreams, and in the minds of other men. In some way or another, man is bound to realize all his fundamental wishes, and these wishes, according to Dr. W. I. Thomas, are four:

He must have (1) security, that is, a home; some place to go out from and return to.

He must have (2) new experience, recreation, adventure, new sensations.

He must have (3) recognition, i.e., he must belong to some society in which he has status, some group in which he is somebody; somewhere or other, in short, he must be a person, rather than a mere cog in the economic or social machine.

Finally (4) he must have affection, intimate association with someone or something, even though it be merely a cat or a dog, for which he feels affection and knows that affection is returned. All special human wishes reduce finally to these four categories, and no human creature is likely to be wholesome and happy unless, in some form or manner, all four of these wishes are more or less adequately realized.[1]

While I was on the Pacific Coast a few months ago, studying what we have called "race relations," I was impressed by the marked differences, as between immigrant groups, with respect to their ability to accommodate themselves to the American environment and, within the limitations imposed upon them by our customs and our laws, to provide for all the interests of life.

---

[1] Robert E. Park, "The Significance of Social Research in Social Service," *Journal of Applied Sociology* (May-June, 1924), pp. 264-65.

Immigrant communities are likely to include within the circle of their interests and their organizations all the interests of life. Every immigrant community will have a religious organization—a synagogue, a temple, or a church—with its related, often dependent, mutual aid and welfare organizations. It will have also its own business enterprises, its clubs, lodges, coffee houses, restaurants and gathering places, and a press. Every immigrant community is likely to have its press in America even if it did not have one in the home country. The immigrant colony is frequently nothing more than a transplanted village, for America actually has been colonized not by races or by nationalities, but by villages.

As to the competence of these immigrant communities to provide an environment in which immigrants can live, Raymond Pearl's paper, "The Racial Origin of Almshouse Paupers in the United States," published in *Science* (October 31, 1924), throws some light.

One paragraph in that paper states the situation as between the nation and the foreign-born. It says:

> While on January 1, 1923, there were in almshouses 59.8 native-born white persons per 100,000 of the same class in the population, the corresponding figure for the foreign-born was 173.6. This is by some regarded as a fact of dread significance. Perhaps it is. To me it seems possibly only an interesting expression of the difficulties which the human organism finds in adapting itself to a new environment.

If these figures may be regarded, as Dr. Pearl suggests that they should, as an index of the difficulties which the human organism finds in adapting itself to a new environment, the more detailed study of the various racial groups exhibits some surprising results.

They show, in the first place, wide divergencies in the capacity of different immigrant groups to adapt themselves to American life; they show, in the second place, that the races and nationalities that have lived here longest are the least able to meet the demands of the new environment. Dr. Pearl states it in this way:

> With a few trifling exceptions, all the countries from which the present law *encourages* immigration contributed to almshouse pauperism in 1923 in *excess* of their representation in the population in 1920. On the other hand, again with a few trifling exceptions, those countries from which the present immigration law was especially framed to *discourage* immigration appear in the lower part of the diagram, because they contribute a *smaller* proportion to almshouse pauperism in 1923 than their representation in the general population in 1920.

Two things strike me as significant in this connection: (1) It is the recent immigrants who contribute least to the almshouse population; (2) among these recent immigrants it is, apparently, those who for one reason or another are least willing or able to participate in American life who contribute the least to our almshouse population.

Why is this true? My own inference is that the decisive factors are not biological, but sociological. The explanation of the almshouse statistics, in other words, is less a matter of racial temperament than of social tradition. It is the immigrants who have maintained in this country their simple village religions and mutual aid organizations who have been most able to withstand the shock of the new environment.

The whole subject needs to be investigated further. What would a comparative study of different racial and language groups with reference to disease, delinquency, and family disorganization show? What would a comparison of the Japanese, Chinese, and Mexicans show with reference to crime? I mention these three groups because they are living and working side by side on the Pacific Coast.

The census of 1910 showed the Mexicans to have the highest crime rate of any immigrant group in the United States. My conviction is that when we obtain the facts we shall find that the Japanese have the lowest crime rate, at least the lowest of any immigrant group on the Coast.

The explanation is that the Japanese—and the same is true of the Chinese—have organized what we may call "control organizations" to deal at once with disputes arising among themselves and with the larger community outside.

The Japanese Association, like the Chinese Six Companies, is organized to keep their nationals out of the courts. But the Japanese Association is more than a court of arbitration and conciliation. Its function is not merely to settle disputes, but to maintain the morale of the local Japanese community and to promote in every practical way, mainly by education, the efforts of the Japanese people to make their way in the communities in which they live. With the possible exception of the Jews, the Japanese are better informed than any other group about the condition of their own people in America.

One thing that has sensibly raised the morale of the Japanese, as it has, indeed of the Jews, is its struggle to maintain its racial status in the United States. Nothing, as Sumner observed, so easily establishes solidarity within the group as an attack from without. Nothing so contributes to the discipline of a racial or national minority as the opposition of the racial or national majority.

The peoples who are making, or have made in recent years, the most progress in America today are, I suspect, the Jews, the Negroes, and the Japanese. There is, of course, no comparison to be made between the Jew, the Japanese, and the Negro as to their racial competence. Of all the immigrant peoples in the United States, the Jews are the most able and the most progressive; the Negro, on the other hand, is just emerging, and is still a little afraid of the consequences of his newly acquired race-consciousness.

What is alike in the case of the Jew, the Negro, and the Japanese is that their conflict with America has been grave enough to create in each a new sense of racial identity, and to give the sort of solidarity that grows out of a common cause. It is the existence in a people of the sense of a cause which finally determines their group efficiency.

In some sense these communities in which our immigrants live their smaller lives may be regarded as models for our own. We are seeking to do, through the medium of our local community organizations, such things as will get attention and interest for the little world of the locality. We are encouraging a new parochialism, seeking to initiate a movement that will run counter to the current romanticism with its eye always on the horizon, one which will recognize limits and work within them.

Our problem is to encourage men to seek God in their own village and to see the social problem in their own neighborhood. These immigrant communities deserve further study.

CHAPTER 4

THE CITY AS A SOCIAL LABORATORY

I. HUMAN NATURE AND THE CITY

THE city has been described as the natural habitat of civilized man. It is in the city that man developed philosophy and science, and became not merely a rational but a sophisticated animal. This means, for one thing, that it is in the urban environment—in a world which man himself has made—that mankind first achieved an intellectual life and acquired those characteristics which most distinguish him from the lower animals and from primitive man. For the city and the urban environment represent man's most consistent and, on the whole, his most successful attempt to remake the world he lives in more after his heart's desire. But if the city is the world which man created, it is the world in which he is henceforth condemned to live. Thus, indirectly, and without any clear sense of the nature of his task, in making the city man has remade himself.

It is in some such sense and in some such connection as this that we may think of the city as a social laboratory.

As a matter of fact civilization and social progress have assumed in our modern cities something of the character of a controlled experiment. Progress tends to assume that character, for example, wherever fact-finding precedes legislation and reforms are conducted

Reprinted by permission of the publisher from T. V. Smith and L. White (Eds.) *Chicago: An Experiment in Social Science Research* (Chicago: University of Chicago Press, 1929), pp. 1-19.

by experts rather than by amateurs. Social surveys and bureaus of municipal research are evidences of a form of politics that has become empirical rather than doctrinaire.

The social problem is fundamentally a city problem. It is the problem of achieving in the freedom of the city a social order and a social control equivalent to that which grew up naturally in the family, the clan, and the tribe.

Civilized man is, so to speak, a late arrival. Viewed in the long perspective of history the appearance of the city and of city life are recent events. Man grew up and acquired most of his native and inheritable traits in an environment in which he lived much as the lower animals live, in direct dependence upon the natural world. In the turmoil of changes which has come with the evolution of city and civil life he has not been able to adapt himself fundamentally and biologically to his new environment.

As long as man lived within the limits of the tribe, custom and tradition provided for all the ordinary exigencies of life and the authority of natural leaders was sufficient to meet the recurrent crises of a relatively stable existence. But the possibilities of human life widened with the rise of the urban community. With the new freedom and the broader division of labor, which the new social order introduced, the city became the center and the focus of social changes that have steadily grown in extent and complexity until every metropolitan city is now a local center of a world-economy, and of a civilization in which local and tribal cultures now in process of fusion will presently disappear altogether.

In a city where custom has been superseded by public opinion and positive law, man has been compelled to live by his wits rather than by his instinct or tradition. The result is the emergence of the individual man as a unit of thought and action.

The peasant who comes to the city to work and live is, to be sure, emancipated from the control of ancestral custom, but at the same time he is no longer backed by the collective wisdom of the peasant community. He is on his own. The case of the peasant is typical. Everyone is more or less on his own in a city. The consequence is that man, translated to the city, has become a problem to himself and to society in a way and to an extent that he never was before.

The older order, based as it was on custom and tradition, was absolute and sacred. It had, besides, something of the character of nature itself; it had grown up, and men took it as they found it, like the climate and the weather, as part of the natural order of things. The new social order, on the other hand, is more or less of an artificial creation, an artifact. It is neither absolute nor sacred, but pragmatic and experimental. Under the influence of a pragmatic point of view education has ceased to be a form of social ritual merely; politics has become empirical; religion is now a quest rather than a tradition, something to be sought rather than to be transmitted.

Natural science came into existence in an effort of man to obtain control over external and physical nature. Social science is now seeking, by the same methods of disinterested observation and research, to give man control over himself. As it is in the city that the political problem, that is, the problem of social control, has arisen, so it is in the city that the problem must be studied.

II. THE FIRST LOCAL STUDIES

It is the detailed and local studies of man in his habitat and under the conditions in which he actually lives, that have contributed most to give the social sciences that realistic and objective character which they have assumed in recent years.

The first of these local studies were, as might be expected, practical rather than theoretic. They were the studies of health and housing; studies of poverty and crime. They became the basis for a whole series of reforms: model tenements, playgrounds, vital statistics. They created a new and romantic interest in the slum. A new literature grew up, telling us how the other half lived, giving us at the same time a new sense of the fact that poor people and immigrants were human like ourselves.

Social settlements, established about near the close of the nineteenth century in England and America, became outposts for observation and for intimate studies of social conditions in regions of the city that up to that time had remained *terra incognita*, except for those pioneer students of urban sociology—politicians and the police. *Hull House Maps and Papers*, published by Jane Addams and her associates, in Chicago, 1895, and *The City Wilderness*, and *Americans in Process*, by Robert Woods, of the South End House, Boston, a few years later, were in the nature of an exploration and recognizance, laying the ground for the more systematic and detailed studies which followed. Notable among these were the series of in-

quiries into housing conditions in Chicago under the direction of
Sophonisba P. Breckinridge and Edith Abbott begun in 1908 at the
request of the chief sanitary inspector of Chicago and under the
auspices of the department of social investigation (Russell Sage
Foundation) of the Chicago School of Civics and Philanthropy.
Early studies included the housing of non-family groups of men;
families in furnished rooms; the Twenty-ninth Ward back of the
yards; the West Side revisited; South Chicago at the gates of the
steel mills; the problem of the Negro; two Italian districts; among
the Slovaks in the Twentieth Ward; Lithuanians in the Fourth
Ward; Greeks and Italians in the neighborhood of Hull House.[1]

Meanwhile Charles Booth had begun, some time about 1888, his
epoch-making study of life and labor in London,[2] followed in 1901
by Rountree's more minute study of poverty in New York.[3] These
were case studies on a grand scale. The thing that characterized
them was a determined and, as it seemed, somewhat pedantic effort
to reduce the descriptive and impressionistic statements of investi-
gators and observers to the more precise and general formulations
of a statistical statement. Booth said: [4]

No one can go, as I have done, over the description of the inhabitants of street after street in this huge district (East London), taken house
by house and family by family—full as it is of picturesque details noted
down from the lips of the visitor to whose mind they have been recalled
by the open pages of their schedules—and doubt the genuine character of
the information and its truth. Of the wealth of my material I have no
doubt. I am indeed embarrassed by its mass and by my resolution to
make use of no fact that I cannot give a quantitative value. The materials for sensational stories lie plentifully in every book of our notes; but,
even if I had the skill to use my material in this way—that gift of the
imagination which is called "realistic"—I should not wish to use it here.
There is struggling poverty, there is destitution, there is hunger, drunk-
enness, brutality and crime; no one doubts that it is so. My object has
been to attempt to show the numerical relation which poverty, misery
and depravity bear to regular earnings and comparative comfort, and to
describe the general conditions under which each class lives.

---

[1] Series of articles on Chicago housing conditions in the *American Journal
of Sociology*, XVI (1910-11), 145-70; 289-308; 433-68; XVII (1911-12), 1-34;
145-76; XVIII (1912-13), 241-57; 509-42; XX (1914-15), 145-69, 289-312; XXI
(1915-16), 285-316.

[2] Charles Booth, *Life and Labor of the People of London*. 9 vols. (London,
1892), p. 97.

[3] B. Seebohm Rountree, *Poverty: A Study of Town Life* (London, 1901).

[4] Booth, *op. cit.*, I, 5-6.

It was not, however, Booth's statistics, but his realistic descriptions of the actual life of the occupational classes—the conditions under which they lived and labored, their passions, pastimes, domestic tragedies, and their life-philosophies with which each class met the crises peculiar to it—which made these studies a memorable and a permanent contribution to our knowledge of human nature and of society. What we have then, finally, in these volumes, is a minute and painstaking account of the phase of modern civilization at the end of the nineteenth century, as manifested in the life of the London laborer. These volumes were a sociological study; they have become a historical document.

The thing which gave the greatest impetus to local studies in the United States was the establishment of the Sage Foundation in 1906, and the publication in the period from 1909 to 1914 of the findings of the Pittsburgh Survey. Pittsburgh was chosen by Paul U. Kellogg and his collaborators for investigation because it was regarded as a particularly flagrant illustration of the working out of forces and tendencies that had their origin in the rapidly expanding industrial life of America. Pittsburgh was conspicuously and exclusively an industrial city. America was in process of industrial transformation. Pittsburgh offered itself as clinical material for a study of American civilization. It seemed possible to exhibit, in a single city, just how the industrial organization of that time affected the personal and cultural life of a people. This was the purpose for which the Survey was undertaken.

The Pittsburgh Survey was timely. It appeared at a moment when, in every part of the United States, thoughtful people were seeking light upon problems that no longer yielded to the traditional technique embodied in the forms and traditions of party politics. It was a time when reformers were seeking to keep reforms out of politics, that is, out of party politics. The Pittsburgh Survey offered a new method for political education and collective action in local affairs, a method that did not raise party issues and did not involve anything so revolutionary as a change in the control of local government.

Social surveys now came into vogue, and local studies of a sort were undertaken in every part of the country. The wide range of interests with which they thought to deal is indicated by the subject matter of some of the more important of them. *The Springfield Survey,* which undertook to cover the whole field of social politics: public health, education, social service in all its various aspects; [5] the *Survey of Criminal Justice in Cleveland*, published in 1922, and the study of race relations in Chicago after the race riot, published in the same year under the title of *The Negro in Chicago*, are examples.

These surveys have, as regional studies invariably do, the characteristics of local and contemporary history. They emphasize what is unique and individual in the situations investigated. But they are at the same time case studies. Conditions in one city are described in terms that make them comparable to conditions in other cities. They do not yield generalizations of wide or general validity, but they have furnished a body of materials that raise issues and suggest hypotheses which can eventually be investigated statistically and stated in quantitative terms.

III. THE URBAN COMMUNITY

In all, or most, of these investigations there is implicit the notion that the urban community, in its growth and organization, represents a complex of tendencies and events that can be described conceptually, and made the object of independent study. There is implicit in all these studies the notion that the city is a thing with a characteristic organization and a typical life-history, and that individual cities are enough alike so that what one learns about one city may, within limits, be assumed to be true of others.

This notion has been the central theme of a series of special studies of the Chicago Urban Community, some of which have already been published, others of which are still in progress.[6] Among these, three, *The Hobo*, by Nels Anderson, *The Ghetto*, by Louis Wirth, and *The Gold Coast and the Slum*, by Harvey W. Zorbaugh, deal each with one of the so-called natural areas of the city. *The Hobo: A Study of the Homeless Man* is unique in so far as it investigates the casual laborer in his habitat, that is to say in the region of the city where the interests and habits of the casual laborer have been, so to speak, institutionalized. *The Ghetto*, on the other hand, is a study of the Jewish quarter, but it is at the same time the natural history of an institution of Jewish life, an institution that

[5] *The Springfield Survey; A Study of Social Conditions in an American City*. Directed by Shelby M. Harrison. 3 vols. (New York: Russell Sage Foundation, 1918-20).

[6] Robert E. Park, E. W. Burgess, *et al.*, *The City* (Chicago, 1925).

grew up and flourished in the Middle Ages but has persisted in some fashion down to the present day. It has persisted, however, because it performed a social function, making it possible for two unassimilated peoples to live together, participating in a single economy, but preserving, at the same time, each its own racial and cultural integrity. *The Gold Coast and the Slum,* finally, is a study of the Lower North Side, which is not so much a natural area, as a congeries of natural areas, including, as it does, "Little Sicily," "The Gold Coast," and an extensive region of rooming-houses between.[7]

A region is called "a natural area" because it comes into existence without design, and performs a function, though the function, as in the case of the slum, may be contrary to anybody's desire. It is a natural area because it has a natural history. The existence of these natural areas, each with its characteristic function, is some indication of the sort of thing the city turns out upon analysis to be—not as has been suggested earlier, an artifact merely, but in some sense, and to some degree, an organism.

The city is, in fact, a constellation of natural areas, each with its own characteristic milieu, and each performing its specific function in the urban economy as a whole. The relation of the different natural areas of the city to one another is typified in the relation of the city and its suburbs. These suburbs are, apparently, mere extensions of the urban community. Every suburb, pushing outward into the open country, tends to have a character which distinguishes it from every other. The metropolis is, it seems, a great sifting and sorting mechanism, which, in ways that are not yet wholly understood, infallibly selects out of the population as a whole the individuals best suited to live in a particular region and a particular milieu. The larger the city, the more numerous and the more completely characterized its suburbs will be. The city grows by expansion, but it gets its character by the selection and segregation of its population, so that every individual finds, eventually, either the place where he can, or the place where he must, live.[8]

Recent studies in Chicago have revealed to what an extraordinary extent this segregation may go. There are regions in Chicago where there are almost no children; regions where half the boys of

---

[7] See *The Gold Coast and the Slum,* pp. 126 and 133 for maps showing the local communities of Chicago.

[8] See the article by E. W. Burgess, "The Growth of the City," in R. E. Park, *et al., The City,* pp. 47-62.

juvenile-court age are recorded, at least once in the course of a year, as delinquents,[9] other regions where there are no divorces, and still others in which the percentage of divorces and desertions is larger, with one exception, than that of any other political unit in the United States.[10]

The proportion of age and sex groups shows extraordinary variations in different parts of the city, and these variations are dependable indices of other cultural and character differences in the population.

It does not follow, from what has been said, that the populations in the different natural areas of the city can be described as homogeneous. People live together on the whole, not because they are alike, but because they are useful to one another. This is particularly true of great cities, where social distances are maintained in spite of geographical proximity, and where every community is likely to be composed of people who live together in relations that can best be described as symbiotic rather than social.

On the other hand, every community is to some degree an independent cultural unit, has its own standards, its own conception of what is proper, decent, and worthy of respect. As individuals rise or sink in the struggle for status in the community they invariably move from one region to another; go up to the Gold Coast, or down to the slum, or perhaps occupy a tolerable position somewhere between the two. In any case, they learn to accommodate themselves more or less completely to the conditions and the code of the area into which they move. The case records of social agencies and institutions make it possible to follow the migrations of individuals and families and learn what has happened to them. It is often possible to carry these studies of individuals and families farther and to get information and insight in regard to their subjective experiences, their attitudes and states of mind, outlook on life, and above all their changing conceptions of themselves incident to their movements from one milieu to another. The numerous life-histories of immigrants that have been published in recent years furnish materials of this sort.

The more we understand the attitudes and personal histories of individuals, the more we can know the community in which these

---

[9] See Clifford R. Shaw, *Delinquency and Crime Areas of Chicago* (Chicago, 1929).

[10] Ernest R. Mowrer, *Family Disorganization*, pp. 116-23.

individuals live. On the other hand, the more knowledge we have of the milieu in which the individual lives, or has lived, the more intelligible his behavior becomes. This is true, because while temperament is inherited, character and habit are formed under the influence of environment.

As a matter of fact, most of our ordinary behavior problems are actually solved, if solved at all, by transferring the individual from an environment in which he behaves badly to one in which he behaves well. Here, again, social science has achieved something that approaches in character a laboratory experiment. For the purpose of these experiments the city, with its natural regions, becomes a "frame of reference," i.e., a device for controlling our observations of social conditions in their relation to human behavior.

IV. THE INDIVIDUAL

It is due to the intrinsic nature of society and of social relations that we ordinarily find our social problems embodied in the persons and in the behavior of individuals. It is because social problems so frequently terminate in problems of individual behavior and because social relations are finally and fundamentally personal relations that the attitude and behavior of individuals are the chief sources of our knowledge of society.

The city always has been a prolific source of clinical material for the study of human nature because it has always been the source and center of social change. In a perfectly stable society where man has achieved a complete biological and social equilibrium, social problems are not likely to arise, and the anxieties, mental conflicts, and ambitions which stimulate the energies of civilized man, and incidentally make him a problem to himself and to society, are lacking.

It was with what Simmel calls inner enemies—the poor, the criminal, and the insane—that personality studies seem to have had their origin. It is, however, within comparatively recent years that poverty and delinquency have come to be reckoned along with insanity as personality and behavior problems. At the present time this is so far true that social service has come to be recognized as a branch of medicine, and the so-called psychiatric social worker has come to replace, or at least supplement, the work of the friendly visitor. The probation officer, visiting teacher, and the public playground director have all achieved a new professional status as the notion has gained recognition that social problems are fundamentally behavior problems.

A new impetus was given to the study of personality problems with the organization in 1899 in Chicago of the first juvenile court of the United States. Juvenile courts became at once, as far as was practicable under the circumstances under which they came into existence, behavior clinics. Putting the delinquent on probation was an invitation to him to participate in an experiment, under the direction of a probation officer, that had as its aim his own rehabilitation.

It was through the establishment of the Juvenile Psychopathic Institute [11] in connection with the Juvenile Court of Chicago that Healy began those systematic studies upon which that notable book, *The Individual Delinquent*, published in 1915, was based. It was followed by similar studies, under the Judge Baker Foundation, in Boston, and by the establishment of other institutes for child study and so-called behavior clinics in every part of the country, notably, the Child Welfare Research Station at the University of Iowa, the Institute of Child Welfare at the University of Minnesota, the Institute for Child Welfare Research at Teachers College, New York City, the Institute for Child Guidance, and locally supported child-guidance clinics established through demonstrations of the Commonwealth Fund Program for the Prevention of Delinquency in St. Louis, Dallas, Los Angeles, Minneapolis, St. Paul, Cleveland, and Philadelphia.[12]

The study of juvenile delinquency and of behavior problems in general was established on a firm basis in Chicago with the organization in May, 1926, by Dr. Herman M. Adler of the Behavior Research Fund. Dr. Adler has brought together a notable group of students and experts and has set up an administrative machinery for making accurate scientific records, both psychiatric and social, which as they have accumulated have created a fund of fact and information that is now being subjected to elaborate statistical analyses which are yielding surprising and important results.

Studies of the Institute of Juvenile Research and of the Behavior Research Fund are in certain respects unique. They are at once psychiatric and social studies, i.e., studies not merely of the individual and his behavior but of the environment and of the situation to

---

[11] Now the Institute for Juvenile Research.

[12] For a review and analysis of the child-study movement see W. I. Thomas and Dorothy S. Thomas, *The Child in America* (New York, 1928).

which the behavior is a response. This realizes, in the form of a definite program, a conception which has been the subject of several conferences between the psychiatrists and representatives of the other social sciences, seeking to define the relation of psychiatric and social studies and to determine the rôle which psychiatry is likely to play in co-operation with the social sciences in the investigation and solution of social problems.

There is not now, if there ever was, any question that the individual's conception of himself, the rôle which he plays in any society, and the character which he eventually acquires are very largely determined by the associations which he makes and, in general, by the world in which he lives. The city is a complex of such worlds—worlds which touch but never completely penetrate.

The differences between urban areas in respect to the type and character of the social life which they support is undoubtedly as great as the standards of living that they maintain, or the price of land on which they are situated. One of the important series of local studies which the University of Chicago has undertaken is that which involves a delimitation and characterization of all the important areas of the city. This study is based on the assumption that more complete knowledge of the localities and of the peoples of the city will throw a new light upon the extraordinary variation, in the different areas of the city in the amount and extent of desertion, divorce, delinquency, crime, and other evidences of social disorganization. In doing this it will be of service to every social agency that is seeking to deal directly or indirectly with these problems. But in determining with more definiteness the conditions under which social experiments are actually being carried on, it will make the city in some more real sense than it has been hitherto a social laboratory.

V. INSTITUTIONS

The city has been made the subject of investigation from many different points of view. There is already a considerable literature on the geography of the city, and there is a vast body of research concerning the city as a physical object, including studies of housing, city planning, and municipal engineering. N. S. B. Gras, in his *Introduction to Economic History*, has made the city the central theme in the history of an economy that has evolved through the stages of village, town, and city to the metropolitan economy of the present day. As a matter of fact economic history assumes a new significance when it is written from the ecological and regional point of view, and when the city, with its market place, is conceived as the focal center of an area of ever widening boundaries over which it is constantly extending and consolidating its dominance and control.

The political and administrative problems of cities have come to occupy a place in political science that has steadily increased in importance as cities have increased in population, in influence, and in complexity.

The urban community is, finally, because it is now as it has always been the melting pot of races and cultures, the region in which new institutions emerge, as earlier ones decline, are modified, and disappear.

The family, in its origin at least, is probably not an institution. It is rather the first and most primitive form of society—a form which has been preserved, although continually modified under all the changing circumstances of man's eventful career. The family has, apparently, formed the basic pattern for every type of civilization except our own. Occidental civilization is based on the city, on the *polis*, as the Greeks called it, and is political rather than familial in origin. It was in the city states of Greece and Rome that society organized on kinship, custom, and the family was superseded by a society based on civil rights and a political organization.

The family is now in process of change and disintegration in every part of the civilized world, including the regions where it has persisted longest in its original form, Japan and China. Changes in the family, however, are taking place more rapidly in cities than elsewhere. Everything that is characteristic of city life, a mobile population, a wide division of labor, and the multiplication of municipal institutions and social conveniences of all sorts have contributed to bring about these changes. Schools, hospitals, and all the numerous agencies for personal service which have taken over, one by one, the functions once performed by the home and in the family have contributed indirectly to undermine that ancient institution and diminish its social importance.

As it is in the urban environment that the older forms of the family have declined, so it is in the city that most of the experiments in new forms of family life are taking place. That is why the institution of the family can be studied to the best advantage in cities rather than elsewhere.

The city and the conditions of life that it imposes have greatly tended to the secularization of all aspects of social life, and this has had profound effect upon the organization of the church. Numerous local studies of city and rural churches have been made in recent years, but as yet no studies have been made to show the extent of changes which involve the structure and function of the church as a social institution.

There is, however, no doubt but that changes are taking place and that as the social sciences develop an interest in and methods for the study of civilized, as they have for primitive, man the changes taking place in contemporary religious institutions will assume an importance that they do not now seem to have.

In recent years, particularly in Chicago, under the inspiration and initiative of Professor Charles E. Merriam, a beginning has been made looking to more realistic studies of the actual workings of the political process as it takes place under the conditions of modern city life.[13]

The political process, broadly conceived, includes much more than the formulation of laws by legislatures and their interpretation by the courts. It includes a whole cycle of events that begins with some sort of general unrest, in which political issues arise, and concludes with the general acceptance into the mores and habits of the community of a new rule of conduct, and—to use an expression which W. I. Thomas has made familiar—a new definition of the situation.

The political process includes public discussion and a definition of issues; the formation and expression of public opinion; the election of legislators; the framing and enactment of legislation; the interpretation and enforcement of the law, and, finally, the general acceptance of and acquiescence in the enforcement of the law by the community. In this way the law eventually passes over into custom and becomes fixed in the habits of the community. The political process covers all the operations of government; and since society is essentially an organization for social control, it involves finally every aspect of social life.

---

[13] See Charles E. Merriam, *New Aspects of Politics* (Chicago, 1925); *Four American Party Leaders* (New York, 1926); *Chicago: A More Intimate View of Urban Politics* (New York, 1929).

The organization in New York City, Chicago, and elsewhere, of bureaus of municipal research and the more recent studies in Cleveland and St. Louis of the administration of criminal justice indicate the direction and progress of research in this field.

The studies of the political science group at the University of Chicago are indicative not only of the trend toward a more realistic perception of the political process but of the attempt to introduce scientific methods into the description and prediction of political behavior, as in the research projects already published of *Non-Voting* by Charles E. Merriam and Harold F. Gosnell, *Getting Out the Vote* by H. F. Gosnell, *The Chicago Primary of 1926: A Study in Election Methods* by Carroll H. Wooddy, *Carter H. Harrison I: A Study in Political Leadership* by C. O. Johnson, and *The City Manager* by Leonard D. White.

Sumner says that there are two kinds of institutions, (1) those which grow, and (2) those which are enacted. But institutions are not merely enacted. Rather, they are discovered and invented. The fact seems to be that institutions always grow, but they grow, ordinarily, by the addition and summation of specific inventions.[14]

One thing that makes the city a peculiarly advantageous place in which to study institutions and social life generally is the fact that under the conditions of urban life institutions grow rapidly. They grow under our very eyes, and the processes by which they grow are open to observation and so, eventually, to experimentation.

Another thing that makes the city an advantageous place to study social life and gives it the character of a social laboratory is the fact that in the city every characteristic of human nature is not only visible but is magnified.

In the freedom of the city every individual, no matter how eccentric, finds somewhere an environment in which he can expand and bring what is peculiar in his nature to some sort of expression. A smaller community sometimes tolerates eccentricity, but the city often rewards it. Certainly one of the attractions of a city is that somewhere every type of individual—the criminal and beggar, as well as the man of genius—may find congenial company and the vice or the talent which was suppressed in the more intimate circle of the family or in the narrow limits of a small community, discovers here a moral climate in which it flourishes.

---

[14] Sumner, *Folkways*, pp. 48-50.

The result is that in the city all the secret ambitions and all the suppressed desires find somewhere an expression. The city magnifies, spreads out, and advertises human nature in all its various manifestations. It is this that makes the city interesting, even fascinating. It is this, however, that makes it of all places the one in which to discover the secrets of human hearts, and to study human nature and society.

CHAPTER 5

Local Communities in the Metropolis

ONE of the pleasures of travel, says Von Ogden Vogt, is that of "discovering communities that are *descript* rather than nondescript." He mentions Oberammergau, Bangkok, Oxford, and adds "or any other place where there has been some sustained attempt to describe all things and set forth the common views in laws, customs, and all the arts of life from house building to worship." A descript community is "a place of unity and charm." A nondescript community is one that lacks these qualities. A nondescript community may be interesting, of course, but it will not be restful, and will not be satisfying merely as an object of contemplation.

The community with which this volume is concerned is nondescript; it is a place of unusual interest, but it has neither the unity nor the charm of a place in which the common view is set forth "in laws, customs, and all the arts of life." There are few customs that are common at once to the "Gold Coast" and to "Little Sicily," and there is certainly no common view which holds the cosmopolitan population of this whole region together in any common purpose. Furthermore, the laws which prevail are not a communal product, and there is no organized public opinion which supports and contributes to their enforcement. In fact, it is doubtful whether, in any proper sense of the word, the "Lower North Side" can be called a community at all. It is a region; one of the characteristic

Reprinted by permission of the publisher from Harvey W. Zorbaugh, *The Gold Coast and the Slum* (Chicago: University of Chicago Press, 1929), pp. vii-x, in which it appeared as the "Introduction."

regions of a metropolitan city, remarkable for the number and kinds of people huddled and crowded together in physical proximity, without the opportunity and, apparently, with very little desire for the intimacies and the mutual understanding and comprehension which ordinarily insure a common view and make collective action possible. It is, however, just this "nondescript" situation, so lacking in "unity and charm," that gives this region its peculiar interest. It is nondescript because it is in process of evolution. It is typically an area of transition, the character of its populations and the problems which it presents are at once a reflection and a consequence of the conditions which this period of transition imposes.

What is true of the region is characteristic of most of the very different classes and kinds of people that inhabit it. From the Gold Coast on the lake front to Little Sicily on the river, they are all in transition. Everywhere the old order is passing, but the new order has not arrived. Everything is loose and free, but everything is problematic.

This is particularly true of the so-called rooming-house area, which occupies the center of the region. Into this area all the young and adventurous people, who come to the city to seek their fortunes, tend to drift. Presently they will find their places somewhere in the broad cadre of occupations which the great city offers them. In this way they will become incorporated into the permanent economic and social order about them. In the meantime they are at large, and in transition. In the rooming-house area there is apparently a larger number of young women than of young men. The Lower North Side is for young women in particular, a kind of Latin Quarter, where students of art and music find places to live in close proximity to the studios. It is this region that supports most of the little theaters, the smart book stores, and the bohemian and radical clubs. Here is Bohemia, which is itself a place of transition, a place in which life is adventurous, to be sure, but often very lonely.

Every great city has its bohemias and its hobohemias; its gold coast and little Sicilies; its rooming-house areas and its slums. In Chicago, and on the Lower North Side, they are in close physical proximity to one another. This gives one an interesting illustration of the situation in which the physical distances and the social distances do not coincide; a situation in which people who live side by side are not, and—because of the divergence of their interests and their heritages—cannot, even with the best of good will, become neighbors.

It is this situation which constitutes the specific problem and the central theme of this study. Our political system is founded upon the conviction that people who live in the same locality have common interests, and that they can therefore be relied upon to act together for their common welfare. This assumption, as it turns out, is not valid for large cities. The difficulty of maintaining in the city the intimate contacts which in the small town insured the existence of a common purpose and made concerted action possible is certainly very great. Particularly is this true of those parts of the city where people live in hotels or lodging houses, where few people own their homes and most people are transient dwellers. Under such circumstances, all the traditional forms of local government fail or break down altogether. The fact that there exists on the Lower North Side a community council which recognizes this problem and has sought to solve it, is itself an evidence of the conditions it seeks to remedy. It was, by the way, this community council and its problems which furnished the original motive for this study.

Perhaps I should add that this volume is not a solution; it is a definition of the problem merely. The statement which it offers has, at any rate, laid the foundation for further study and experiment. Furthermore, it offers an example of a kind of investigation of urban life which is at least comparable with the studies that anthropologists have made of the cultures of primitive peoples. It is upon studies of this general character, I am convinced, that we must base our programs for the reorganization of our own political and collective life.

CHAPTER 6

THE MIND OF THE HOBO: REFLECTIONS UPON THE RELATION BETWEEN MENTALITY AND LOCOMOTION

IN the evolutionary hierarchy, as Herbert Spencer has sketched it for us, the animal series occupied a higher position than that of the plants. But in spite of all the progress represented in the long march from the amoeba to man, it is still true that the human creature is a good deal of a vegetable. This is evident in the invincible attachment of mankind to localities and places; in man's, and particularly woman's, inveterate and irrational ambition to have a home—some cave or hut or tenement—in which to live and vegetate; some secure hole or corner from which to come forth in the morning and return to at night.

As long as man is thus attached to the earth and to places on the earth, as long as nostalgia and plain homesickness hold him and draw him inevitably back to the haunts and places he knows best, he will never fully realize that other characteristic ambition of mankind, namely, to move freely and untrammeled over the surface of mundane things, and to live, like pure spirit, in his mind and in his imagination alone.

I mention these things merely to emphasize a single point,

Reprinted by permission of the publisher from R. E. Park, E. W. Burgess and R. D. McKenzie, *The City* (Chicago: University of Chicago Press, 1925), pp. 156-160.

namely, mind is an incident of locomotion. The first and most convincing indication of mind is not motion merely, but, as I have said, locomotion. The plants don't locomote, don't move through space; they respond more or less to stimulation, even though they have no nerves, but they do not move through space, certainly not of their own motion. And when they do move, they have no goal, no destination, and that is because they have no imagination.

Now it is characteristic of animals that they can and do change their spots. The ability to do this implies that they are able not merely to wag a tail or move a limb, but that they are able to co-ordinate and mobilize the whole organism in the execution of a single act. Mind, as we ordinarily understand it, is an organ of control. It does not so much initiate new movements as co-ordinate impulses, and so mobilize the organism for action; for mind, in its substantive aspect, is just our disposition to act; our instincts and attitudes, in other words.

Mental activity begins on the periphery, with stimuli which are antecedent to, but ultimately discharged in, actions. But mind in the transitive, verbal aspect is a process by which, as we say, we "make up our minds" or change them; that is to say, it is a process by which we define the direction in which we are going to move, and locate in imagination the goal that we intend to seek.

Plants carry on, apparently, all the processes of metabolism which are characteristic of animals—these are, in fact, what we mean by the vegetative processes—but they do not go anywhere. If the plants have minds, as some people assume they do, they must be of that brooding, vegetative sort characteristic of those mystics who, quite forgetful of the active world, are absorbed in the contemplation of their own inner processes. But the characteristic of the animal, and of the higher types of animal—everything above the oyster, in fact—is that they are made for locomotion and for action. Furthermore, it is in the processes of locomotion—involving, as they do, change of scene and change of location—that mankind is enabled to develop just those mental aptitudes most characteristic of man, namely, the aptitude and habit of abstract thought.

It is in locomotion, also, that the peculiar type of organization that we call "social" develops. The characteristic of a social organism—if we may call it an organism—is the fact that it is made up of individuals capable of independent locomotion. If society were, as some individuals have sought to conceive it, an organism in the biological sense—if it were made up of little cells all neatly and safely inclosed in an outer integument, or skin, in which all cells were so controlled and protected that no single cell could by any chance have any adventures or new experience of its own—there would be no need for men in society to have minds, for it is not because men are alike that they are social, but because they are different. They are moved to act by individual purposes, but in doing so they realize a common end. Their impulses are private, but actions are public.

In view of all this we may well ask ourselves what, if anything, is the matter with the hobo's mind. Why is it that with all the variety of his experiences he still has so many dull days? Why, with so much leisure, has he so little philosophy? Why, with so wide an acquaintance with regions, with men, and with cities, with life in the open road and in the slums, has he been able to contribute so little to our actual knowledge of life?

We need not even pause for a reply. The trouble with the hobo mind is not lack of experience, but lack of a vocation. The hobo is, to be sure, always on the move, but he has no destination, and naturally he never arrives. Wanderlust, which is the most elementary expression of the romantic temperament and the romantic interest in life, has assumed for him, as for so many others, the character of a vice. He has gained his freedom, but he has lost his direction. Locomotion and change of scene have had for him no ulterior significance. It is locomotion for its own sake. Restlessness and the impulse to escape from the routine of ordinary life, which in the case of others frequently marks the beginning of some new enterprise, spends itself for him in movements that are expressive merely. The hobo seeks change solely for the sake of change; it is a habit, and, like the drug habit, moves in a vicious circle. The more he wanders, the more he must. It is merely putting the matter in an another way to say that the trouble with the hobo, as Nels Anderson has pointed out in his recent volume, *The Hobo*, is that he is an individualist. He has sacrificed the human need of association and organization to a romantic passion for individual freedom. Society is, to be sure, made up of independent, locomoting individuals. It is this fact of locomotion, as I have said, that defines the very nature of society. But in order that there may be permanence and progress in society the individuals who compose it must be located; they must be located, for one thing, in order to maintain communication, for it is only through communication that the moving equilibrium which we call society can be maintained.

All forms of association among human beings rest finally upon locality and local association. The extraordinary means of communication that characterize modern society—the newspaper, the radio, and the telephone—are merely devices for preserving this permanence of location and of function in the social group, in connection with the greatest possible mobility and freedom of its members.

The hobo, who begins his career by breaking the local ties that bound him to his family and his neighborhood, has ended by breaking all other associations. He is not only a "homeless man," but a man without a cause and without a country; and this emphasizes the significance, however futile, of the efforts of men like James Eads. How to establish hobo colleges in different parts of the country, places where hobos can meet to exchange experiences, to discuss their problems, and all of the problems of society; places, also, where they can maintain some sort of corporate existence and meet and exchange views with the rest of the world on a basis of something like equality and with some hope of understanding.

The same thing may be said of the Industrial Workers of the World, the only labor organization that has persistently sought and to some extent succeeded in organizing the unorganizable element among laboring men, namely, the seasonal and casual laborers. The tendency of their efforts to organize the hobo in his own interest has been, so far as they have been successful, to give him what he needed most, namely, a group-consciousness, a cause, and a recognized position in society.

If they have failed, it is due in part to the fact that so large a part of modern industry is organized in a way which tends inevitably to the casualization of labor. It is due, in part, to the fact that the hobo, in so far as he is a congenital type, finds in casual and seasonal labor a kind of occupation congenial to his temperament, for the hobo is the bohemian in the ranks of common labor. He has the artistic temperament. Aside from the indispensable labor of his hands, the only important contribution which he has made to the permanent common fund of our experience which we call our culture has been his poetry. It is an interesting fact, however, that some of the best of this poetry has been produced in jail. During these periods of enforced quietude, when he could no longer move,

the hobo has vented his habitual restlessness in songs, songs of pro-
test, the hymns of the rebllious I.W.W., tragic little ballads describing some of the hardships and tragedies of life on the long, gray
road.

There have been many hobo poets. The most eminent of them,
Walt Whitman, reflected the restlessness and rebelliousness and
individualism of the hobo mind not only in the content but in the
very formlessness of his verse.

What do you suppose will satisfy the soul, except to walk free and
own no superior?

Nothing could better express the spirit of the old frontier which,
more than any other feature in American life, has served to characterize American institutions and American mores. The hobo is, in
fact, merely a belated frontiersman, a frontiersman at a time and in
a place when the frontier is passing or no longer exists.

CHAPTER 7

THE HABITAT OF THE GANG

THE title of this book does not quite describe it. It is a study of the gang, to be sure, but it is at the same time a study of "gangland"; that is to say, a study of the gang and its habitat, and in this case the habitat is a city slum.

Gangs are not confined to cities, nor to the slums of cities. Every village has at least its boy gang, and in the village, as in the city, it is composed of those same foot-loose, prowling, and predacious adolescents who heard and hang together, after the manner of the undomesticated male everywhere. Gangs flourish on the frontier, and the predatory bands that infest the fringes of civilization exhibit, on the whole, the same characteristic traits displayed by the groups studied in this volume. The thirteen hundred gangs investigated in Chicago are typical of gangs elsewhere. Gangs are gangs, wherever they are found. They represent a specific type or variety of society, and one thing that is particularly interesting about them is the fact that they are, in respect to their organization, so elementary, and in respect to their origin, so spontaneous.

Formal society is always more or less conscious of the end for which it exists, and the organization through which this end is achieved is always more or less a product of design. But gangs grow like weeds, without consciousness of their aims, and without administrative machinery to achieve them. They are, in fact, so spontaneous in their origin, and so little conscious of the purposes for which they exist, that one is tempted to think of them as predeter-

Reprinted by permission of the publisher from Frederick M. Thrasher, *The Gang* (Chicago: University of Chicago Press, 1927), pp. ix-xii, in which it appeared as the "Editor's Preface."

mined, foreordained, and "instinctive," and so, quite independent of the environment in which they ordinarily are found.

Indeed, social life is so necessary and so fundamental to the existence of human nature that society has sometimes been conceived to be an innate trait of the individual man. This is so far true that human beings have at any rate shown themselves capable of creating a society out of the most unpromising materials. Children, abandoned to their own resources, find companionship in dolls, make friends with dogs and cats, and, if necessary, create imaginary personalities, with whom they are able to live on the very best of terms. Solitary persons, on the other hand, establish intimate and personal relationships with their physical environment and find "sermons in stones, books in running brooks."

It is therefore to a certain extent true that the society in which we live is predetermined and innate. We spin our social relations, somewhat as the spider spins its web, out of our own bodies.

On the other hand, the specific character of our society, the type, is always more or less determined by the sort of world, physical and social, in which we happen to live.

And so gangs, like most other forms of human association, need to be studied in their peculiar habitat. They spring up spontaneously, but only under favoring conditions and in a definite milieu. The instincts and tendencies that find expression in any specific form of association are no doubt fundamentally human, but it is only under specific conditions that they assume the forms and exhibit the traits that are characteristic of any existing type. And this is true of gangs. It is this that makes them worth studying; it is this that assures us that they are not incorrigible and that they can be controlled.

It is not only true that the habitat makes gangs, but what is of more practical importance, it is the habitat which determines whether or not their activities shall assume those perverse forms in which they become a menace to the community. Village gangs, because they are less hemmed about by physical structures and social inhibitions of an urban environment, ordinarily do not become a social problem, certainly not a problem of the dimensions and significance of those which constitute so obvious and so obdurate a feature of city life.

The gangs here studied are not a product of the city merely, but they are at the same time the product of a clearly defined and well-recognized area of the city, particularly of the modern American city. It is the slum, the city wilderness, as it has been called, which provides the city gang its natural habitat. The slum is a wide region, which includes various other characteristic areas, each inhabited by its own specific type. The slum is not simply the habitat of gangs, but it is the rendezvous of the hobo, and Hobohemia, already described by Nels Anderson, in an earlier volume of this series, is a minor division of the city slum.

The slum includes also the areas of first settlement to which the immigrants inevitably gravitate before they have found their places in the larger urban environment. The racial "ghettos," which now shelter and set apart from the rest of the community Negroes and Chinese as they once sheltered and segregated Jews, are invariably located in the slum. The Jewish ghetto still exists, but the slum, as far as the Jew is concerned, is at present only an area of first settlement. Negroes and Chinese, on the other hand, still find it difficult to live beyond the pale.

It is because this study of the gang is at the same time the study of an urban area and of a type of urban life, that it falls naturally within the series of "Studies in Urban Sociology."

CHAPTER 8

THE GHETTO

THE ghetto seems to have been originally a place in Venice, a quarter of the city in which the first Jewish settlement was located. It became, in the course of time, an institution recognized in custom and defined in law. It became, in short, not merely the place in which Jews lived, but the place in which they were compelled to live. The walls of that ghetto have long since crumbled, but the ghost of the ancient institution lingers. It is still a place of refuge for the masses of the Jewish people and still imposes upon them, for good and for ill, something of the ancient isolation.

Meanwhile other alien peoples have come among us who have sought, or had imposed upon them, the same sort of isolation. Our great cities turn out, upon examination, to be a mosaic of segregated peoples—differing in race, in culture, or merely in cult—each seeking to preserve its peculiar cultural forms and to maintain its individual and unique conceptions of life. Every one of these segregated groups inevitably seeks, in order to maintain the integrity of its own group life, to impose upon its member some kind of moral isolation. So far as segregation becomes for them a means to that end, every people and every cultural group may be said to create and maintain its own ghetto. In this way the ghetto becomes the physical symbol for that sort of moral isolation which the "assimilationists," so called, are seeking to break down.

It is in this sense that the word is used in this volume. "Ghetto," as it is here conceived, is no longer a term that is limited in its appli-

Reprinted by permission of the publisher from Louis Wirth, *The Ghetto* (Chicago: University of Chicago Press, 1928), pp. ix-xi, in which it appeared as the "Foreword."

cation to the Jewish people. It has come into use in recent times as a common noun—a term which applies to any segregated racial or cultural group. The ghetto, as it is here conceived, owes its existence, not to legal enactment, but to the fact that it meets a need and performs a social function. The ghetto is, in short, one of the so-called "natural areas" of the city.

The casual observer, looking over this vast complex, the modern metropolitan city, is likely to see it as a mere congeries of physical structures, institutions, and peoples contiguous in space, bound together in some sort of mechanical fashion, but in no sense a whole consisting of organically related parts. This impression finds an indirect expression in the familiar statement "God made the country, but man made the town." Nowhere else, in fact, is the order which exists so manifestly the order imposed by man's intelligence and design; nowhere else has man shown himself more completely the master of the world in which he lives.

On the other hand, nothing is more certain, as recent studies of the urban community have shown, than the fact that the city as it exists is very largely the product of tendencies of which we have as yet little knowledge and less control. Under the influence of these forces, and within the limitation which geography and historical accident impose, the city is steadily assuming a form that is not conventional merely, but typical. In short, the city is not merely an artifact, but an organism. Its growth is, fundamentally and as a whole, natural, i.e., uncontrolled and undesigned. The forms it tends to assume are those which represent and correspond to the functions that it is called upon to perform.

What have been called the "natural areas of the city" are simply those regions whose locations, character, and functions have been determined by the same forces which have determined the character and functions of the city as a whole. The ghetto is one of those natural areas. The historical ghetto, with which this study is mainly concerned, is merely the one most striking example of a type. It is in the history of the Jews, in the Diaspora, that we have access to a body of facts which exhibit in convincing detail the moral and cultural consequences of that isolation which the ghetto enforced; consequences that touch both those who live within and those who live without the pale. The history of the ghetto is, in large measure, the history, since the dispersion, of the Jewish people.

The ghetto has been the center of all that may be described as sectarian and provincial of Jewish life. It has put its imprint, not only upon the manners of the Jew, but upon his character. It is the interaction of this culture of the ghetto and that of the larger gentile community outside, involving the more or less complete participation of Jews in both worlds, that is the source of most that is problematic and enigmatic in the situation of the Jew of today, as of yesterday. And so it has turned out that this attempt to investigate, in its more fundamental and permanent aspects, one of the typical local areas of the Chicago urban community has led to the exploration of one of the most fundamental problems in sociology, and in doing this it has thrown a new light upon one of the puzzling and tragic situations in history.

CHAPTER 9

M AGIC, MENTALITY, AND CITY LIFE

I. MAGIC AND PRIMITIVE MENTALITY

FEW words of African origin have survived and found a permanent place in the popular speech of the English West Indies. One of these is "obeah." Of this word, J. Graham Cruickshank in a little pamphlet entitled *Black Talk* says:

> *Obeah*—which is Negro witchcraft, and whose worst aspect was the poisonous *idea* put into the mind of the subject—has gone under to a great extent. Extraordinary cases of it crop up now and again in the newspapers. It is the most difficult of all anthropological data on which to "draw" the old Negro. Burton gives an Old Calabar proverb: "Ubio nkpo ono onya" (They plant Obeah for him) and adds this note: " 'Ubio' means any medicine or charm put in the ground to cause sickness or death. It is manifestly the origin of the West Indian 'obeah.' We shall be the less surprised to hear that the word has traveled so far when told by Clarkson, in his *History of the Slave Trade*, that when the traffic was a legitimate branch of commerce as many slaves were annually exported from Bonny and the Old Calabar River as from all the rest of the West African Coast." [1]

Obeah is Negro magic. The paper which follows was suggested by observation on Negro magic during a recent visit to the English Islands in the Carribean.

Reprinted by permission of the publisher from *Publications of The American Sociological Society*, XVIII (1923), pp. 102-115. This was later reprinted in R. E. Park, E. W. Burgess and R. D. McKenzie, *The City* (Chicago: University of Chicago Press, 1925), pp. 121-141.

[1] J. Graham Cruickshank, *Black Talk*, p. 8.

During the past year two very important books have been published, in English, dealing with the subject of magic. The first is a translation of Lévy-Bruhl's *La Mentalité Primitive*, and the other is Lynn Thorndyke's *A History of Magic and Experimental Science during the First Thirteen Centuries of the Christian Era.*

In venturing to include two volumes so different in content and point of view in the same general category, I have justified myself by adopting Thorndyke's broad definition, which includes under "magic" "all occult arts and sciences, superstition and folklore."

Lévy-Bruhl's book is an attempt, from a wide survey of anthropological literature, to define a mode of thought characteristic of primitive peoples.

Thorndyke, on the other hand, is interested mainly, as the title of his volume indicates, in the beginnings of empirical science. The points of view are different, but the subject-matter is the same, namely, magical beliefs and practices, particularly in so far as they reflect and embody a specific type of thought.

Lévy-Bruhl has collected, mainly from the writings of missionaries and travelers, an imposing number of widely scattered observations. These have been classified and interpreted in a way that is intended to demonstrate that the mental life and habits of thought of primitive peoples differ fundamentally from those of civilized man.

Thorndyke, on the other hand, has described the circumstances under which, during the first thirteen centuries of our era, the forerunners of modern science were gradually discarding magical practices in favor of scientific experiment.

There is, of course, no historical connection between the culture of Europe in the thirteenth century and that of present-day savages, although the magical beliefs and practices of both are suprisingly similar and in many cases identical, a fact which is intelligible enough when we reflect that magic is a very ancient, widespread, characteristically human phenomenon, and that science is a very recent, exceptional, and possibly fortuitous manifestation of social life.

Lévy-Bruhl described the intelligence and habits of thought characteristic of savage peoples as a type of mentality. The civilized man has another and a different mentality. "Mentality," used in this way, is an expression the precise significance of which is not at once clear. We use the expression "psychology" in a similar but somewhat different way when we say, for example, that the rural and urban populations "have a different 'psychology,' " or that such and such a one has the "psychology" of his class—meaning that a given individual or the group will interpret an event or respond to a situation in a characteristic manner. But "mentality," as ordinarily used, seems to refer to the form, rather than to the content, of thought. We frequently speak of the type or grade of mentality of an individual, or of a group. We would not, however, qualify the word "psychology" in any such way. We would not, for example, speak of the grade or degree of the bourgeoisie, or the proletarian "psychology." The things are incommensurable and "psychology," in this sense, is a character but not a quantity.

The term "mentality," however, as Lévy-Bruhl uses it, seems to include both meanings. On the whole, however, "primitive mentality" is used here to indicate the form in which primitive peoples are predisposed to frame their thoughts. The ground pattern of primitive thought is, as Lévy-Bruhl expresses it, "pre-logical."

As distinguished from Europeans and from some other peoples somewhat less sophisticated than ourselves, the primitive mind "manifests," he says, "a decided distaste for reasoning and for what logicians call the discursive operations of thought. This distaste for rational thought does not arise out of any radical incapacity or any inherent defect in their understanding," but is simply a method—one might almost say a tradition—prevalent among savage and simple-minded people of interpreting as wilful acts the incidents, accidents, and unsuspected changes of the world about them.

What is this pre-logical form of thought which characterizes the mentality of primitive people? Lévy-Bruhl describes it as "participation." The primitive mind does not know things as we do, in a detached objective way. The uncivilized man enters, so to speak, into the world about him and interprets plants, animals, the changing seasons, and the weather in terms of his own impulses and conscious purposes. It is not that he is lacking in observation, but he has no mental patterns in which to think and describe the shifts and changes of the external world, except those offered by the mutations of his own inner life. His blunders of interpretation are due to what has been described as the "pathetic fallacy," the mistake of attributing to other persons, in this case, to physical nature and to things alive and dead, the sentiments and the motives which they inspire in him. As his response to anything sudden and strange is more likely to be one of fear than of any other emotion, he interprets the strange and unfamiliar as menacing and malicious. To the civilized observer it seems as if the savage lived in a world peopled with devils.

One difference between the savage and the civilized man is that the savage is mainly concerned with incidents and accidents, the historical, rather than scientific, aspects of life. He is so actively engaged in warding off present evil and meeting his immediate needs that he has neither time nor inclination to observe routine. It is the discovery and explanation of this routine that enables natural science to predict future consequences of present action and so enable us to prepare today for the needs of tomorrow. It is the discovery and explanation, in terms of cause and effect, of this routine that constitutes, in the sense in which Lévy-Bruhl uses the term, rational thought.

What the author of primitive mentality means by "participation" is familiar enough, though the expression itself is unusual as description of a form of thought. Human beings may be said to know one another immediately and intuitively by "participation." Knowledge of this kind is dependent, however, upon the ability of human beings to enter imaginatively into one another's minds and to interpret overt acts in terms of intentions and purposes. What Lévy-Bruhl's statement amounts to, then, is that savage people think, as poets have always done, in terms of wills rather than forces. The universe is a society of wilful personalities, not an irrefragable chain of cause and effect. For the savage, there are events, but neither hypotheses nor facts, since facts, in the strict sense of the word, are results of criticism and reflection and presuppose an amount of detachment that primitive man does not seem to possess. Because he thinks of his world as will rather than force, primitive man seeks to deal with it in terms of magic rather than of mechanism.

II. MAGIC AS A FORM OF THOUGHT

Thorndyke's *History of Magic* is an account of the manner and circumstances under which, within the period it covers, not all at once, but gradually, first in one field of knowledge and practice, and then in another—haltingly, painfully, and step by step—the transition from magic to science was made.

Anthropologists have not always agreed as to the precise relation between magic and science. Is magic to be regarded as an earlier and more primitive form of science, or is it not? It is at least true that science, as means of control of the external world, has always found some form of magic in existence, and has always displaced it. But magic is probably never *merely* a tool or a technique which men use to control and fashion the world after their desire. It is primarily a form of emotional expression, a gesture, or dramatic performance. It has something, also, of the character of a prayer or solemn formulation of a wish, but always with the hope that in some—not quite intelligible—way the formulation of the wish will bring its own fulfilment. Magic ceases to interest us where the relation of the means to ends assumes the definiteness and certainty of a scientific demonstration.

Farmers in some parts of the country still pray for rain—at least they did so up to a few years ago. They will quit doing so, however, as soon as someone invents a sure-fire device for making it.[2]

We still believe in magic in medicine and in politics—partly, I suspect, because in those fields science has not been able to give us the positive knowledge it has in other regions of our experience, and partly because in the field of medicine and of politics our solemn formulations of our wishes so frequently bring the results desired. In many cases the method of social reformers in dealing with social evils is not unlike the technique of Christian Science in dealing with bodily and spiritual ailments; it consists mainly in solemnly and ceremonially asserting that a given evil no longer exists. Society formulates its wish, consecrates it—through the solemn referendum of a popular election, perhaps—and writes it on the statute books. As far as the public is concerned, the thing is then finished. Fortunately, this form of magic often works—but unfortunately, it does not work so often as it used to.[3]

---

[2] Archbishop E. J. Hanna, head of the Catholic diocese of California, recently, during the drouth on the Pacific Coast, issued formal instructions to the pastors of all Catholic churches to offer the following prayer immediately after mass: "O God, in whom we live and move and are, grant us seasonal rain that we, enjoying a sufficiency of support in this life, may with more confidence strive after things eternal."—From *Los Angeles Evening Herald*, January 17, 1924.

[3] Thomas and Znaniecki, *The Polish Peasant in Europe and America* (Boston, 1918), I, 3: "The oldest but most persistent form of social technique is that of 'ordering-and-forbidding'—that is, meeting a crisis by an arbitrary act of will decreeing the disappearance of the undesirable or the appearance of the desirable phenomena, and the using arbitrary physical action to enforce

What has been said indicates that magic may be regarded as a form of thought characteristic of, but not confined to, primitive—or what Professor Ellsworth Faris has called preliterate—man. It suggests, also, that primitive thought and primitive mentality are ordinarily associated with a definite organization of life and experience, perhaps even a definite economic organization of society. We all are disposed to think in magical terms in those regions of our experience that have not been rationalized, and where our control is uncertain and incomplete. The stock exchange and the golf course, where success is uncertain and fortuitous, all tend to breed their own superstition.

"Magic," as Thorndyke says, "implies a mental state, and so may be viewed from the standpoint of the history of thought." But magic, if it is a form of thought, is not science; neither is it art. The arts may be said to begin with the lower animals. But in the art with which the beaver constructs a dam and the bird builds a nest there is neither magic nor science.

We can best understand magic and its relation to science if we recall that thought is itself an interrupted act, "a delayed response," to use the language of the behaviorists. There is the impulse to act, which is interrupted by reflection, but eventually the impulse completes itself in action. Magic has the character of thought in so far as it is an impulse that is interrupted and so becomes conscious. But it is not rational thought because it does not foresee and seek to define the relation between the end it seeks and the means necessary to achieve that end. Between ends and means there is always a hiatus in which there is feeling but not clear intuition of how that end is to be achieved.

All human activities tend to assume the character of magic in so far as they become purely traditional and conventional, defined in some sacred formula piously transmitted. It is peculiarly characteristic of modern life, however, that all our inherited forms of behavior tend to become rationalized. It is characteristic of modern

_____

the decree. This method corresponds exactly to the magical phase of natural technique. In both, the essential means of bringing a determined effect is more or less consciously thought to reside in the act of will itself by which the effect is decreed as desirable, and of which the action is merely an indispensable vehicle or instrument; in both, the process by which the cause (act of will and physical action) is supposed to bring its effect to realization remains out of reach of investigation."

life that nothing is accepted merely on authority, every tradition is subject to criticism.

It is only in very recent years that we have achieved scientific agriculture and scientific cooking. On the other hand we have already scientific advertising and scientific "cheering." "Yelling" at ball games, once so spontaneous, has now become an art, if not a duty.[4]

III. MENTALITY AND CITY LIFE

The reason the modern man is a more rational animal than his more primitive ancestor is possibly because he lives in a city, where most of the interests and values of life have been rationalized, reduced to measurable units, and even made objects of barter and sale. In the city—and particularly in great cities—the external conditions of existence are so evidently contrived to meet man's clearly recognized needs that the least intellectual of peoples are inevitably led to think in deterministic and mechanistic terms.

The embodiment of rational thought is the tool, the machine, in which all the parts are manifestly designed to achieve a perfectly intelligible end. The primitive man lives in a vastly different world, where all the forces about him are mysterious and uncontrollable, and where nature seems as wild, as romantic, and as unpredictable as his own changing moods. The primitive man has almost no machinery, and relatively few tools.

The mentality of the modern man, on the other hand, is based upon the machine and upon the application of science to all the interests of life—to education, to advertising, and, presently, perhaps, to politics. The culture of the modern man is characteristically urban, as distinguished from the folk culture, which rests on personal relations and direct participation in the common life of the family, the tribe, and the village community.

In fact, if we define them strictly, as Lévy-Bruhl seems to do, we may say that reason and reflective thinking were born in the city. They came, if not into existence, at least into vogue, in Athens, in

---

[4] The following telegram was recently in the *San Francisco Bulletin:* "Stanford University, Jan. 24, 1924—Stanford has established what is termed a unique course in the curriculum of western universities. It teaches scientific yell-leading, according to the rally committee, which sponsors the course. The course is open to sophomores only. Practices will be held in Encina gymnasium."

the time of Socrates and the Sophists. The Sophists were, in fact, a distinctly urban phenomenon, and we owe to Socrates—who was one of them—the first clear recognition of conceptional, as distinguished from perceptional, knowledge. We owe to Plato, Socrates' disciple, the definition of the most fundamental tool of modern scientific thought, namely, the concept, i.e., the Platonic idea.

Magic may be regarded, therefore, as an index, in a rough way, not merely of the mentality, but of the general cultural level of races, peoples, and classes. It is even possible that a more thoroughgoing analysis of the mental processes involved in magic and rational thought will permit us to measure the mentalities of social groups with as much precision, at least, as we now measure and grade—with the aid of the Binet-Simon tests—the intelligence of individuals. At least we should know in this case what we were measuring, namely, the extent and degree to which a given group or class had acquired the ability and the habit of thinking in rational rather than magical terms.

With a more precise conception of the nature of magic and of the mechanisms of prelogical thinking, we shall, no doubt, be able not merely to compare and perhaps measure with a certain degree of accuracy and objectivity the mentality and cultural levels of different cultural groups, but we shall be able also to describe the process by which races and peoples make the transition from one cultural level to another. This transition, which Thorndyke has described in his history of magic, is everywhere in progress. These changes in a contemporary and living society are open and accessible to investigation, now that history has enabled us to see them, as they can never see them later, when they have become history.

In a recent paper in the *American Journal of Sociology*, Professor U. G. Weatherly has called attention to the advantages of the West Indies as a sociological laboratory.

Islands are peculiarly interesting sociologically, provided, of course, that they are inhabited. For one thing, they are physically defined. The island community is, for this reason, invariably isolated, geographically and socially, and because the means of communication are known, the extent of isolation can be reduced to relatively measurable terms.

This isolation tends to give to each separate island community an individuality that one rarely finds elsewhere. Because islands are geographically limited and isolated, the influence of climate and physiographic characteristics, as well as of economic organization, in defining cultural traits, can be estimated and assessed with greater accuracy than elsewhere. Until one has visited some of the Lesser Antilles, he is not likely to understand or appreciate Frederick A. Ober's rather drastic summary of their history—"Discovered by the Spaniards, appropriated by the Dutch, Danish, or English, and finally abandoned to the semi-barbarous blacks from Africa, this has been the usual succession in the islands." [5]

The rather bitter note of this statement probably reflects the tone of the white planters, whose position in the islands has gradually declined since the emancipation of the slaves.

It directs attention, however, to what is, from the point of view of the student of human nature and of society, the most interesting and unique feature of the islands, namely, the racial situation. As Professor Weatherly has said, "Perhaps nowhere else is there a better opportunity for securing definite evidence bearing on the opposing theories of race and contact as factors in cultural growth." Every island, in fact, is a separate racial melting-pot in which the mingled cultures and races of Europe, Africa, and Asia seem to be gradually, very gradually, simmering down to a single cultural, and eventually, also, to a single racial, blend.

IV. OBEAH: THE MAGIC OF THE BLACK MAN

Outside the Spanish Islands, Negroes are the dominant race in the West Indies. In regions where they have not been replaced by Hindus, as they have been in Trinidad and Demerara, British Guiana, they constitute 90 per cent of the population. They are, in fact, the only people who regard themselves as natives. The Asiatics and the Europeans are, for the most part, mere sojourners.

So far as the islands now have a native culture it is the culture of the Negro folk. It is, at the same time, the most characteristic manifestation of the mentality of the West Indian black man, so far as he has preserved what Lévy-Bruhl describes as the mentality of primitive man.

What is more interesting about obeah is that while as a practice and a belief it is universal among the uneducated classes of the black population in the islands, it is everywhere different, and everywhere

---

[5] Frederick A. Ober, *A Guide to the West Indies Bermudas*, New York, 1908, p. 351.

in process of change. Practices that were originally imported from Africa tend to assimilate and fuse with related practices and traits of the European and Hindu cultures wherever the Africans have come into contact with them.

This is evident, in the first place, from the fact that the obeah man is not always a Negro; he may be, and not infrequently is, a Hindu. In the second place, the ritual of obeah may include anything from patent medicine to Guinea pepper. Among the instruments of obeah in the possession of the police of Trinidad recently were a stone image, evidently of Hindu origin, and a book of magic ritual published in Chicago, which pretended to be, and no doubt had been, translated originally from the writings of Albertus Magnus, the great medieval writer on magic. A book called *Le Petit Albert* is said to be extremely popular among obeah men in the French Islands.

The favorite decoctions in use among witch doctors consist of bones, ashes, "grave dirt," human nail parings—mixed, perhaps, with asafetida or any other substance having a pungent odor. But in addition to these, obeah men in the West Indies use the candles, the little shrines, or "chapels," as they call them, and various other portions of the ritual of the Catholic church.

In January, 1917, a woman known as Valentine Sims, a native of St. Lucia, was convicted, in Port-of-Spain, Trinidad, of obtaining money by the assumption of supernatural powers. The testimony in the case showed that, among other things, she attended the Roman Catholic church, and, on pretense of receiving holy communion, took the altar bread distributed to the worshipers during the communion, and used it in practicing obeah.

All this suggests that obeah, as one finds it in the West Indies, is not so much a tradition and a cultural inheritance as it is an innate predisposition, like a sense of humor, or "the will to believe," as James describes it. Behind these practices, and supporting them, are all sorts of fears and a general sense of insecurity in regard to the physical and spiritual environment that more cultivated persons either do not feel, or find escape from in quite different practices.

This is clearly indicated in the letters found among the papers of obeah adepts which have been confiscated from time to time by the police. From these letters one gains an insight into the nature and extent of the terrors, anxieties, and perils of the soul which trouble the dreams and imaginations of the black man, whom we ordinarily think of as roaming, cheerful, care-free, and unconcerned in a worried and troubled world.

The black man in the West Indies is greatly troubled about a great many things. He has more than the usual number of obscure pains and aches, which he worries about a great deal, and for which he, like most of us, is in search of some sovereign remedy. He is disturbed about his relations with his employer. Not that, like the workingman we know, he talks or thinks about his rights and the rights of labor. He is not class-conscious. Quite the contrary, he is constantly worried because he is not in favor with his employer. If he is scolded or scowled at, he is troubled. His first assumption, in such circumstances, is that some fellow-employee in some dark way is influencing his employer against him, and he seeks the obeah charm which will discover and circumvent his enemy and win back his employer's good will.

If he gets into a quarrel with the family next door, if his sweetheart looks coldly upon him, if his wife deserts him, he inevitably assumes that there are personal and magical influences at work, seeking to undermine otherwise sweet and happy relations. Frequently he is right. At any rate the obeah man exploits these suspicions, and that is the reason strenuous efforts are being made in the British Islands to stamp the superstition out.

Visiting the police courts in the English islands, one is profoundly impressed by the patient efforts of most of the judges to discover and apply the rules of law to the petty personal and neighborhood difficulties that the natives are so fond of airing in the courts. One gets the impression that the most difficult thing for the primitive mind to conceive and administer for himself is justice. On the other hand, the Negro, at least, knows and appreciates justice when he meets it. That is probably one reason why he likes to take his troubles to court.

V. FASHIONS IN OBEAH

One gets the impression that there are fashions in obeah. Dominica, for example, is noted for its use of love-philters; in Montserrat, obeah is mainly a protection against evil spirits and a means of communication with the dead; in Antigua, obeah is most generally a form of medicine. Amulets, "guards," as they are popularly called, intended to ward off evil spirits or protect one against the ill-will of an evil-minded neighbor are also popular. Nevis has a reputation for "black magic."

The older generation of obeah men were supposed to have a knowledge of vegetable poisons the effects of which cannot be detected on postmortem. In Nevis the older tradition has apparently lingered longer than elsewhere. At any rate, magical practices seem to have assumed a more malignant form in Nevis than in some of the other islands.

In 1916 an old woman, Rose Eudelle, deaf and bedridden, was convicted of practicing obeah. She seems to have been one of the few witch doctors who believed sincerely in the efficacy of their own practices. She had a great reputation, and boasted that she had killed one man and sent another to the asylum. Curiously enough, she practiced obeah mainly through correspondence, and when she was finally arrested, some fifty letters from clients in various islands, one of them in New York City, were discovered. There was great excitement in Nevis when she was arrested. As she had solemnly threatened the colored police sergeant who arrested her, the whole black population was confidently expecting that some dramatic misfortune would overtake him. Here there seemed to be something more nearly approaching primitive and African magic than in any of the other thirty-eight cases of which I obtained some sort of record.

Not only is the fashion in obeah different in the different islands, but interest in magic, which is said to be declining everywhere, is less modified in some islands than in others. In Barbados, though the practices still persist, prosecutions for obeah have almost entirely ceased. In the police station at Castries, St. Lucia, on the other hand, there are still preserved the heart and hand of a Negro boy who was killed some years ago to furnish an obeah man with the instruments of magic to enable him to open the vaults of the local bank and rob it of the treasure which was supposed to be amassed there.

The fact is, then, that the mentality of the black population of the West Indies, as that of Africa, is changing under the influence of contact with the white man's culture, and particularly under the influence of the very energetic prosecution which not only have made the profession less profitable, but by undermining faith in his supernatural powers, have robbed the obeah man of the terror which he at one time inspired.

Aside from the superficial changes in the original superstition and the gradual decline of interest and belief in magic, it seems as if certain more fundamental changes, reflected in these practices, were taking place. First, the obeah man tends to become, on the one hand, a sort of unlicensed physician, as in the case of Percival Duval, an obeah man who maintained regular office hours, wrote prescriptions, and prescribed medicines. Actually, Duval seems to have used a little less medicine and a little more hocus pocus than the average medical practitioner in our own country did a few years ago. But he was convicted, and upon appeal to the higher court his conviction was confirmed. Another obeah man in St. John's, Antigua, was found to be dealing, along with the other instruments of obeah, very largely in patent medicines and homely household remedies. Among the instruments of obeah taken from his office when it was raided were the following: (1) Exhibit labeled "ground bones and ashes." The sample consisted of a mixture of calcium compound and probably lime, wood-ashes, and incense. The incense content was 26.3 per cent. (2) Exhibit labeled "ground glass and smith coal." This sample consisted of a coarse commercial oxygen mixture. (3) Yellow powder. This consisted of a cheap, scented starch powder. (4) Supposed dog's tongue. This consisted entirely of vegetable matter composed principally of starch cells. (5) Exhibit labeled "ashes and incense." The sample consisted of incense, wood-ashes, and charcoal, earth, and small pebbles, with a small proportion of oxygen mixture. It contained 17.3 per cent of incense in lump and powdered form. (6) Exhibit "vial with yellow liquid." The sample consisted of ordinary commercial oil of anise. (7) Vial with brownish liquid. The sample consisted of a solution of iodine in potassium iodide of approximately 15 per cent strength.

The fact is, the obeah man in the West Indies is in a way to become a quack doctor. This represents one direction in which change is taking place.

On the other hand, there is a disposition of the obeah man to become a sort of confessor and privy counselor in all the intimate and personal affairs of the common people. The black people—and not only black, but occasionally Portuguese, who are the traders in the smaller islands—go to him with affairs of business and of the heart. They write him long personal letters, and he sends them a magical prayer or incantation to cure them of bodily ailments, to protect them from dangers of travel, and to insure general good fortune. In an affair of the heart, the witch doctor frequently prescribes a magic powder, sweetly scented, to accompany and lend a delicate and stimulating fragrance to a love letter. In principle, this aspect of the obeah man's practice is like Mr. Coué's—"Every day, in every way, I am better and better"—only that the uses of obeah are more specific. In any case, there is here a very evident tendency of the practice to assume a form in which the ritual of obeah is merely a device, like the prayers of primitive folk, for magically reinforcing the expression of a wish. So closely are the magical practices of the obeah man connected—in the mind of the ordinary black man—with religion that in one case, at any rate, he pretended to cure a boy of insanity by making believe that he was operating as the agent or proxy of the priest.

This, then, represents a second tendency to change in the practices of magic by the black man. If obeah in some instances seems to be taking the form of popular medicine, in others it tends to assume the form of a pagan religious ceremony, adapting itself to the forms and the ritual of the local church.

VI. THE PROBLEM STATED

In a recent volume, *Studies in Human Nature*, Mr. J. R. Baillie has suggested that the disposition and the ability to think abstractly, disinterestedly, and scientifically is not only a relatively recent acquisition of the human race, but at the same time is a local phenomenon.

This geographical limitation of science is indeed a remarkable fact, the importance of which our familiarity with the scientific mood and our insularity of mind constantly tend to obscure. . . . . We should not forget that millions of human beings have no interest in the scientific mood at all, and seem by constitution to have no capacity for it. . . . . Some individuals among these non-scientific peoples may, and do, assimilate the science of the West. But experience seems to show that such acquisition is at best a mere accomplishment, and leaves the racial structure and composition of their minds unaffected. . . . . The non-scientific peoples take up science as they put on Western clothes. One may change one's clothes, but there is no changing the skin. The fact is that the scientific mood arises from a peculiar attitude of the mind to the world found amongst certain peoples of the globe; and without this attitude science will always appear a curiosity or an irrelevance.[6]

---

[6] J. B. Baillie, *Studies in Human Nature*, p. 242.

The author assumes that the disposition to think rationally and to cultivate abstract and scientific thought is a racial attribute. Perhaps a more accurate statement of the matter would take account of the fact that even within the comparatively limited area where science is in vogue, there are large numbers of people who still—even while using the language of science—think in the more elementary forms of folk-thought. This seems to be true wherever large masses of the population are still illiterate, or where, for any reason, even when able to read, they habitually think in terms of the spoken language, rather than in the language of the printed page. Literacy itself is very largely a product of modern city life. Books and reading which used to be, and to a certain extent are yet, a luxury in the country, become a necessity in the city.

The Negroes migrating in such large numbers from the West Indies to the United States are bringing with them habits of thought which have largely disappeared among the Negro population native to this country. The obeah men of the West Indies have many clients in the United States, and a recent issue of the *New York Age* announced that the Negro quarter around 135th Street, New York, was overrun with fortune tellers and witch doctors, many or most of them from the West Indies.

Within a few years, however, most of these superstitions will have disappeared, or at any rate will have assumed those more conventional forms with which we are familiar and have learned to tolerate. This is certainly true of the city population.

Great changes are taking place, with the introduction of modern methods of education, in our own insular possessions. Mr. Axel Holst, of the National Bank of the Danish West Indies, who has been a close and assiduous student of Negro folklore in the Virgin Islands, says that the effect of the American system of education will within a few years totally change the mental habits of the natives of St. Thomas. Since the younger generation have begun to read books, they are not so interested as they were in the Nansi stories, which correspond to the Bre'r Rabbit stories of the States. Since the introduction of American rule, newspapers have come into vogue, and the young men have taken to political discussion.

The changes in the "mentality" of the Negro population are, Mr. Holst says, going on visibly, and at a surprising rate. These changes, if they are actually taking place, should be made the subject of further investigation. Such study should enable us to determine, among other things, more precisely than we have been able to determine hitherto, the rôle which cultural contacts, social heritages, and racial temperament play in the whole cultural process.

It is evident that we are not to assume, as otherwise we might, that there is no area of experience in which primitive or preliterate people think realistically and rationally. On the other hand, in contrasting primitive mentality with that of civilized man, we need not assume—except for the sake of the contrast—that the thinking of civilized man is always and everywhere either rational or scientific. As a matter of fact, there are still wide areas of our experience that have not as yet been fully rationalized, notably the fields of medicine and religion. In medicine, at least—if we are to believe a recent medical critic of what, in imitation of Lévy-Bruhl, we might call "medical mentality"—the majority of practitioners still think of diseases as morbid entities instead of convenient labels for groups of symptoms.

The following paragraph from a recent writer states the matter from the point of view of a critic of "medical mentality."

It is not to be thought that any educated medical man indeed believes "a disease" to be a material thing, although the phraseology in current use lends colour to such supposition. Nevertheless, in hospital jargon, "diseases" are "morbid entities," and medical students fondly believe that these "entities" somehow exist in *rebus Naturae* and were discovered by their teachers, much as was America by Columbus. . . . . In fact, for these gentlemen "diseases" are Platonic realities; universals *ante rem*. This unavowed belief, which might be condoned were it frankly admitted, is an inheritance from Galen, and carries with it the corollary that our notions concerning this, that, or the other "diseases" are either absolutely right or absolutely wrong, and are not merely matters of mental convenience.

But if the practitioners think of diseases in pre-logical terms what can we expect of the layman, whose medical education has been largely confined to the reading of patent medicine advertisements? What has been said suggests a problem which may be perhaps stated in this way: How far is the existence of magic and magical mode of thought a measure of the mentality of a racial or cultural group in which it is found to persist? How far is what Ballie calls "the scientific mood" an effect of the urban environment?

THE CITY AS A NATURAL PHENOMENON

THERE are obviously several points of view from which a city or any other territorially organized society, for that matter, may be properly conceived for the purpose of investigation. It may be conceived, (1) as a mere territorial aggregate, as it tends to be in the census of population. In that case no account is taken of the manifold ways in which the individual units of which this aggregate is composed are related to and dependent, one upon the other. It may be regarded (2) as a kind of physical and conceptual artifact, in which the physical structure of the city is completed by a framework of legal concepts within which the lives of individuals who compose the community are regimented and controlled. The city may (3) finally be regarded as a functional unit in which the relations among individuals that compose it are determined, not merely by the conditions imposed by the city's physical structure, nor even by the formal regulations of a local government, but rather more by the direct and indirect interaction of individuals one upon the other.

Considered from this point of view the urban community turns out to be something more than a mere congeries of peoples and institutions. On the contrary its component elements, institutions and persons are so intimately bound up that the whole tends to assume the character of an organism, or to use Herbert Spencer's term, a super-organism. Conceived in this way the limits of the urban com-

---

This unpublished essay was evidently written as a critique of E. L. Thorndike's attempt to measure the goodness of cities, in *Your City* (New York, 1939).

munity are not likely to be identified with the city as an administrative unit, but rather with the metropolitan region, the boundaries of which are not arbitrarily fixed but coextensive with the area within which the city, as a natural phenomenon, actually functions or, perhaps, with the area within which it exercises a dominant economic and a somewhat less obvious cultural influence.

The studies of plant and animal ecologists have familiarized us with the fact that plants and animals, living together in a common habitat, invariably tend to develop a natural economy and to form, as an incident of such economic interdependence, a biotic community in which the different species are able to live more securely and prosperously together than they can apart. This is the situation where different species, occupying the same habitat, make different demands upon the soil or where their joint occupations of a habitat tends, for any reason, to diminish competition and, in that way insure for their *habitants*, if we may apply that term to plants, a greater degree of cooperation. The biotic community, as described by plant and animal ecologists, is an example of what one means by the term super-organism.

Competition, which is the fundamental organizing principle in the plant and animal community, plays a scarcely less important role in the human community. In the plant and animal community it has tended to bring about (1) an orderly distribution of the population, and (2) a differentiation of the species within the habitat.

The same principles operate in the case of human population, with the exception that in the latter case the habitat is the economic region and competition achieves and maintains a relatively stable equilibrium, not by a differentiation of the species, but by a division of labor and a differentiation of function or of occupation among individual organisms.

The function of competition in the biotic community, as in human society, seems to be that of differentiation and individuation and in so far as it performs that function it enters into the very constitution of the community or society in which it operates.

There is, however, in human society another fundamental form of interaction or process. This is communication. It is the function of communication, or one of its functions, to bring about those understandings among members of a society which eventually take the form of custom, folkways and other more intimate and personal forms of solidarity. It is these that enable us to maintain, even in the midst of the distractions and confusions of this modern world of ours, the concert, cooperation and the *rapport* necessary to effective collective action.

If the function of competition, including under that term not merely economic competition but the more fundamental struggle for existence, has been, as I have said, not only to distribute and redistribute but by differentiation of their functions to individuate the individual units of which a community is composed, the function of communication, on the contrary, has been to integrate, synthesize and consolidate the functions of individuals and groups into something like an organic or superorganic unit.

Let me elaborate upon the conception of the community,—and particularly of the urban community—to which I have referred. This will permit me to indicate more specifically the relation of the physical structure and the technological devices by which relations between individual organisms, of which the super-organism is composed, are maintained.

The modern city has long since ceased to be what the peasant village was, or appeared to be, an agglomeration of individual persons and habitations. Rather, it is like the civilization of which it is the center and focus, a vast physical and institutional structure in which men live, like bees in a hive, under conditions such that their activities are considerably more regulated, regimented and conditioned than is likely to appear to the spectator or be perceived by the inhabitant.

The types of association which we expect to find in a city as in any other forms of society organized on a territorial and economic basis are: (1) territorial, (2) economic and (3) cultural.

The territorial order. Geography and the territorial organization of society get their importance from the facts that social relations are determined largely by physical distances and that social stability is insured when human beings are rooted in the soil. On the other hand, the most drastic changes in society are likely to be those that involve mobility and, particularly, mass migrations of peoples. This is so true that Frederick Teggart, who has given much attention to the subject, believes that most of the great advances in civilization are due, directly or indirectly, to the migration of peoples and the catastrophic changes which have accompanied them.

From this point of view it seems that every technical device, from the wheelbarrow to the airplane, which provided a new and more effective means of locomotion, has, or should have, marked an epoch in history. It is said that every civilization carries in itself the seeds of its own destruction. Such seers are likely to be the technical devices that introduce a new social order and usher out the old.

The economic or competitive order. Living creatures not only attract and repel each other as physical objects, but they also interact in ways which are peculiar to living organisms, that is to say they compete. Economic relations and an economic order, wherever they exist, are the products of competition, but of a competition which eventually brings about some sort of cooperation. In the case of human beings, this cooperation takes the form of an exchange of goods and services. The economic order is the product of trade. The market and the area over which exchange takes place mark the centers and limits of an economic society.

Technologic devices have profoundly affected economic relations. In improving the means of transportation they have progressively extended the limits of the world market and of economic society. They have made mass production and mass distribution possible and are directly responsible for the existence of the capitalistic system as we know it. Insofar as they have brought the diverse peoples of the earth into a world-wide web of economic relations, technologic devices, which provided the means of transportation and communication, have laid the basis for a world-wide political society and eventually of a moral and cultural order that will presumably include all mankind.

The cultural order. The thing we call the city is, obviously, something more than a population aggregate having a territorial configuration; something more than a "geographical expression," or even an association for the exchange of goods and services. The city, like other forms of society, is not only a political but a moral order. As such it tends to impose upon the free play of economic and egoistic forces the restraints of custom, conventions and law. All of these forms of control turn out finally, however, to be the products of communication. Communication is, as Bridgman defined it in his recent volume *The Intelligent Individual and Society*, "a device by which one endeavors as far as possible to anticipate the probable future actions of his fellows and so put himself in a position to make the necessary preparations." [1]

---

[1] P. W. Bridgman, *The Intelligent Individual and Society*. New York: The Macmillan Company, 1938.

But communication is something more than Bridgman's description indicates. It is a social-psychological process by which one individual is enabled to assume, in some sense and to some degree, the attitudes and the point of view of another; it is the process by which a rational and moral order among men is substituted for one that is merely physiological and instinctive. Communication "spins a web of custom and mutual expectation which binds together social entities as diverse as the family group, a labor organization, or the haggling participants in a village market." [2] Communication and competition are elementary social processes by which the continued existence of the urban community, as an organic and functional unit, is insured and maintained.

The conception which emerges from a consideration of this kind is a conception of the city which conforms, in a general way, to every other form of association in which individual organisms, occupying the same habitat, carry on a common life. The types of associations we expect to find in human society differ from those which we find in plant and animal communities mainly in that the relations among human beings are controlled by tradition, culture and law rather than, as in the case of the lower animals, by instinct.

It is not at once obvious that Professor Thorndike's "three years study of the recorded facts of 310 cities in the United States" has any very definite relation to the conception of the city here outlined. He is not interested in the natural history of cities but in their contributions to human welfare, and he has devised a scale for measuring these.

In view of the fact that cities are the centers and foci of most of the problems and processes involved in the evolution of a civilized existence one might expect an analysis of the available facts about them,—even though collected for purely administrative purposes—to throw some light on the nature of the functions they perform in the economic and cultural life of a people. But the purpose of this volume is not to describe and explain, but to measure and assess values.

However, values are notoriously subjective and personal and even in America, where most everything else is standardized, individuals and even communities have their own peculiar notions of what is essential to the good life.

The problem of devising a standard for the comparison of the

<hr />

[2] Robert E. Park, "Reflections on Communication and Culture," *The American Journal of Sociology*, Vol. XLIV, September, 1938, No. 2.

culture of cities is made more difficult by the fact that the actual operation of social processes is to multiply the existing diversity in the functions of cities as well as in the occupations of their inhabitants.

Particularly in a cosmopolitan country like our own, where the individuals vary so widely in respect to their cultural backgrounds, as well as in their vocations, things do not have for each and every individual, no more than for each and every community, the same relative value.

The fact that cities have widely different functions in the national economy and that the progressive solution of the economic problem invariably brings about an ever wider differentiation of these functions, as well as a more thoroughgoing segregation of their population suggests the necessity of some classification of their different functions before attempting to assess their contributions to the good life. The assumption that it is either possible or desirable to measure the welfare of communities as different as Pasadena and Newport News, or Oak Park and East Chicago, by the same yardstick is certainly, as Professor Thorndike has recognized, a debatable question.

Professor Thorndike might have very properly applied his measuring rod to "the general goodness of life" in different sections of metropolitan cities. It would be interesting to compare with reference to the thirty-seven traits which, as Professor Thorndike remarks, "all reasonable persons will regard as significant for the goodness of good people," sections so different as Morningside Heights and Hell's Kitchen in New York, or regions as different as the so-called Gold Coast and the Hobohemia of West Madison Street, Chicago. It would be even more interesting perhaps to compare, with respect to "the goodness of life for good people," sections of the country as different as the Sea Islands off the coast of South Carolina and Georgia, the Ozark Mountains in Missouri and the Berkshire country in western Massachusetts, or the East Coast of Florida.

I shall not attempt to analyze or criticize the procedure by which the scale for measuring "the general goodness of life" was devised. That is a technical procedure for which I profess no competence. The manipulation of statistical data by which such scales are contrived and applied has always impressed me a good deal like parlor magic. One is frequently startled by the results but is mainly interested to discover by what sleight of hand the trick was turned.

In any case I am disposed to question the value of a standard of goodness which when applied leads to the conclusion that goodness and the good people always tend to turn up in the same places. It is not clear, in the first place, to what extent "the good people" are the product of "the good life" or vice versa "the good life" makes "the good people." However, in view of the fact that the welfare of every community requires that every individual should find himself finally in the place and in the vocation in which he will contribute most to the common good it seems certain that many perfectly good people must live in hard spots.

The devising and application of a scale or a standard for measuring excellence, or goodness or anything so subjective and imponderable as value is always, it seems, a ticklish affair. For one thing the indices, by which a value is measured, tend to be identified with the things they measure. Thus, as in the case of the intelligence tests, so "the goodness of life" comes to be identified with the indices of goodness, that is to say with bath tubs, telephones, radios, etc., always of course, with the saving clause, "other things being equal." But of course other things are never equal and this is particularly the case when southern cities like Nashville, Tennessee, or Charleston, South Carolina, are given a lower rating by the Thorndike index than cities like Cicero, Illinois, or Wichita, Kansas,—because, among other things, they have more Negroes, more churches and fewer dentists.

But Negroes, like dentists, tend on the whole to go where they can make a living and where they are permitted to live, and it is probably good for society on the whole that each of us should live where he can rather than where he would choose to live. Besides I am not at all certain that more dentists and fewer Negroes would make either Nashville or Charleston better places to live than they are. I doubt it for one reason because I cannot foresee all the consequences that these improvements might bring. They might make Charleston and Nashville more like Cicero or Wichita. Not that Cicero is as bad as the reputation it gained when it was the headquarters of Al Capone and his gang, and Wichita evidently possesses more of the indices of a good life than its proximity to the Dust Bowl of western Kansas would suggest.

The difficulty of devising a scale which can be applied, in a way to bring into relief significant differences, in cities whose functions in the whole economic and cultural complex are as diverse as in the case of the cities I have cited, led Professor Thorndike to put in a separate category, (a) residential suburbs, (b) cities of the old South and (c) giant cities, and to limit comparisons to 200 cities, where conditions are such as seem likely to make comparisons not only interesting but instructive. However, when he later included these, making the total number of cities studied 310, the results tended to confirm his earlier conclusions.

Professor Thorndike was by no means unaware of either of the difficulties or the shortcomings of his effort to standardize and measure both the "material" and "spiritual" traits of cities. The fundamental objection to this sort of procedure is, as it seems to me, that it necessitates the substitution of a frigid and artificial construction, a sort of logical artifact, like the economic man, for the actual living object in which we are interested. Such artificial constructions may, perhaps, serve the purposes of an administrative agency for whom the "goodness of life," and particularly collective life, has no mysteries. It cannot serve the purpose of a science that is not satisfied with a precision that is gained by definition, merely, or with a procedure that substitutes correlations and logical relations for real causes.

It is this that tends to give social studies based on statistics the character of a purely scholastic exercise in which the answers to all the questions are already implicit in the conceptions and assumptions with which the inquiry started. It tends to give social studies the character of a game like chess, in which the pieces are concepts and the rules those of a mathematical or formal logic.

Thus it appears from Professor Thorndike's analysis of the statistics that Negroes, poverty, large families and churches are indices of a low grade community. On the other hand, dentists, cigar stores, home ownership and low birthrate are—I am choosing a few samples at random—indices of a high grade community. I believe, as Professor Thorndike seems to, that the connection of these different items or communal traits is a little mystifying and deserves, therefore, more investigation than a statistician, without going out of his laboratory, is likely to give them.

It is an interesting if somewhat discouraging fact that in high grade communities, where otherwise everything seems to be for the best in the best of all possible worlds, the population does not reproduce itself and must depend therefore upon the low grade communities to insure its survival. I would like to know what is the underlying connection between this and other traits of high grade communities.

I am intrigued, also, by the connection between churches and Negroes. They are both indices of low grade communities, it seems. That is not, of course, because churches or Negroes are bad in themselves. Both are often so much a source of comfort that many good people in the South would not like to dispense with either. As for the Negroes, even when they are not a comfort, they are always interesting, so interesting in fact that it is hard to understand just what life in the South would be without them.

I do not want to seem to diminish the importance of the statistics and correlations which Professor Thorndike has been at such an expense of time and patience to gather. I simply mean that by themselves and in the form in which they are presented they raise more questions than they answer.

In order to arrive at a satisfactory explanation of the facts about cities, and one that would insure effective action based on sound policy, we need something less precise, perhaps, and more empirical than the statistics and the formulas on which the conclusions in this study are based.

In order to grasp the significance of the facts about cities that Professor Thorndike has analyzed we should know what were the forces that operated to bring about the distribution of peoples, of institutions and of incomes in the different cities studied. We would want to know, in regard to the good people who make their residences in the seclusion and comfort of some residential suburb, not merely the conditions in the cities where they sleep but in the cities where they work. We should want to know not merely where they raised their families but where these families got their incomes. We want to know not merely the character of the communities which consumed the wealth of the country but the characters of the communities which produced it. We should want to know why, if dentists, and doctors and school marms do so much to determine the character of the good people and the good communities, they are so unequally distributed.

To me this volume reads like the introduction to a very interesting and far reaching inquiry. But as I have read Professor Thorndike's conclusions, I confess I have been somewhat disappointed.

What does he tell us finally? Does he tell us now just how, in view of the conditions under which this unequal, unwholesome and, I suspect uneconomic, distributions of peoples and the goods of life took place, how we could, if at all, change the situation? No, he does not even give us the assurance that if we understood better than we do, they would not seem to the good people in the good communities as bad as they now do. There are some compensations in the life of the slums that the people who live in the residential suburbs do not understand. In the immigrant areas it is, for example,—children.

All that we seem to get out of all these ingenious statistics in which the author has contrived to put down with some show of precision, but not with any sort of completeness, what we already in a general way know, is the assurance that if we had the necessary will and intelligence we could do better. All these statistics are not a contribution to the solution of a problem, it seems, but the prelude to a sermon.

"Improve your city," he urges. "Any city can improve itself! Now, however, as this attempt to standardize values would suggest, by trying to become something which it is not fitted to be."

This is, indeed, an instance of knowledge for what?

CHAPTER II

THE CITY AND CIVILIZATION

I. THE BRIEF PERIOD OF CIVILIZATION

CIVILIZATION, as has been frequently pointed out, is a comparatively recent manifestation of human nature and one that is, perhaps, not destined to endure the strains and stresses of its continued existence. The word itself is new, so new in fact, that it did not find a place in Samuel Johnson's dictionary published in 1755.

Professor James Harvey Robinson, seeking to visualize for us the brief span of man's history, proposed that we represent the possible 500,000 years of man's life upon the planet and the 4,000 years of his recorded history by the divisions of time on the face of a clock. Let us assume that man first appeared upon earth, say, last night at midnight and that we are now at high noon. In that case the period of man's recorded history has occupied something less than the last ten minutes.

Professor Robinson has, as a matter of fact, stated the matter a little more elaborately. He says: "To get the matter before one, let us imagine that 500,000 years of developing culture were compressed into 50 years. On this scale mankind would have required 49 years to learn enough to desert, here and there, his inveterate hunting habits and settle down in villages. Half through the 50th year writ-

Reprinted by permission of the publisher from *Syllabus and Selected Reading*, Social Science II, University of Chicago Press. Fifth Edition, 1936, pp. 204-220.

ing was discovered and practiced within a limited area, thus supplying one of the chief means of perpetuating and spreading culture. The achievements of the Greeks would be but three months back, the prevailing Christianity two; the printing press would be a fortnight old and man would have been using steam hardly a week. The peculiar conditions under which we live today did not come about until December 31 of the fiftieth year." [1] This suggests how young and fragile civilization is, and justifies to that extent Oswald Spengler's prophecy of *Der Untergang des Abendlandes*.

II. THE BEGINNING OF CIVILIZATION

Anthropologists have recently called attention to the fact that civilization is not exclusively, as has been assumed, a creation of historic peoples. Civilization of some sort existed before men established permanent settlements or invented a calendar or kept records of their collective life. If, however, we are disposed, as historians are, to locate in time and in space the point at which civilization, "true civilization," as they describe it, had its origin, we may say civilization began in Egypt, somewhere about the time that the Egyptian calendar was inaugurated. This date has been fixed. The oldest date in history, according to Edward Meyer, is July 19, 4241 B.C.

Since that time civilizations have risen, declined and disappeared. Much has been gained in the process, but somewhat has been lost, for civilization seems to be, on the whole, a cyclical rather than a secular process, each succeeding civilization reproducing more or less completely the conditions, and repeating more or less precisely the successive phases of its predecessors. This is in fact the basis of Spengler's prophecy, to which I have just referred.

It has been said that each new civilization began with a new migration, that is to say with a movement that widened man's intellectual horizon and extended the area of his competition and cooperation with other men. Modern civilization, for example, which began with the discovery of America may be said to have achieved its characteristic form with the application of steam power to locomotion and to industry.

It is, however, quite as true that each new civilization has been accompanied by the rise of new cities. For the expansion of man's

---

[1] *Encyclopaedia Britannica*, 14th Ed. 1929.

corporate and collective existence has been made possible only by new cities. For the expansion of man's corporate and collective existence has been made possible only by new concentrations of population and a more complex organization of those populations at the centers. These centers have been cities.

Thus civilization, or true civilization, as the historians describe it, began in Egypt when the nomadic peoples left the tablelands, now the deserts of North Africa, to establish themselves in permanent settlements along the Nile, and when they began at the same time to substitute a territorial and communal organization of society for the familial, totemic and clan organizations of primitive man. This seems, according to the historians of civilization, to have been one of the really great facts, marking one of the great epochs in history.

Later these territorial units were consolidated under the Pharaohs and the Egyptian Empire was established in two cities. This empire, however, was not an aggregation of tribes but of territories. It was, moreover—measured either in territory or in population—a very little empire as empires go. For the arable surface of Egypt is scarcely as large as Sicily, and while the length of the Nile Valley, from the first cataract to the Delta, is 490 miles—that is to say, as far as from Chicago to Pittsburgh—the distance between the Nile and the desert on either bank does not exceed nine and two-thirds miles.

III. THE ORIGINS OF STATES

What took place first in Egypt seems to have been repeated later in other parts of the world where and when new civilizations and new cities came into existence. What existed before the advent of the city was a congeries of more or less primitive societies; sometimes little settled communities of peasants; more often wandering herdsmen and nomads, widely scattered, living in comparative isolation in close contact with the soil and in immediate dependence upon their natural environment and upon their local habitat.

The transition from nomadic and sedentary life seems to have taken place at that time much as it does in North Africa today. A clan or a tribe or some portion of it, lingers at a spring where there is water for their flocks, or settles down at a ford or a crossroad where there is opportunity for trade. Where water is abundant, agriculture springs up. Where a market is established, workshops make their appearance, and commodities of various sorts are imported to supply the demands of the market. The necessity of protection against marauding nomads leads to a federation of villages, and to the building of a fortification, around which a city eventually springs up.

More often, perhaps, wandering nomads invade the settlements, conquer the sedentary people, establish themselves in a fortified position and remain as rulers of the country. This is, in fact, the way in which most states seem to have had their origin. The origin of the state is one of the classic problems of the history of civilization.

"The war-like character of nomads," says Ratzel, in his *History of Mankind*, "is a great factor in the creation of Asia, controlled by nomad dynasties and nomad armies, such as Persia, ruled by the Turks; China, conquered and governed by the Mongols and the Manchus, and in the Mongol and Rajaputa states of India. . . . . For this reason, the desert-born lords of the Sudan rule over the Negro folk just as the Manchus rule (or did when this was written) their Chinese subjects."

"This," he adds, "takes place pursuant to a law valid from Timbuktu to Pekin, whereby advantageous state formations arise in rich peasant lands; where a high material culture of sedentary peoples is violently subjugated to the service of prairie-dwellers, having energy, war-like capacity, and desire to rule." [2] Thus the city and the state grew up together.

Note in this connection that the state is invariably a territorial rather than a tribal unit, that within its limits a new power, a political power, arises to protect its boundaries and to administer its affairs. This new power is not merely superior to that of the tribe and the clan but eventually supplants them, substituting for the authority of the elders the rule of a monarch; for the tribal fetishes a provincial god, and for the primitive communism of the clan an organization based on caste and class.

"Every state in history," says Oppenheimer, "was or is a state of classes, a polity of superior and inferior groups, based upon distinctions of rank or of property. This phenomenon must then be called the state." There are no classes in primitive society. There are merely age and sex groups.

---

[2] Quoted by Oppenheimer, *The State; Its History and Development Viewed Sociologically*. Indianapolis, 1914, pp. 55, 56.

IV. THE STATE AND THE CITY

Within the limits of the state there arises, out of the same imminent necessity, cities which are at once the seat of political power and centers of trade. Many of the early cities, like the imperial cities of Nanking and Peking in China today, bear witness in their very structure to the conditions under which the imperial and political authority was established. Nanking contains within its walls the ruins of a fortified Tartar city, once occupied by the Mongol conquerors of China, and Peking, which exists today in a condition much like that described by Marco Polo in the days of Kubla Khan, is really four cities: there is a Chinese city, Tartar city, and within the limits of the latter an imperial and a Forbidden City, each with its own wall and its separate circle of Defenses, indicating that the conquerors had to protect themselves from within as well as without.

The first states were city states, and the word policy, politics, and political are derived from the Greek word for the city, *polis;* just as the word city and civilization are derived from the Latin word *civitas*. Originally the city was the state; thus politics, civilization, and the city may be said to have come into existence together and to represent different elements in one single complex.

V. CIVILIZATION AND RACIAL CULTURAL TRAITS

It is worth noting in this connection that while the different races of mankind grew up in comparative isolation and acquired their distinctive racial characteristics by adaptation and inbreeding, civilization seems to owe its existence to the coming together of peoples of different cultures and different racial stocks. In other words, racial differences and man's biological inheritance—the slow accumulation of successive generations—are the result of the efforts of mankind to adapt itself to conditions which his physical environment imposes. Civilization, on the other hand, is the result of man's effort to use the resources of his environment in order to change nature and, where possible, make it less raw, more comfortable and less difficult to endure.

It has been said that God made the country and man made the town. So far as this is true, cities and civilization may be regarded as man's irreverent attempt to improve on nature and create a world more after his heart's desire. In any case, what we call civilization is measured and estimated not by man's conformity to nature but by his triumph over it, less by his religions and his mores than by his tools and his artifacts.

Cities, and particularly the great metropolitan cities of modern times, so far as they can be regarded as the product of art and design rather than the effect of natural forces, are, with all their complexities and artificialities, man's most imposing creation, the most prodigious of human artifacts. We must conceive of our cities, therefore, not merely as centers of population, but as the workshops of civilization, and, at the same time, as the natural habitat of civilized man.

VI. MODERN AND ANCIENT CIVILIZATION

The difference between modern civilization, and those civilizations that preceded it, is that modern civilization is prospectively at least world-wide in extent. It has drawn and is drawing together in a wide embrace the most distant regions and the most isolated peoples. Its limits of expansion are fixed and insurmountable until we get interplanetary communication.

If the limits of modern civilization are measured by the area within which the products of modern machine industry are distributed, we may indeed say that modern civilization is world-wide. There seems to be almost no part of the world, for example, to which the Singer sewing machine, the automobile, the cinema, and the aeroplane have not penetrated. The tin cans in which the Standard Oil Company distributes its product have become a familiar and indispensable household utensil among the most inaccessible peoples of the world. The automobile is not only urbanizing rural America but it is transforming Africa and Asia.

On the other hand, modern, as contrasted with ancient civilization, has, or seems to have, no metropolis, no dominant center such as Athens was in the Aegean world and Rome in the Mediterranean. In the ancient world the centers of civilization were unmistakably fixed. The margins were undefined. In the modern world the opposite is the case. The modern world, it would appear, has not one but many metropolitan centers, and every great commercial city today is a world-city. Cities like London, New York, San Francisco, Yokohama, Osaka, Shanghai, Singapore, and Bombay are not merely centers of a wide regional commerce. They are, by their position on the great ocean highway which now circles the earth, integral parts of a system of international commerce. They are way-stations and shopping centers, so to speak, on the main street of the world.

Politically and administratively, these cities are of course independent of one another, but commercially they are all bound up together and as interdependent as the spokes of a wheel.

It is an interesting fact, that in this modern world, and in this machine age, all metropolitan cities, oriental and occidental, turn out upon observation to be very much alike. Every great city counts among its habitants representatives of all of the races and most of the peoples of the world. Just as there are Chinatowns in New York and San Francisco, so there are American colonies in Tokyo and Shanghai. Everywhere there are European banks and European hotels. Everywhere people ride in automobiles, speak through telephones, follow the same fashions, attend the same cinemas, and read, in different languages, the same news. Shanghai is like London just as London is like New York. Everywhere one meets evidence of the integration and interpenetrations of peoples and cultures.

On the other hand, these great metropolitan cities, particularly in the Orient, impress one, as R. D. McKenzie has said, like a modern façade erected upon an ancient structure. If one seeks to penetrate behind these new faces through which ancient peoples are looking out upon the modern world, one discovers evidences of cultures that are changing, to be sure, but are still very far removed from the civilization of the great port cities. This is particularly true in Asia but is also true in Europe and to a less extent in America.

The Lithuanian peasant, whose life is still bounded by the narrow limits of his ancestral village, or the Appalachian mountaineer, who has never seen a city, is likely to be less at home in Paris or Berlin than a traveling salesman from New York or Chicago would be in Tokyo.

VII. MODERN CIVILIZATION AND ITS ECONOMIC BASE

One reason why there is, or seems to be, no city that occupies the position in the modern world, comparable to that of Rome or Athens in the ancient, is that empires based on conquest and colonization are now in process of dissolution and political powers, far from being concentrated, are being dispersed. Nevertheless, commerce is steadily expanding and there is nothing that has more clearly demonstrated the interdependence of all the peoples of the world— not even the world war—than the present world-wide economic depression, and the curious results of various attempts to fix prices in the world-market.

In 1920, you may remember, the price of rubber rose suddenly to unprecedented levels in the world-market, and the price of rubber tires mounted in America. It appears that this was due to a maneuver of the government of the Straits Settlements in the Malay Peninsula, where most of the rubber plantations are located. The result was a vast expansion of the rubber plantations in Sumatra; a feverish search by American tire manufacturers for new sources of supply, a search which terminated in a political scandal in Liberia. More recently the attempt to fix the price of coffee eventuated in a political revolution in Brazil. What the ultimate effect upon the American farmer and American farming of the efforts of the farm board to stabilize the price of wheat in the United States remains to be seen.

It is evident, at any rate, that the forces which bind the world together today are economic rather than political. They are, specifically, commerce and communication, banks and newspapers, money and the news. This statement may sound a little cryptic and is likely to be misunderstood. However, when I speak of the influence of banks I do not mean the influence of bankers merely, and when I speak of the power of the press I do not mean the persuasiveness of the editorial writers. It is difficult to recognize that social forces, as we call them, may be, and sometimes are, impersonal in character. When we speak of banks and newspapers we usually think of them as benevolent or malevolent monsters, rather than as social agencies and institutions. However, banking institutions and the press do probably, at this moment, exercise, directly and indirectly, a larger measure of influence in human affairs than any existing government, and their influence, unlike that of government, is exercised on the whole impersonally.

Walter Lippmann expressed, some years ago, his sense of the new and impersonal power of the press in a very shrewd phrase, "Freedom and the news." This phrase suggested at least what is a fact, that the power of the press today is incorporated less in the editor than in the news, and the direct and indirect consequences of the publication of the news is so pervasive and intangible that no editor can any longer make himself responsible for it. The old editor held himself responsible for everything he printed and if God let something happen that should not have happened he suppressed any mention of it.

The forces that control the destinies of the world are, however, not less real because they are less visible. I have suggested that they are bound up with exchange and communication, that is to say, with the international money market and the international news. So far as this is true, these powers are very largely centered in four or five cities, perhaps finally, in one.

The news centers and the money centers, furthermore, are very intimately related. This is the reason they are never likely to be very far apart. It is the news that determines the value of securities and the price of money on the exchanges. That is the reason Wall Street in New York and Lombard Street in London are so close to the news tickers. Finally it is the price of securities and money on the international exchanges that determines, in the long run, the prices of every other commodity that enters into the world-market. All this tends to make Paris, Berlin, New York, and finally London the centers of the modern world.

VIII. THE PATTERN OF ORGANIZATION OF THE CITY AND OF CIVILIZATION

I have called attention earlier in this paper to the fact that every extension of the periphery of a civilization or a cultural area involves a new concentration at the center. But in the modern world there are, as I have pointed out, not one but many centers, and not all of them are concerned with commerce. It will be possible to present this relation between the centers and the circumference of the modern world a little more clearly, and a little more abstractly, if we look for a moment at the cities themselves, and consider how they are organized and how they are related to one another.

There seems to be a very direct relation between the size of the city and the area which it dominates, politically, culturally, or commercially. In fact, cities as well as the areas of which they are the centers grow at the same time and in something like the same extent on the peripheries and at the centers. Thus there is a very definite relation between the height of buildings at the business center and the limits of the surrounding suburban areas, between land values and trading areas.

The patterns which metropolitan regions assume are due in the main to geography and to transportation, but also to the differing functions which the different suburbs, in the metropolitan economy, perform. Thus we have residential suburbs, industrial suburbs, and satellite cities, because the industrial laborer wants to live next to his work, while the business and professional man prefers to work at the center and live at the periphery, making his residence in the so-called dormitory suburb.

There is a constant movement outward of industry and population; but there is, at the same time, a constant concentration of professional and special services, of office buildings, and of everything that involves control at the center. The chain store and the branch bank are illustrations of this double movement. The function of distribution moves out but control and management move in.

Precisely the same thing takes place, with the improvement of transportation and communication in that larger unit, the world. Capital moves out—is exported to South America, to China, to the ends of the world—but control remains in London and New York. Thus London became the world financial center, not because English bankers had the most money, but because they invested the most money abroad. If it continues to be the world's financial center, it will probably do so not merely because it has the largest foreign investment but because it has the most information; is better able to interpret the news, and to make the proper responses to events.

The city is the microcosm in which is reflected, often in advance of their actual appearance, changes impending in the macrocosm. This means that London, New York, Chicago have completed changes in their internal organization that are still in progress in Shanghai, Bombay, and Constantinople. It means, further, in all probability, that changes in international relations, in what Graham Wallis calls "The Great Society," will eventually assume a pattern not unlike that of a metropolis and its suburbs.

Just as in the United States the different cities and different suburbs tend to specialize, each performing in the metropolitan or national economy some special function, so the different cities of the world, no longer in direct competition to the extent that they once were, are finding their special place and peculiar function in the world-economy, and in that larger cultural unit we call civilization.

IX. CULTURAL CENTERS NOT ECONOMIC

This position is not always determined by what are ordinarily described as economic forces. Why is Mecca the center of the Mohammedan world? It was once, to be sure, an important trading center. It is so no longer.

Why did the Bishop of Rome become the Pope, and Rome the Catholic capital of the world? Because Rome was at one time the center of the civilized world. It has long since ceased to occupy that position.

Why has Paris so long been able to dictate the fashions? Why has New York become the publication center of the United States, although it is no longer the center of the printing trade, the result being that journals published in New York are printed in Chicago, even when that involves the added expense of sending copy to the printer by telegraph? *Time*, for example, is published in New York but printed and distributed in Chicago.

One may state the matter in more general terms. Why does every cultural area, as Clark Wissler pointed out, have a center and a circumference? [3]

His explanation of the fact is geographical. The reason why every cultural area has a center is that the conditions of organic life of the area is richer at the center and the conditions for human adjustment are better there.[4] The point is, that it is at the centers of a cultural area that you get the novelties and the new inventions.

This principle does not seem to explain either Paris, Rome, or Mecca. Besides, as it has been pointed out by Dixon, changes take place on the periphery as well as at the center, in an expanding cultural area.[5]

X. THE EXPLANATION OF THE DOMINANCE OF CITIES

The reason why Rome is the center of the Catholic world and Paris dictates the fashions to Europe and to America seems to be because both Rome and Paris, in respect to the specific cultural interests they represent, are, at the same time, each the locus of tradition and the center of news.

This means that it is possible in these cities to act more promptly

---

[3] Clark Wissler, *Relation of Nature to Man in Aboriginal America*, N. Y., 1926, p. 41.
[4] *Ibid.*, p. 219.
[5] Roland Burrage Dixon, *The Building of Cultures*.

and with greater precision with respect to the special interests with which these cities elsewhere are concerned. It is not the authority vested in the Pope that makes or has made Rome the center of the Catholic world. It is because there is at Rome a tradition and a group of individuals, a faculty, whose experience, knowledge, and sources of information with respect to that world have enabled the church to maintain its various functions through all the exigencies and vicissitudes of a changing world. The authority of the Pope and the dominance of Rome itself (in its own religious world) are but the incidental products of this functioning through a long period of time. It is not the Pope that made Rome. Rather one might say: "Rome made the Pope."

In the same way the dominance that New York has achieved in finance, in the publication of books, and in the theatrical world is due to the fact that in these different lines of interest New York brought together a larger number of competent persons in these several fields than any other part of the country has been able to do; that out of the competition and cooperation of these individuals in their several fields there has grown up a tradition which has served as a basis for innovations, improvements, and inventions which not only preserve the existing tradition but perfect it.

It is thus that fruitful inventions come into existence everywhere. They are always modifications, more or less thoroughgoing, of what already exists. Each new invention rests on all the inventions that preceded it.

It is the essence of fashion to change, but not to change too much or too abruptly. Cultural changes take place like changes in fashion, with relatively little break in the existing tradition. It is in the cultural centers also, that is to say, in the cities, that new inventions and new specializations of existing cultural traits appear, but these changes tend to be orthogenic in character, that is to say, progressive.

This explanation seems to hold equally of Mecca, the center of Mohammedan culture, and of London, the present financial center of the world. It is the existence in these cities of a tradition, in the light of which the news has a significance it would not otherwise have that has enabled not only Mecca but London, in spite of the shifts and changes in every part of the world, to maintain their prestige and to remain the seat of powers that are certainly very great even if quite incalculable.

Viewed abstractly, dominance in the social world seems to be very much the same as dominance in the biological organism as Child describes that phenomenon in his *Physiological Foundations of Behavior*. Dominance, as he says, is related to excitement and transmission, that is to say, related to what might be described as organic news and communication. In the biological, as in the social organism, dominance begins at the point at which the organism is most responsive to stimulus. The different sense organs are those parts of the body that have in the course of the growth and evolution of the organism become most sensitive to certain types of stimulation, i.e., the eye to light waves and the ear to sound waves. Control in the organism is, finally, centered at the point where these sense organs are located.

It is precisely the same with respect to the functions which different cities perform in this social organism we call civilization. They become dominant in certain parts of the world and in certain regions of the general collective life because, for some reason, they are more responsive to certain kinds of stimulation than to others. Paris is keen on the fashions, Hollywood on the moving picture and because they are responsive to everything that concerns these specific interests they gradually acquire a prestige and tradition which defines their function and their special role in respect to other cities and to civilization in general.

CONCLUSION

In conclusion, I may say that the contributions which cities have made to civilization have not been in the preservation nor perfection of any specific racial stock or any particular cultural type. On the whole, the influence of cities has been to destroy the existing racial stock by interbreeding; and in other respects the influence of the urban environment has been dysgenic than otherwise. Cities and civilizations have grown at the expense of existing cultures. Neither have the cities made any considerable contribution to morals as we ordinarily understand that term. Quite the contrary. Cities have been proverbially and very properly described as "wicked."

What cities have done have been (1) to bring together people from the ends of the earth, not because they were like-minded or of the same racial stock but simply because they were useful to one another, and useful, in all probability, because they were different.

At any rate, great cities have always been cosmopolitan. They have always been the melting pots for races and cultures.

(2) To bring people of different races, cultures, and individual capacities into competition with one another for a livelihood, the effect of which has been to destroy the older kinship and cultural groups and to sort out and place every individual into the position and in the occupation, irrespective of race or previous condition, where he was likely to be most efficient, that is to say, to make the largest contribution to the common good. This process has been interrupted from time to time where occupations have been inherited and classification on the basis of occupation has hardened into caste. Still, the effect of city life has always been to break up classes and castes in the interest of economic efficiency.

(3) To greatly extend the division of labor, and by multiplying occupations and professions, to enable every individual, by concentrating on some single task, to make a greater contribution to the common fund of values than he otherwise would have been able to do.

(4) To break what Bagehot calls the "cake of custom," thus freeing the individual from the routine which tradition imposes, stimulating his ambition and his energy for new and strange inventions and achievements.

(5) To diffuse these inventions and achievements by providing a market-place and a medium of exchange and thus, indirectly, standardizing local cultural traits or eventually incorporating them as integral parts of a common and world-wide culture which we call civilization.

It is in some such fashion, it seems to me, that we must view the city if we are to understand its importance as an instrument in the evolution and extension of civilization.

PART TWO: *Human Ecology*

CHAPTER 12

Human Ecology

I. THE WEB OF LIFE

NATURALISTS of the last century were greatly intrigued by their observation of the interrelations and co-ordinations, within the realm of animate nature, of the numerous, divergent, and widely scattered species. Their successors, the botanists and zoölogists of the present day, have turned their attention to more specific inquiries, and the "realm of nature," like the concept of evolution, has come to be for them a notion remote and speculative.

The "web of life," in which all living organisms, plants and animals alike, are bound together in a vast system of interlinked and interdependent lives, is nevertheless, as J. Arthur Thomson put it, "one of the fundamental biological concepts" and is "as characteristically Darwinian as the struggle for existence."[1]

Darwin's famous instance of the cats and the clover is the classic illustration of this interdependence. He found, he explains, that humblebees were almost indispensable to the fertilization of the heartsease, since other bees do not visit this flower. The same thing is true with some kinds of clover. Humblebees alone visit red clover, as other bees cannot reach the nectar. The inference is that if the humblebees became extinct or very rare in England, the heartsease and red clover would become very rare, or wholly disappear. However, the number of humblebees in any district depends in a great

---

Reprinted by permission of the publisher from the *American Journal of Sociology*, XLII (July, 1936), pp. 1-15.

[1] *The System of Animate Nature* (Gifford Lectures, 1915-16), II (New York, 1920), 58.

measure on the number of field mice, which destroy their combs and nests. It is estimated that more than two-thirds of them are thus destroyed all over England. Near villages and small towns the nests of humblebees are more numerous than elsewhere and this is attributed to the number of cats that destroy the mice.[2] Thus next year's crop of purple clover in certain parts of England depends on the number of humblebees in the district; the number of humblebees depends upon the number of field mice, the number of field mice upon the number and the enterprise of the cats, and the number of cats—as someone has added—depends on the number of old maids and others in neighboring villages who keep cats.

These large food chains, as they are called, each link of which eats the other, have as their logical prototype the familiar nursery rhyme, "The House that Jack Built." You recall:

> The cow with the crumpled horn,
> That tossed the dog,
> That worried the cat,
> That killed the rat,
> That ate the malt
> That lay in the house that Jack built.

Darwin and the naturalists of his day were particularly interested in observing and recording these curious illustrations of the mutual adaptation and correlation of plants and animals because they seemed to throw light on the origin of the species. Both the species and their mutual interdependence, within a common habitat, seem to be a product of the same Darwinian struggle for existence.

It is interesting to note that it was the application to organic life of a sociological principle—the principle, namely, of "competitive co-operation"—that gave Darwin the first clue to the formulation of his theory of evolution.

"He projected on organic life," says Thomson, "a sociological idea," and "thus vindicated the relevancy and utility of a sociological idea within the biological realm." [3]

The active principle in the ordering and regulating of life within the realm of animate nature is, as Darwin described it, "the struggle for existence." By this means the numbers of living organisms are regulated, their distribution controlled, and the balance of nature

---

[2] J. Arthur Thomson, *Darwinism and Human Life* (New York, 1911), pp. 52-53.

[3] *Ibid.*, p. 72.

maintained. Finally, it is by means of this elementary form of competition that the existing species, the survivors in the struggle, find their niches in the physical environment and in the existing correlation or division of labor between the different species. J. Arthur Thomson makes an impressive statement of the matter in his *System of Animate Nature*. He says:

The hosts of living organisms are not . . . . isolated creatures, for every thread of life is intertwined with others in a complex web. . . . . Flowers and insects are fitted to one another as hand to glove. Cats have to do with the plague in India as well as with the clover crop at home. . . . . *Just as there is a correlation of organs in the body, so there is a correlation of organisms in the world of life.* When we learn something of the intricate give and take, supply and demand, action and reaction between plants and animals, between flowers and insects, between herbivores and carnivores, and between other conflicting yet correlated interests, we begin to get a glimpse of a vast self-regulating organization.

These manifestations of a living, changing, but persistent order among competing organisms—organisms embodying "conflicting yet correlated interests"—seem to be the basis for the conception of a social order transcending the individual species, and of a society based on a biotic rather than a cultural basis, a conception later developed by the plant and animal ecologists.

In recent years the plant geographers have been the first to revive something of the earlier field naturalists' interest in the interrelations of species. Haeckel, in 1878, was the first to give to these studies a name, "ecology," and by so doing gave them the character of a distinct and separate science, a science which Thomson describes as "the new natural history." [4]

The interrelation and interdependence of the species are naturally more obvious and more intimate within the common habitat than elsewhere. Furthermore, as correlations have multiplied and competition has decreased, in consequence of mutual adaptations of the competing species, the habitat and habitants have tended to assume the character of a more or less completely closed system.

Within the limits of this system the individual units of the population are involved in a process of competitive co-operation, which has given to their interrelations the character of a natural economy.

---

[4] "Ecology," says Elton, "corresponds to the older terms Natural History and Bionomics, but its methods are now accurate and precise." See article, "Ecology," *Encyclopaedia Britannica* (14th ed.).

To such a habitat and its inhabitants—whether plant, animal, or human—the ecologists have applied the term "community."

The essential characteristics of a community, so conceived, are those of: (1) a population, territorially organized, (2) more or less completely rooted in the soil it occupies, (3) its individual units living in a relationship of mutual interdependence that is symbiotic rather than societal, in the sense in which that term applies to human beings.

These symbiotic societies are not merely unorganized assemblages of plants and animals which happen to live together in the same habitat. On the contrary, they are interrelated in the most complex manner. Every community has something of the character of an organic unit. It has a more or less definite structure and it has "a life history in which juvenile, adult and senile phases can be observed." [5] If it is an organism, it is one of the organs which are other organisms. It is, to use Spencer's phrase, a superorganism.

What more than anything else gives the symbiotic community the character of an organism is the fact that it possesses a mechanism (competition) for (1) regulating the numbers and (2) preserving the balance between the competing species of which it is composed. It is by maintaining this biotic balance that the community preserves its identity and integrity as an individual unit through the changes and the vicissitudes to which it is subject in the course of its progress from the earlier to the later phases of its existence.

II. THE BALANCE OF NATURE

The balance of nature, as plant and animal ecologists have conceived it, seems to be largely a question of numbers. When the pressure of population upon the natural resources of the habitat reaches a certain degree of intensity, something invariably happens. In the one case the population may swarm and relieve the pressure of population by migration. In another, where the disequilibrium between population and natural resources is the result of some change, sudden or gradual, in the conditions of life, the pre-existing correlation of the species may be totally destroyed.

Change may be brought about by a famine, an epidemic, or an invasion of the habitat by some alien species. Such an invasion may result in a rapid increase of the invading population and a sudden decline in the numbers if not the destruction of the original popula-

---

[5] Edward J. Salisbury, "Plants," *Encyclopaedia Britannica* (14th ed.).

tion. Change of some sort is continuous, although the rate and pace of change sometimes vary greatly. Charles Elton says:

> The impression of anyone who has studied animal numbers in the field is that the "balance of nature" hardly exists, except in the minds of scientists. It seems that animal numbers are always tending to settle down into a smooth and harmonious working mechanism, but something always happens before this happy state is reached.[6]

Under ordinary circumstances, such minor fluctuations in the biotic balance as occur are mediated and absorbed without profoundly disturbing the existing equilibrium and routine of life. When, on the other hand, some sudden and catastrophic change occurs—it may be a war, a famine, or pestilence—it upsets the biotic balance, breaks "the cake of custom," and releases energies up to that time held in check. A series of rapid and even violent changes may ensue which profoundly alter the existing organization of communal life and give a new direction to the future course of events.

The advent of the boll weevil in the southern cotton fields is a minor instance but illustrates the principle. The boll weevil crossed the Rio Grande at Brownsville in the summer of 1892. By 1894 the pest had spread to a dozen counties in Texas, bringing destruction to the cotton and great losses to the planters. From that point it advanced, with every recurring season, until by 1928 it had covered practically all the cotton producing area in the United States. Its progress took the form of a territorial succession. The consequences to agriculture were catastrophic but not wholly for the worse, since they served to give an impulse to changes in the organization of the industry long overdue. It also hastened the northward migration of the Negro tenant farmer.

The case of the boll weevil is typical. In this mobile modern world, where space and time have been measurably abolished, not men only but all the minor organisms (including the microbes) seem to be, as never before, in motion. Commerce, in progressively destroying the isolation upon which the ancient order of nature rested, has intensified the struggle for existence over an ever widening area of the habitable world. Out of this struggle a new equilibrium and a new system of animate nature, the new biotic basis of the new world-society, is emerging.

It is, as Elton remarks, the "fluctuation of numbers" and "the

---

[6] "Animal Ecology," *ibid.*

failure" from time to time "of the regulatory mechanism of animal increase" which ordinarily interrupts the established routine, and in so doing releases a new cycle of change. In regard to these fluctuations in numbers Elton says:

These failures of the regulating mechanism of animal increase—are they caused by (1) internal changes, after the manner of an alarm clock which suddenly goes off, or the boilers of an engine blowing up, or are they caused by some factors in the outer environment—weather, vegetation, or something like that? [7]

and he adds:

It appears that they are due to both but that the latter (external factor) is the more important of the two, and usually plays the leading rôle.

The conditions which affect and control the movements and numbers of populations are more complex in human societies than in plant and animal communities, but they exhibit extraordinary similarities.

The boll weevil, moving out of its ancient habitat in the central Mexican plateau and into the virgin territory of the southern cotton plantations, incidentally multiplying its population to the limit of the territories and resources, is not unlike the Boers of Cape Colony, South Africa, trekking out into the high veldt of the central South African plateau and filling it, within a period of one hundred years, with a population of their own descendants.

Competition operates in the human (as it does in the plant and animal) community to bring about and restore the communal equilibrium, when, either by the advent of some intrusive factor from without or in the normal course of its life-history, that equilibrium is disturbed.

Thus every crisis that initiates a period of rapid change, during which competition is intensified, moves over finally into a period of more or less stable equilibrium and a new division of labor. In this manner competition brings about a condition in which competition is superseded by co-operation.

It is when, and to the extent that, competition declines that the kind of order which we call society may be said to exist. In short, society, from the ecological point of view, and in so far as it is a territorial unit, is just the area within which biotic competition has

[7] *Ibid.*

declined and the struggle for existence has assumed higher and more sublimated forms.

III. COMPETITION, DOMINANCE AND SUCCESSION

There are other and less obvious ways in which competition exercises control over the relations of individuals and species within the communal habitat. The two ecological principles, dominance and succession, which operate to establish and maintain such communal order as here described are functions of, and dependent upon, competition.

In every life-community there is always one or more dominant species. In a plant community this dominance is ordinarily the result of struggle among the different species for light. In a climate which supports a forest the dominant species will invariably be trees. On the prairie and steppes they will be grasses.

Light being the main necessity of plants, the dominant plant of a community is the tallest member, which can spread its green energy-trap above the heads of the others. What marginal exploitation there is to be done is an exploitation of the dimmer light below this canopy. So it comes about in every life-community on land, in the cornfield just as in the forest, that there are layers of vegetation, each adapted to exist in a lesser intensity of light than the one above. Usually there are but two or three such layers; in an oak-wood for example there will be a layer of moss, above this herbs or low bushes, and then nothing more to the leafy roof; in the wheat-field the dominating form is the wheat, with lower weeds among its stalks. But in tropical forests the whole space from floor to roof may be zoned and populated.[8]

But the principle of dominance operates in the human as well as in the plant and animal communities. The so-called natural or functional areas of a metropolitan community—for example, the slum, the rooming-house area, the central shopping section and the banking center—each and all owe their existence directly to the factor of dominance, and indirectly to competition.

The struggle of industries and commercial institutions for a strategic location determines in the long run the main outlines of the urban community. The distribution of population, as well as the location and limits of the residential areas which they occupy, are determined by another similar but subordinate system of forces.

The area of dominance in any community is usually the area of

---

[8] H. G. Wells, Julian S. Huxley, and G. P. Wells, *The Science of Life* (New York, 1934), pp. 968-69.

highest land values. Ordinarily there are in every large city two such positions of highest land value—one in the central shopping district, the other in the central banking area. From these points land values decline at first precipitantly and then more gradually toward the periphery of the urban community. It is these land values that determine the location of social institutions and business enterprises. Both the one and the other are bound up in a kind of territorial complex within which they are at once competing and interdependent units.

As the metropolitan community expands into the suburbs the pressure of professions, business enterprises, and social institutions of various sorts destined to serve the whole metropolitan region steadily increases the demand for space at the center. Thus not merely the growth of the suburban area, but any change in the method of transportation which makes the central business area of the city more accessible, tends to increase the pressure at the center. From thence this pressure is transmitted and diffused, as the profile of land values discloses, to every other part of the city.

Thus the principle of dominance, operating within the limits imposed by the terrain and other natural features of the location, tends to determine the general ecological pattern of the city and the functional relation of each of the different areas of the city to all others.

Dominance is, furthermore, in so far as it tends to stabilize either the biotic or the cultural community, indirectly responsible for the phenomenon of succession.

The term "succession" is used by ecologists to describe and designate that orderly sequence of changes through which a biotic community passes in the course of its development from a primary and relatively unstable to a relatively permanent or climax stage. The main point is that not merely do the individual plants and animals within the communal habitat grow but the community itself, i.e., the system of relations between the species, is likewise involved in an orderly process of change and development.

The fact that, in the course of this development, the community moves through a series of more or less clearly defined stages is the fact that gives this development the serial character which the term "succession" suggests.

The explanation of the serial character of the changes involved in succession is the fact that at every stage in the process a more or less stable equilibrium is achieved, which in due course, and as a result of progressive changes in life-conditions, possibly due to growth and decay, the equilibrium achieved in the earlier stages is eventually undermined. In such case the energies previously held in balance will be released, competition will be intensified, and change will continue at a relatively rapid rate until a new equilibrium is achieved.

The climax phase of community development corresponds with the adult phase of an individual's life.

In the developing single organism, each phase is its own executioner, and itself brings a new phase into existence, as when the tadpole grows the thyroid gland which is destined to make the tadpole state pass away in favour of the miniature frog. And in the developing community of organisms, the same thing happens—each stage alters its own environment, for it changes and almost invariably enriches the soil in which it lives; and thus it eventually brings itself to an end, by making it possible for new kinds of plants with greater demands in the way of mineral salts or other riches of the soil to flourish there. Accordingly bigger and more exigent plants gradually supplant the early pioneers, until a final balance is reached, the ultimate possibility for that climate.[9]

The cultural community develops in comparable ways to that of the biotic, but the process is more complicated. Inventions, as well as sudden or catastrophic changes, seem to play a more important part in bringing about serial changes in the cultural than in the biotic community. But the principle involved seems to be substantially the same. In any case, all or most of the fundamental processes seem to be functionally related and dependent upon competition.

Competition, which on the biotic level functions to control and regulate the interrelations of organisms, tends to assume on the social level the form of conflict. The intimate relation between competition and conflict is indicated by the fact that wars frequently, if not always, have, or seem to have, their source and origin in economic competition which, in that case, assumes the more sublimated form of a struggle for power and prestige. The social function of war, on the other hand, seems to be to extend the area over which it is possible to maintain peace.

IV. BIOLOGICAL ECONOMICS

If population pressure, on the one hand, co-operates with changes in local and environmental conditions to disturb at once the

---

[9] *Ibid.*, pp. 977-78.

biotic balance and social equilibrium, it tends at the same time to intensify competition. In so doing it functions, indirectly, to bring about a new, more minute and, at the same time, territorially extensive division of labor.

Under the influence of an intensified competition, and the increased activity which competition involves, every individual and every species, each for itself, tends to discover the particular niche in the physical and living environment where it can survive and flourish with the greatest possible expansiveness consistent with its necessary dependence upon its neighbors.

It is in this way that a territorial organization and a biological division of labor, within the communal habitat, is established and maintained. This explains, in part at least, the fact that the biotic community has been conceived at one time as a kind of superorganism and at another as a kind of economic organization for the exploitation of the natural resources of its habitat.

In their interesting survey, *The Science of Life,* H. G. Wells and his collaborators, Julian Huxley and G. P. Wells, have described ecology as "biological economics," and as such very largely concerned with "the balances and mutual pressures of species living in the same habitat." [10]

"Ecology," as they put it, is "an extension of Economics to the whole of life." On the other hand the science of economics as traditionally conceived, though it is a whole century older, is merely a branch of a more general science of ecology which includes man with all other living creatures. Under the circumstances what has been traditionally described as economics and conceived as restricted to human affairs, might very properly be described as Barrows some years ago described geography, namely as human ecology. It is in this sense that Wells and his collaborators would use the term.

The science of economics, at first it was called Political Economy—is a whole century older than ecology. It was and is the science of social subsistence, of needs and their satisfactions, of work and wealth. It tries to elucidate the relations of producer, dealer, and consumer in the human community and show how the whole system carries on. Ecology broadens out this inquiry into a general study of the give and take, the effort, accumulation and consumption in every province of life. Economics, therefore, is merely Human Ecology, it is the narrow and special study of

---

[10] *Ibid.*

the ecology of the very extraordinary community in which we live. It might have been a better and brighter science if it had begun biologically.[11]

Since human ecology cannot be at the same time both geography and economics, one may adopt, as a working hypothesis, the notion that it is neither one nor the other but something independent of both. Even so the motives for identifying ecology with geography on the one hand, and economics on the other, are fairly obvious.

From the point of view of geography, the plant, animal, and human population, including their habitations and other evidence of man's occupation of the soil, are merely part of the landscape, of which the geographer is seeking a detailed description and picture.

On the other hand ecology (biologic economics), even when it involves some sort of unconscious co-operation and a natural, spontaneous, and non-rational division of labor, is something different from the economics of commerce; something quite apart from the bargaining of the market place. Commerce, as Simmel somewhere remarks, is one of the latest and most complicated of all the social relationships into which human beings have entered. Man is the only animal that trades and traffics.

Ecology, and human ecology, if it is not indentical with economics on the distinctively human and cultural level is, nevertheless, some thing more than and different from the static order which the human geographer discovers when he surveys the cultural landscape.

The community of the geographer is not, for one thing, like that of the ecologist, a closed system, and the web of communication which man has spread over the earth is something different from the "web of life" which binds living creatures all over the world in a vital nexus.

V. SYMBIOSIS AND SOCIETY

Human ecology, if it is neither economics on one hand nor geography on the other, but just ecology, differs, nevertheless, in important respects from plant and animal ecology. The interrelations of human beings and interactions of man and his habitat are comparable but not identical with interrelations of other forms of life that live together and carry on a kind of "biological economy" within the limits of a common habitat.

---

[11] H. H. Barrows, "Geography as Human Ecology," *Annals Association American Geographers*, XIII (1923), 1-14. See H. G. Wells, *et al., op. cit.,* pp. 961-62.

For one thing man is not so immediately dependent upon his physical environment as other animals. As a result of the existing world-wide division of labor, man's relation to his physical environment has been mediated through the intervention of other men. The exchange of goods and services have co-operated to emancipate him from dependence upon his local habitat.

Furthermore man has, by means of inventions and technical devices of the most diverse sorts, enormously increased his capacity for reacting upon and remaking, not only his habitat but his world. Finally, man has erected upon the basis of the biotic community an institutional structure rooted in custom and tradition.

Structure, where it exists, tends to resist change, at least change coming from without; while it possibly facilitates the cumulation of change within.[12] In plant and animal communities structure is biologically determined, and so far as any division of labor exists at all it has a physiological and instinctive basis. The social insects afford a conspicuous example of this fact, and one interest in studying their habits, as Wheeler points out, is that they show the extent to which social organization can be developed on a purely physiological and instinctive basis, as is the case among human beings in the natural as distinguished from the institutional family.[13]

In a society of human beings, however, this communal structure is reinforced by custom and assumes an institutional character. In human as contrasted with animal societies, competition and the freedom of the individual is limited on every level above the biotic by custom and consensus.

The incidence of this more or less arbitrary control which custom and consensus imposes upon the natural social order complicates the social process but does not fundamentally alter it—or, if it does, the effects of biotic competition will still be manifest in the succeeding social order and the subsequent course of events.

---

[12] Here is, obviously, another evidence of that organic character of the interrelations of organisms in the biosphere to which J. Arthur Thomson and others have referred. It is an indication of the way in which competition mediates the influences from without by the adjustment and readjustment of relations within the community. In this case "within" coincides with the orbit of the competitive process, at least so far as the effects of that process are substantive and obvious. See Simmel's definition of society and the social group in time and space quoted in Park and Burgess, *Introduction to the Science of Sociology* (2d ed.), pp. 348-56.

[13] William Morton Wheeler, *Social Life among the Insects* (Lowell Institute Lectures, March, 1922), pp. 3-18.

The fact seems to be, then, that human society, as distinguished from plant and animal society, is organized on two levels, the biotic and the cultural. There is a symbiotic society based on competition and a cultural society based on communication and consensus. As a matter of fact the two societies are merely different aspects of one society, which, in the vicissitudes and changes to which they are subject remain, nevertheless, in some sort of mutual dependence each upon the other. The cultural superstructure rests on the basis of the symbiotic substructure, and the emergent energies that manifest themselves on the biotic level in movements and actions reveal themselves on the higher social level in more subtle and sublimated forms.

However, the interrelations of human beings are more diverse and complicated than this dichotomy, symbiotic and cultural, indicates. This fact is attested by the divergent systems of human interrelations which have been the subject of the special social sciences. Thus human society, certainly in its mature and more rational expression, exhibits not merely an ecological, but an economic, a political, and a moral order. The social sciences include not merely human geography and ecology, but economics, political science, and cultural anthropology.

It is interesting also that these divergent social orders seem to arrange themselves in a kind of hierarchy. In fact they may be said to form a pyramid of which the ecological order constitutes the base and the moral order the apex. Upon each succeeding one of these levels, the ecological, economic, political, and moral, the individual finds himself more completely incorporated into and subordinated to the social order of which he is a part than upon the preceding.

Society is everywhere a control organization. Its function is to organize, integrate, and direct the energies resident in the individuals of which it is composed. One might, perhaps, say that the function of society was everywhere to restrict competition and by so doing bring about a more effective co-operation of the organic units of which society is composed.

Competition, on the biotic level, as we observe it in the plant and animal communities, seems to be relatively unrestricted. Society, so far as it exists, is anarchic and free. On the cultural level, this freedom of the individual to compete is restricted by conventions, understandings, and law. The individual is more free upon the economic level than upon the political, more free on the political than the moral.

As society matures control is extended and intensified and free commerce of individuals restricted, if not by law then by what Gilbert Murray refers to as "the normal expectation of mankind." The mores are merely what men, in a situation that is defined, have come to expect.

Human ecology, in so far as it is concerned with a social order that is based on competition rather than consensus, is identical, in principle at least, with plant and animal ecology. The problems with which plant and animal ecology have been traditionally concerned are fundamentally population problems. Society, as ecologists have conceived it, is a population settled and limited to its habitat. The ties that unite its individual units are those of a free and natural economy, based on a natural division of labor. Such a society is territorially organized and the ties which hold it together are physical and vital rather than customary and moral.

Human ecology has, however, to reckon with the fact that in human society competition is limited by custom and culture. The cultural superstructure imposes itself as an instrument of direction and control upon the biotic substructure.

Reduced to its elements the human community, so conceived, may be said to consist of a population and a culture, including in the term culture (1) a body of customs and beliefs and (2) a corresponding body of artifacts and technological devices.

To these three elements or factors—(1) population, (2) artifact (technological culture), (3) custom and beliefs (non-material culture)—into which the social complex resolves itself, one should, perhaps, add a fourth, namely, the natural resources of the habitat. It is the interaction of these four factors that maintain at once the biotic balance and the social equilibrium, when and where they exist.

The changes in which ecology is interested are the movements of population and of artifacts (commodities) and changes in location and occupation—any sort of change, in fact, which affects an existing division of labor or the relation of the population to the soil.

Human ecology is, fundamentally, an attempt to investigate the processes by which the biotic balance and the social equilibrium (1) are maintained once they are achieved and (2) the processes by which, when the biotic balance and the social equilibrium are disturbed, the transition is made from one relatively stable order to another.

CHAPTER 13

DOMINANCE

THE CONCEPT: ITS ORIGIN AND NATURAL HISTORY

THE simplest way in which to conceive the dominance with which we are here concerned is in the sense in which geographers or descriptive writers sometimes use the term in describing some of the more obvious and outstanding features of a landscape. In this sense we may say that the mountain dominates the plain; or that the castle or fortress, buttressed and protected by the cliffs upon which it stands, dominates the valley. In the latter case the notion of dominance is not confined to the mere pictorial aspects of the scene but includes a reference to the obvious value of the location as a vantage point from which to resist and attack or to survey a wide area of potential action. In any case, orientation, as well as security and the permanence that security ensures, seem to be factors in every form of dominance, which involves administration and control of people or affairs.

Dominance is, however, a term which applies not merely to persons but to things, and it is as a thing, acting upon other things, and not as a mere pictorial feature of the landscape, that constitutes the geographer's ultimate interest in the mountain. The mountain may and ordinarily will exert an influence on the direction and movement of the prevailing winds: determine the amount of clouds and sunshine, the extent of rainfall, and so determine finally the char-

Reprinted by permission of the publisher from R. D. McKenzie (ed.), *Readings in Human Ecology* (Ann Arbor, Michigan: Geo. Wahr, 1934), pp. 381-385.

acter of the soil and the vegetation, within the limits of the area in which the mountain may be said to be dominant, or within which it exercises a measurable influence.

This suggests that any feature in the landscape that, in the general flux, offers a point of resistance may serve as a rallying point where living things that would otherwise drift may gain a foothold and by the mutual support which, in this precarious situation, each affords the other, may succeed in maintaining some sort of common household and economy.

As a matter of fact this is just what happens in the so-called plant community, the difference being in the case of the plant community that the dominant factor in the situation is not some physical object outside the household, so to speak, but is one of the several species of plants of which the community is composed.

This characteristic of the plant community is such that it appears at first blush and is ordinarily conceived as a mere aggregate or a complex of individuals that are, to be sure, mutually dependent but do not stand in relations to one another that can be described as organic, as in the case of a plant or animal organism, where the parts not only act in concert but are at the same time connected, no matter how tenuously, by living tissue. It is not customary to describe as an organism a collective unit, no matter to what extent the functions of the different parts are integrated, since the parts are not, like the Siamese twins, actually joined.

The function of the dominant species in the plant community seems to be to impose a sort of order in the numbers, kinds and distribution of the plants and species which constitute the community. As a consequence of this dominance and the integration it imposes upon the cooperating and competing units of which it is composed, the community as a whole behaves in many respects more like an organism than would be possible in the case of a mere aggregation.

The term dominance is used very little in animal ecology, one reason being that such organization as exists in the animal and more particularly in insect communities, rests on a territorial rather than a familial basis. It is organized for collective action, in attack and defense, rather than for competitive cooperation as in the case of the plants.

The concept dominance is used in a very interesting way in physiology in describing the processes of growth and the integration of the different functions of the physiological organization in such way as to achieve coordination and concert. It is this which makes possible the behavior that Child describes as organismic as contrasted with segmental behavior. Organismic behavior is behavior of the organism as a whole. Organismic behavior in the individual corresponds to collective behavior in the group.

Child attempts to interpret so-called organismic behavior in social and political terms. (See Child's *Physiological Foundations of Behavior.*) Dominance as he conceives it includes all the processes by which the organism is enabled to concert and control its responses to external environment, and the growth and structure of the organism is the form in which these responses are progressively formed and made more effective. The location of dominance is that portion of the body of the organism that is most responsive to stimuli from within and without the organism.

Human society, so far as it can be described as a biotic rather than a social organism, exhibits forms of organization and of dominance which exhibit a character somewhere between that of the plant community and of the physiological organism. From the point of view of its territorial or communal organization, society may be conceived as a form of symbiosis.

So far as dominance in a community arises out of what Sumner calls the competition of life, it results in the regulation of numbers, the distribution of vocations, putting every individual and every race into the particular niche where it will meet the least competition and contribute most to the life of the community, the function of dominance in human society is not different from the function it performs in the plant community. It determines the orderly distribution upon the soil and in the occupational pyramid of all the individuals which society, as organized, can support, and disposes of those for which it has no place.

On the other hand as soon as society achieves a structure and its activities become institutionalized, there dominance, with reference to that structure and institution, assumes a form which is comparable with the role of dominance as Child describes it in the physiological organism. Even in the plant community it is not merely the individuals but the community, particularly in its climax phase, which reacts to intrusion of alien species and change.

An institution embodies a social function. It is the form in which the individuals who constitute society seek to act collectively for the common, rather than the individual welfare. Neither plants nor animals have institutions, but plant communities do have structure.

The function of dominance in the case of the institution is to so modify and adapt the institution as to meet most effectively the demands upon it which changing conditions impose. In this case dominance functions in the human community in much the same way as it does in the individual organism.

Thus the fundamental function of dominance seems to be everywhere the same. It is to stabilize, to maintain order, and permit the growth of structure in which that order and the corresponding functions are embodied.

In the realm of the social, as distinct from the biological, the conception of dominance has a wide application. One may speak, for example, of (1) economic, (2) political and military and of (3) cultural and moral dominance.

In human society dominance not infrequently tends to become embodied in the persons of individuals, in a chief, king, a pope, in a Stalin, Hitler, Gandhi, the Wahabi, and a Mrs. Eddy. But eventually the functions performed by individuals in times of crisis tend to become institutionalized, so that the function becomes in time identified with the office rather than the individual who occupied it. Thus the name of the first Caesar, Julius the dictator, adopted as a title by the first Roman Emperor, has been preserved in the title of the German Kaiser and the Russian Czar.

Once a function has achieved an institutional form, however, it inevitably tends to become localized and eventually identified with the place from which, as a matter of tradition or of convenience, it is ordinarily exercised. Thus London has been and still is, in spite of the competition in recent years of New York City, the dominant money market of the world. Paris is in the same sense the fashion center of the Western World. The United States dominates the Caribbean. Italy, France and England are competing for dominance in the Mediterranean. Rome, Mecca and now Moscow are the centers of three great militant and missionary religions, Catholicism, Mohammedanism, and Communism, now struggling for the hegemony of the world.

Protestant Christianity, which has had in the past the character of a group of dissenting and more or less warring sects, is militant and evangelical in character but has in recent years, since sects have begun to be denominations, begun to assume the character of a religion distinct from that of Catholicism, but it has not yet achieved sufficient unity so that it has become identified with any single local center so outstanding that it can be said to dominate the world.

This suggests, what seems to be the fact, that dominance, whether economic, political or cultural, ordinarily implies the existence at the same time of (1) a central or focal point from which control and direction emanates and (2) a domain within which this control and direction is operative. Furthermore, the limits of this area of dominance are not always clearly defined and never wholly fixed. On the contrary they are continually in process of expansion or contraction, in response to the operation of forces within and without the area of dominance.

On the other hand, as has already been suggested, in human society at least, we may expect to meet dominance on different levels: (1) the biotic, or ecological, (2) economic, (3) political, (4) cultural. All these represent forms of association which grow, expand and decline, in relative independence of one another, but are nevertheless and finally all involved in the same social complex.

Population expands, trade precedes or follows, political control arises to administer the area thus appropriated. Missions and schools accompany this expansion or eventual contraction of the domain thus appropriated and dominated.

Although these processes of expansion and of dominance proceed, on the whole, simultaneously and more or less independently, on the other hand they represent, from the point of view of logic if not in time, a definite succession. Thus the biotic association in which man lives, not only with man but other animals, is relatively at least a purely external, free and impersonal relationship. Man's economic relations, however, involve personal relations so that trade and commercial relations are free only within the limitation imposed by custom and usage. In his political association man is free only so far as his freedom is defined and guaranteed to him as constitutional rights or as his personal liberties are maintained by tradition and custom. Otherwise his relations in society take the form of personal duties and social obligations. Finally, in his more intimate relations he is limited not merely by what is customary and proper but by notions of equity, what the Chinese call *li*, and this is simply what the people in the community, or at any rate the people immediately concerned, expect of him under the circumstance.

It will be apparent that as the relations become more intimate the circle of relations becomes narrower. On the other hand the extent of the claims which the community makes upon its members becomes more pressing as the association becomes more intimate. These are, however, the conditions under which domination is exercised at the different levels mentioned.

Another distinction with reference to the character of dominance and the manner in which it is enforced upon the four different levels, is that the territorial factor which is of first importance on the biotic level, where competition is very largely a struggle for space and a spot in the sun, assumes less and less importance as relations assume a more and more personal character, as they do in proportion as one approaches the cultural level.

It is with the spatial, the local and territorial aspect of dominance that human ecology is concerned.

The assumption is that even such intimate and subjective matters as love and religion may and do have their spatial aspects, and as a matter of fact we do know that love is very largely a matter of propinquity. One interesting effect of the automobile, as Burgess points out, is increase of the area over which intermarriage ordinarily extends in rural and small town communities.

But to expand the area over which intermarriage takes place is to extend the area of personal dominance; i.e., the dominance of parents, teachers, and pastors. The offset of this extension upon personal dominance is, ordinarily, to diminish its intensity or modify its character.

CHAPTER 14

THE URBAN COMMUNITY AS A SPATIAL PATTERN AND A MORAL ORDER

SOME thirty years ago Professor Eugenius Warming, of Copenhagen, published a little volume entitled *Plant Communities* (*Plantesamfund*). Warming's observations called attention to the fact that different species of plants tend to form permanent groups, which he called communities. Plant communities, it turned out, exhibit a good many of the traits of living organisms. They come into existence gradually, pass through certain characteristic changes, and eventually are broken up and succeeded by other communities of a very different sort. These observations later become the point of departure for a series of investigations which have since become familiar under the title "Ecology."

Ecology, in so far as it seeks to describe the actual distribution of plants and animals over the earth's surface, is in some very real sense a geographical science. Human ecology, as the sociologists would like to use the term, is, however, not identical with geography, nor even with human geography. It is not man, but the community; not man's relation to the earth which he inhabits, but his relations to other men, that concerns us most.

Reprinted by permission of the publisher from *Publications of the American Sociological Society*, XX (1925), pp. 1-14, where it was published under the title "The Concept of Position in Sociology." Later it was reprinted under the present title in E. W. Burgess (ed.) *The Urban Community* (Chicago: University of Chicago Press, 1926), pp. 3-20.

Within the limits of every natural area the distribution of population tends to assume definite and typical patterns. Every local group exhibits a more or less definite constellation of the individual units that compose it. The form which this constellation takes, the position, in other words, of every individual in the community with reference to every other, so far as it can be described in general terms, constitutes what Durkheim and his school call the morphological aspect of society.[1]

Human ecology, as sociologists conceive it, seeks to emphasize not so much geography as space. In society we not only live together, but at the same time we live apart, and human relations can always be reckoned, with more or less accuracy, in terms of distance. In so far as social structure can be defined in terms of position, social changes may be described in terms of movement; and society exhibits, in one of its aspects, characters that can be measured and described in mathematical formulas.

Local communities may be compared with reference to the areas which they occupy and with reference to the relative density of population distribution within those areas. Communities are not, however, mere population aggregates. Cities, particularly great cities, where the selection and segregation of the population has gone farthest, display certain morphological characteristics which are not found in smaller population aggregates.

One of the incidents of size is diversity. Other things being equal, the larger community will have the wider division of labor. An examination a few years ago of the names of eminent persons listed in *Who's Who* indicated that in one large city (Chicago) there were, in addition to the 509 occupations listed by the census, 116 other occupations classed as professions. The number of professions requiring special and scientific training for their practice is an index and a measure of the intellectual life of the community. For the intellectual life of a community is measured not merely by the scholastic attainments of the average citizen, nor even by the communal intelligence-quotient, but by the extent to which rational

---

[1] Geographers are probably not greatly interested in social morphology as such. On the other hand, sociologists are. Geographers, like historians, have been traditionally interested in the actual rather than the typical. Where are things actually located? What did actually happen? These are the questions that geography and history have sought to answer. See *An Introduction to Geographical History*, by M. Lucien Febre.

methods have been applied to the solution of communal problems —health, industry, and social control, for example.

One reason why cities have always been the centers of intellectual life is that they have not only made possible, but have enforced, an individualization and a diversification of tasks. Only as every individual is permitted and compelled to focus his attention upon some small area of the common human experience, only as he learns to concentrates his efforts upon some small segment of the common task, can the vast co-operation which civilization demands be maintained.

In an interesting and suggestive paper read before the American Sociological Society at its meeting in Washington in 1922, Professor Burgess sketched the processes involved in the growth of cities. The growth of cities has usually been described in terms of extensions of territory and increase in numbers. The city itself has been identified with an administrative area, the municipality; but the city, with which we are here concerned, is not a formal and administrative entity. It is rather a product of natural forces, extending its own boundaries more or less independently of the limits imposed upon it for political and administrative purposes. This has become to such an extent a recognized fact that in any thoroughgoing study of the city, either as an economic or a social unit, it has been found necessary to take account of natural, rather than official, city boundaries. Thus, in the city-planning studies of New York City, under the direction of the Russell Sage Foundation, New York City includes a territory of 5,500 square miles, including in that area something like one hundred minor administrative units, cities, and villages, with a total population of 9,000,000.

We have thought of the growth of cities as taking place by a mere aggregation. But an increase in population at any point within the urban area is inevitably reflected and felt in every other part of the city. The extent to which such an increase of population in one part of the city is reflected in every other depends very largely upon the character of the local transportation system. Every extension and multiplication of the means of transportation connecting the periphery of the city with the center tends to bring more people to the central business district, and to bring them there oftener. This increases the congestion at the center; it increases, eventually, the height of office buildings and the values of the land on which these buildings stand. The influence of land values at the business center radiates from that point to every part of the city. If the growth at the center is rapid it increases the diameter of the area held for speculative purposes just outside the center. Property held for speculation is usually allowed to deteriorate. It easily assumes the character of a slum; that is to say, an area of casual and transient population, an area of dirt and disorder, "of missions and of lost souls." These neglected and sometimes abandoned regions become the points of first settlement of immigrants. Here are located our ghettos, and sometimes our bohemias, our Greenwich Villages, where artists and radicals seek refuge from the fundamentalism and the Rotarianism, and, in general, the limitations and restrictions of a Philistine World. Every large city tends to have its Greenwich Village just as it has its Wall Street.

The growth of the city involves not merely the addition of numbers, but all the incidental changes and movements that are inevitably associated with the efforts of every individual to find his place in the vast complexities of urban life. The growth of new regions, the multiplication of professions and occupations, the incidental increase in land values which urban expansion brings—all are involved in the processes of city growth, and can be measured in terms of changes of position of individuals with reference to other individuals, and to the community as a whole. Land values can be reckoned, for example, in terms of mobility of population. The highest land values exist at points where the largest number of people pass in the course of twenty-four hours.

The community, as distinguished from the individuals who compose it, has an indefinite life-span. We know that communities come into existence, expand and flourish for a time, and then decline. This is as true of human societies as it is of plant communities. We do not know with any precision as yet the rhythm of these changes. We do know that the community outlives the individuals who compose it. And this is one reason for the seemingly inevitable and perennial conflict between the interests of the individual and the community. This is one reason why it costs more to police a growing city than one which is stationary or declining.

Every new generation has to learn to accommodate itself to an order which is defined and maintained mainly by the older. Every society imposes some sort of discipline upon its members. Individuals grow up, are incorporated into the life of the community, and eventually drop out and disappear. But the community, with the moral order which it embodies, lives on. The life of the community therefore involves a kind of metabolism. It is constantly assimilating new individuals, and just as steadily, by death or otherwise, eliminating older ones. But assimilation is not a simple process, and, above all else, takes time.

The problem of assimilating the native-born is a very real one; it is the problem of the education of children in the homes and of adolescents in the schools. But the assimilation of adult migrants, finding for them places in the communal organization, is a more serious problem: it is the problem of adult education, which we have just in recent years begun to consider with any real sense of its importance.

There is another aspect of the situation which we have hardly considered. Communities whose population increase is due to the excess of births over deaths and communities whose increase is due to immigration exhibit important differences. Where growth is due to immigration, social change is of necessity more rapid and more profound. Land values, for one thing, increase more rapidly; the replacement of buildings and machinery, the movement of population, changes in occupation, increase in wealth, and reversals in social position proceed at a more rapid tempo. In general, society tends to approach conditions which are now recognized as characteristic of the frontier.

In a society in which great and rapid changes are in progress there is a greater need for public education of the sort that we ordinarily gain through the public press, through discussion and conversation. On the other hand, since personal observation and tradition, upon which common sense, as well as the more systematic investigations of science, is finally based, are not able to keep pace with changes in conditions, there occurs what has been described by Ogburn as the phenomenon of "cultural lag." Our political knowledge and our common sense do not keep up with the actual changes that are taking place in our common life. The result is, perhaps, that as the public feels itself drifting, legislative enactments are multiplied, but actual control is decreased. Then, as the public realizes the futility of legislative enactments, there is a demand for more drastic action, which expresses itself in ill-defined mass movements and, often, in mere mob violence. For example, the lynchings in the southern states and the race riots in the North.

So far as these disorders are in any sense related to movements of population—and recent studies of race riots and lynchings indicate that they are—the study of what we have described as social metabolism may furnish an index, if not an explanation, of the phenomenon of race riots.

One of the incidents of the growth of the community is the social selection and segregation of the population, and the creation, on the one hand, of natural social groups, and on the other, of natural social areas. We have become aware of this process of segregation in the case of the immigrants, and particularly in the case of the so-called historical races, peoples who, whether immigrants or not, are distinguished by racial marks. The Chinatowns, the Little Sicilies, and the other so-called "ghettos" with which students of urban life are familiar are special types of a more general species of natural area which the conditions and tendencies of city life inevitably produce.

Such segregations of population as these take place, first, upon the basis of language and of culture, and second, upon the basis of race. Within these immigrant colonies and racial ghettos, however, other processes of selection inevitably take place which bring about segregation based upon vocational interests, upon intelligence, and personal ambition. The result is that the keener, the more energetic, and the more ambitious very soon emerge from their ghettos and immigrant colonies and move into an area of second immigrant settlement, or perhaps into a cosmopolitan area in which the members of several immigrant and racial groups meet and live side by side. More and more, as the ties of race, of language, and of culture are weakened, successful individuals move out and eventually find their places in business and in the professions, among the older population group which has ceased to be identified with any language or racial group. The point is that change of occupation, personal success or failure—changes of economic and social status, in short—tend to be registered in changes of location. The physical or ecological organization of the community, in the long run, responds to and reflects the occupational and the cultural. Social selection and segregation, which create the natural groups, determine at the same time the natural areas of the city.

The modern city differs from the ancient in one important respect. The ancient city grew up around a fortress; the modern city has grown up around a market. The ancient city was the center of a region which was relatively self-sufficing. The goods that were produced were mainly for home consumption, and not for trade beyond the limits of the local community. The modern city, on the other hand, is likely to be the center of a region of very highly specialized production, with a corresponding widely extended trade area. Under these circumstances the main outlines of the modern city will be determined (1) by local geography and (2) by routes of transportation.

Local geography, modified by railways and other major means of transportation, all connecting, as they invariably do, with the larger industries, furnish the broad lines of the city plan. But these broad outlines are likely to be overlaid and modified by another and a different distribution of population and of institutions, of which the central retail shopping areas is the center. Within this central downtown area itself certain forms of business, the shops, the hotels, theaters, wholesale houses, office buildings, and banks, all tend to fall into definite and characteristic patterns, as if the position of every form of business and building in the area were somehow fixed and determined by its relation to every other.

Out on the periphery of the city, again, industrial and residential suburbs, dormitory towns, and satellite cities seem to find, in some natural and inevitable manner, their predetermined places. Within the area bounded on the one hand by the central business district and on the other by the suburbs, the city tends to take the form of a series of concentric circles. These different regions, located at different relative distances from the center, are characterized by different degrees of mobility of the population.

The area of greatest mobility, i.e., of movement and change of population, is naturally the business center itself. Here are the hotels, the dwelling-places of the transients. Except for the few permanent dwellers in these hotels, the business center, which is the city *par excellence*, empties itself every night and fills itself every morning. Outside the city, in this narrower sense of the term, are the slums, the dwelling-places of the casuals. On the edge of the slums there are likely to be regions, already in process of being submerged, characterized as the "rooming-house areas," the dwelling-places of bohemians, transient adventurers of all sorts, and the unsettled young folk of both sexes. Beyond these are the apartment-house areas, the region of small families and delicatessen shops. Finally, out beyond all else, are the regions of duplex apartments and of single dwellings, where people still own their homes and raise children, as they do, to be sure, in the slums.

The typical urban community is actually much more complicated than this description indicates, and there are characteristic variations for different types and sizes of cities. The main point, however, is that everywhere the community tends to conform to some pattern, and this pattern invariably turns out to be a constellation of typical urban areas, all of which can be geographically located and spatially defined.

Natural areas are the habitats of natural groups. Every typical urban area is likely to contain a characteristic selection of the population of the community as a whole. In great cities the divergence in manners, in standards of living, and in general outlook on life in different urban areas is often astonishing. The difference in sex and age groups, perhaps the most significant indexes of social life, are strikingly divergent for different natural areas. There are regions in the city in which there are almost no children, areas occupied by the residential hotels, for example. There are regions where the number of children is relatively very high: in the slums, in the middle-class residential suburbs, to which the newly married usually graduate from their first honeymoon apartments in the city. There are other areas occupied almost wholly by young unmarried people, boy and girl bachelors. There are regions where people almost never vote, except at national elections; regions where the divorce rate is higher than it is for any state in the Union, and other regions in the same city where there are almost no divorces. There are areas infested by boy gangs and the athletic and political clubs into which the members of these gangs or the gangs themselves frequently graduate. There are regions in which the suicide rate is excessive; regions in which there is, as recorded by statistics, an excessive amount of juvenile delinquency, and other regions in which there is almost none.

All this emphasizes the importance of location, position, and mobility as indexes for measuring, describing, and eventually explaining social phenomena. Bergson has defined mobility as "just the idea of motion which we form when we think of it by itself, when, so to speak, from motion we abstract mobility." Mobility measures social change and social disorganization, because social change almost always involves some incidental change of position in space, and all social change, even that which we describe as progress, involves some social disorganization. In the paper already referred to, Professor Burgess points out that various forms of social disorganization seem to be roughly correlated with changes in city life that can be measured in terms of mobility. All this suggests a further speculation. Since so much that students of society are ordinarily interested in seems to be intimately related to position, distribution, and movements in space, it is not impossible that all we ordinarily conceive as social may eventually be construed and described in terms of space and the changes of position of the individuals within the limits of a natural area; that is to say, within the limits of an area of competitive co-operation. Under such interesting conditions as these all social phenomena might eventually become subject to measurement, and sociology would become actually what some persons have sought to make it, a branch of statistics.

Such a scheme of description and explanation of social phenomena, if it could be carried out without too great a simplification of the facts, would certainly be a happy solution of some of the fundamental logical and epistemological problems of sociology. Reduce all social relations to relations of space and it would be possible to apply to human relations the fundamental logic of the physical sciences. Social phenomena would be reduced to the elementary movements of individuals, just as physical phenomena, chemical action, and the qualities of matter, heat, sound, and electricity are reduced to the elementary movements of molecules and atoms.

The difficulty is that in kinetic theories of matter, elements are assumed to remain unchanged. That is, of course, what we mean by element and elementary. Since the only changes that physical science reckons with are changes in space, all qualitative differences are reduced to quantitative differences, and so made subject to description in mathematical terms. In the case of human and social relations, on the other hand, the elementary units—that is to say, the individual men and women who enter into these different combinations—are notoriously subject to change. They are so far from representing homogeneous units that any thoroughgoing mathematical treatment of them seems impossible.

Society, as John Dewey has remarked, exists in and through communication, and communication involves not a translation of energies, such as seems to take place between individual social units, for example, in suggestion or imitation, two of the terms to which sociologists have at various times sought to reduce all social phenomena;

but rather communication involves a transformation in the individuals who thus communicate. And this transformation goes on unceasingly with the accumulation of individual experiences in individual minds.

If human behavior could be reduced again, as some psychologists have sought to reduce it, to a few elementary instincts, the application of the kinetic theories of the physical sciences to the explanation of social life would be less difficult. But these instincts, even if they may be said to exist, are in constant process of change through the accumulation of memories and habits. And these changes are so great and continuous that to treat individual men and women as constant and homogeneous social units involves too great an abstraction. That is the reason why we are driven finally, in the explanation of human conduct and society, to psychology. In order to make comprehensible the changes which take place in society it is necessary to reckon with the changes which take place in the individual units of which society seems to be composed. The consequence is that the social element ceases to be the individual and becomes an attitude, the individual's tendency to act. Not individuals, but attitudes, interact to maintain social organizations and to produce social changes.

This conception means that geographical barriers and physical distances are significant for sociology only when and where they define the conditions under which communication and social life are actually maintained. But human geography has been profoundly modified by human invention. The telegraph, telephone, newspaper, and radio, by converting the world into one vast whispering-gallery, have dissolved the distances and broken through the isolation which once separated races and people. New devices of communication are steadily multiplying, and incidentally complicating, social relations. The history of communication is, in a very real sense, the history of civilization. Language, writing, the printing press, the telegraph, telephone, and radio mark epochs in the history of mankind. But these, it needs to be said, would have lost most of their present significance if they had not been accompanied by an increasingly wider division of labor.

I have said that society exists in and through communication. By means of communication individuals share in a common experience and maintain a common life. It is because communication is fundamental to the existence of society that geography and all the other factors that limit or facilitate communication may be said to enter into its structure and organization at all. Under these circumstances the concept of position, of distance, and of mobility have come to have a new significance. Mobility is important as a sociological concept only in so far as it insures new social contact, and physical distance is significant for social relations only when it is possible to interpret it in terms of social distance.

The social organism—and that is one of the most fundamental and disconcerting things about it—is made up of units capable of locomotion. The fact that every individual is capable of movement in space insures him an experience that is private and peculiar to himself, and this experience, which the individual acquires in the course of his adventures in space, affords him, in so far as it is unique, a point of view for independent and individual action. It is the individual's possession and consciousness of a unique experience, and his disposition to think and act in terms of it, that constitutes him finally a person.

The child, whose actions are determined mainly by its reflexes, has at first no such independence and no such individuality, and is, as a matter of fact, not a person.

It is this diversity in the experiences of individual men that makes communication necessary and consensus possible. If we always responded in like manner to like stimulation there would not be, as far as I can see, any necessity for communication, nor any possibility of abstract and reflective thought. The demand for knowledge arises from the very necessity of checking up and funding these divergent individual experiences, and of reducing them to terms which make them intelligible to all of us. A rational mind is simply one that is capable of making its private impulses public and intelligible. It is the business of science to reduce the inarticulate expression of our personal feelings to a common universe of discourse, and to create out of our private experiences an objective and intelligible world.

We not only have, each of us, our private experiences, but we are acutely conscious of them, and much concerned to protect them from invasion and misinterpretation. Our self-consciousness is just our consciousness of these individual differences of experience, together with a sense of their ultimate incommunicability. This is the basis of all our reserves, personal and racial; the basis, also, of our opinions, attitudes, and prejudices. If we were quite certain that everyone was capable of taking us, and all that we regard as personal to us, at our own valuation; if, in other words, we were as naïve as children, or if, on the other hand, we were all as suggestible and lacking in reserve as some hysterics, we should probably have neither persons nor society. For a certain isolation and a certain resistance to social influences and social suggestion is just as much a condition of sound personal existence as of a wholesome society. It is just as inconceivable that we should have persons without privacy as it is that we should have society without persons.

It is evident, then, that space is not the only obstacle to communication, and that social distances cannot always be adequately measured in purely physical terms. The final obstacle to communication is self-consciousness.

What is the meaning of this self-consciousness, this reserve, this shyness, which we so frequently feel in the presence of strangers? It is certainly not always fear of physical violence. It is the fear that we will not make a good impression; the fear that we are not looking our best; that we shall not be able to live up to our conception of ourselves, and particularly, that we shall not be able to live up to the conception which we should like other persons to have of us. We experience this shyness in the presence of our own children. It is only before our most intimate friends that we are able to relax wholly, and so be utterly undignified and at ease. It is only under such circumstances, if ever, that communication is complete and that the distances which separate individuals are entirely dissolved.

This world of communication and of "distances," in which we all seek to maintain some sort of privacy, personal dignity, and poise, is a dynamic world, and has an order and a character quite its own. In this social and moral order the conception which each of us has of himself is limited by the conception which every other individual, in the same limited world of communication, has of himself, and of every other individual. The consequence is—and this is true of any society—every individual finds himself in a struggle for status: a struggle to preserve his personal prestige, his point of view, and his self-respect. He is able to maintain them, however, only to the extent that he can gain for himself the recognition of everyone else whose estimate seems important; that is to say, the estimate of everyone else who is in his set or in his society. From this struggle for status no philosophy of life has yet discovered a refuge. The individual who is not concerned about his status in some society is a hermit, even when his seclusion is a city crowd. The individual whose conception of himself is not at all determined by the conceptions that other persons have of him is probably insane.

Ultimately the society in which we live invariably turns out to be a moral order in which the individual's position, as well as his conception of himself—which is the core of his personality—is determined by the attitudes of other individuals and by the standards which the group uphold. In such a society the individual becomes a person. A person is simply an individual who has somewhere, in some society, social status; but status turns out finally to be a matter of distance—social distance.

It is because geography, occupation, and all the other factors which determine the distribution of population determine so irresistibly and fatally the place, the group, and the associates with whom each one of us is bound to live that spatial relations come to have, for the study of society and human nature, the importance which they do.

It is because social relations are so frequently and so inevitably correlated with spatial relations; because physical distances so frequently are, or seem to be, the indexes of social distances, that statistics have any significance whatever for sociology. And this is true, finally, because it is only as social and psychical facts can be reduced to, or correlated with, spatial facts that they can be measured at all.

CHAPTER 15

SOCIOLOGY, COMMUNITY AND SOCIETY

I. THE COMMUNITY

TEGGART has stated the difference between history and the other sciences in one fine phrase. "Science," he says, "deals with objects, entities, things, and their relations; history concerns itself with events." [1] Events happen; things do not. On the contrary, they come into existence, change, and disappear in orderly ways, each in accordance with a rule that is characteristic of the class and type to which it belongs, or of which each is an individual example. That is what is meant by describing things as natural phenomena. The nature of a thing is, in fact, just the rule or law by which it moves or changes. [2]

Scientific method, methods of research at any rate, cannot be studied in a vacuum, quite apart from any reference to things. There is, as a matter of fact, no general science of method. Mathematics makes the nearest approach to it, and has been the model of exactness to which the other sciences have invariably striven to attain. The conceptual exactness of mathematics and the wide application that it has found in the other sciences is due to the fact that it

---

Reprinted by permission of the editor from Wilson Gee (ed.), *Research in the Social Sciences* (New York: Macmillan Co., 1929), pp. 3-49.

[1] Teggart, Frederick J. *Theory of History*. New Haven, 1925, p. 71.

[2] Rickert, Heinrich. *Die Grenzen der naturwissenschaftlichen Begriffsbildung. Eine logische Einleitung in die historischen Wissenschaften.* Leipzig, 1902, p. 212.

has limited itself to the most obvious characteristics of things; namely, their form and sequence. Form and ordered sequence are, in fact, the "things" of mathematics. And this suggests the further observation that what things are for any special science or for common sense, for that matter, is determined largely by the point of view from which they are looked at. Our original datum is always an event. Every science more or less creates its own objects out of events which are a part of the common experience of mankind.[3] The first task of every science is to convert events into things, the particular things it proposes to study.

Statistics has been the method *par excellence* of the social sciences where they have sought to become systematic and attained anything like quantitative exactness.[4] The difficulty has been that statisticians have applied their technique to social phenomena as if the social sciences did not exist, or as if they were mere compendiums of common-sense facts.

Statisticians, for example, have usually treated persons as if they were mere physical units, and societies as if they were mere physical aggregates. But the social sciences—some of them at least—have begun to define conceptually the "things" which are the objects of their investigations. Sociology is not concerned with individuals as such, but with a special type of relation, not fundamentally physical, existing between individuals, and which constitutes them persons. Societies, in the strict sense of the word, are composed of persons, and persons are individuals who have status in some society. Looked at from this point of view, societies themselves become things; things with a natural history and with characteristics which are determined by the interactions and mutual relations of the persons who compose them.

Societies are composed of individuals having status, but sociological writers have not always agreed as to the nature of the relations which bind individuals together in such a way as to constitute

---

[3] Whitehead, Alfred North. *The Concept of Nature*. Cambridge, England, 1920.

[4] "Where there is quantity," says Tarde, "there is science." "Social science," he adds, "will have achieved autonomy as soon as it is able to point to a rhythm (*un mode repetition*) peculiarly its own." Scientific facts, in other words, are facts that are capable of repetition. They can therefore be tested, checked up, counted, reduced to classes and in general treated quantitatively. *See* Gabriel Tarde, *Études de Psychologie Sociale*, Paris, 1898, pp. 41-2. *See, also,* by the same author, *Essais et mélanges sociologiques*, Paris, 1895, pp. 230-308, where he reviews the attempts to apply statistics to the study of attitudes (*Croyances et desirs*).

them a society. Sociologists are still not agreed as to what, precisely, the relation is which they call "social."

The earlier writers like Comte and Spencer described society as a "social organism." This was one way, at any rate, of expressing their conviction that it was possible to look at societies—composed of units so visibly independent of one another—as something more than mere formal and statistical entities. But Comte and Spencer, looking at the social complex from somewhat different points of view, described it in different terms. The essential relations between men which constitute them a society is best represented, Spencer said, in the *division of labor*. Society is essentially an economic organization. Men live and work together because they are useful to one another. Competition, which is the fundamental fact of social life, enforces coöperation, and society is the outcome.[5]

Comte, on the other hand, regarded *consensus*, rather than the division of labor, as the fundamental fact about society. Society is primarily a cultural group, having common customs, language, and institutions. The relations of individuals in a society—in the family, for example, which Comte regards as the unit and model of all other forms of society—are closer and more intimate than those which exist between the organs of a plant or of an animal. They are more intimate, and, as Comte probably would have said, more completely organic, because the solidarity of the group is based upon consensus, i.e., understanding. In a society minds interpenetrate, and individuals live and act on the basis of a common experience.[6]

Now, it is an indubitable fact that societies do have this double aspect. They are composed of individuals who act independently of one another, who compete and struggle with one another for mere existence, and treat one another, as far as possible, as utilities. On the other hand, it is quite as true that men and women are bound together by affections and common purposes; they do cherish traditions, ambitions, and ideals that are not all their own, and they maintain, in spite of natural impulses to the contrary, a discipline and a moral order that enables them to transcend what we ordinarily call nature and, through their collective action, recreate the world in the image of their collective aspirations and their common will.

---

[5] Spencer, Herbert. *The Principles of Sociology*. London, 1893, Vol. I, pp. 437, 579-80.

[6] Lévy-Bruhl, L. *The Philosophy of August Comte*, authorized translation, with an introduction by Frederick Harrison. New York, 1903, p. 337.

There are no words that accurately or exactly describe these different aspects of collective life. The words society and community, as they are used in common parlance, suggest differences, but do not define them. The word community, however, more accurately describes the social organism, as Spencer conceived it. Comte's conception, on the other hand, comes nearer to describing what we ordinarily mean by society.

Community, in the broadest sense of that term, has a spatial and a geographical connotation. Every community has a location, and the individuals who compose it have a place of residence within the territory which the community occupies. Otherwise they are transients and are not reckoned as members. They also have an occupation in the local economy. Towns, cities, hamlets, and, under modern conditions, the whole world, with all its differences of race, of culture, and of individual interests—all these are communities. They are all communities in just so far as, through the exchange of goods and services, they may be regarded as coöperating to carry on a common life.

Society, however, always includes something more than competitive coöperation and its resulting economic interdependence. The existence of a society presupposes a certain amount of solidarity, consensus, and common purpose. The image of society, in the narrower sense of that term, is best reflected in the family, the tribe, the nation. Societies are formed for action and in action. They grow up in the efforts of individuals to act collectively. The structures which societies exhibit are on the whole the incidental effects of collective action. Living in society, the individual gets his interests defined in reference to the larger aims of the group of which he is a member. In this sense, and to this extent, society controls the individuals who compose it. Law, custom, convention "define," as Thomas says, "the situation," and in this and in other ways impose a discipline upon all who seek to participate in the common life.

The term community is employed in a wider connotation. It has been applied to plants and animals, where individuals and species seem to carry on some sort of group economy. In such cases there is, however, no society, in the sense in which Comte would use that term, because in such communities there is no consensus, no conventions, and no moral order. Such order as exists is the order of nature.

It is evident that the two terms do not, in all respects, correspond, and society and community are, strictly speaking, different things. It is probably true, however, that so long as the term is limited in its applications to human beings, every community is, in some sense and to some degree, a society. Man has never quite succeeded in practice and for long in treating other men as he has the lower animals, as part of the fauna, mere physical objects in the landscape.[7] On the other hand, it is certainly true that not every society is a community.

The community, if not always identical with society, is, at the very least, the habitat in which alone societies grow up. It provides the economic organization and the necessary conditions in which societies are rooted; upon which, as upon a physical base, they can be established.

This is one reason why sociological research may very properly begin with the community. A more practical reason is the fact that the community is a visible object. One can point it out, define its territorial limits, and plot its constituent elements, its population, and its institutions on maps. Its characteristics are more susceptible to statistical treatment than society, in the sense of Comte.

II. POPULATION PYRAMIDS

The community, in its most obvious aspect, i.e., as the statistician is likely to conceive it, is, as has been said, a mere numerical aggregate, a population group defined by the space it occupies. The simplest method of investigating a society conceived so abstractly is to enumerate the individuals of which it is composed. It is primarily the task of human geography to determine the present distribution of the earth's population and to discover the relative densities of those populations in every geographical region and in every local community within these regions. But density of population, because it is related to so much else that is significant in the life of every community, is itself an important sociological datum. Ross, in recognition of this fact, makes population studies the introduction to his textbook on sociology.[8]

The noted French sociologist, Durkheim, and his school give a prominent place to population studies in their conception of sociology, under the title of social morphology.[9]

Size and numbers are so significant an aspect, not merely of the

---

[7] Dewey, John. *Education and Democracy*. New York, 1916, p. 6.

[8] Ross, Edward A. *Principles of Sociology*. New York, 1920.

[9] *See* Durkheim, Émile. *L'Année Sociologique*, pp. 520-21.

community, but of any society, that attempts have been made to classify and define cities and minor population aggregates in purely numerical terms.[10]

Enumeration ordinarily involves, however, a division of the population into age classes and sex, in the form of a pyramid; what is called the population pyramid. It appears that the populations of different communities exhibit a variety of deviations which characterize and are typical of the communities whose populations they represent.

Populations, it has been assumed, and recent investigations support the thesis, invariably tend to achieve, in response to the physical and human environment, a stable equilibrium. Malthus thought that population increase was limited only by the food supply, and in the long run perhaps this is true. More recent studies indicate, however, that, for certain populations and for certain classes, the standard of living and other more obscure causes play an important rôle.[11]

Actually, at certain times and in response to certain conditions, populations increase rapidly, either by natural reproduction or by immigration. At other times, and in response to other conditions, they either decline or remain stationary. In any case, new individuals are inevitably introduced into and incorporated in the population group, in order to replace those who have been eliminated by death or by emigration. As a matter of fact, the process by which new elements are incorporated into an old population is a good deal more elaborate than it seems. And this is true whether the new elements are recruited from the native or from the immigrant stocks. The new generation has to be educated and the immigrants have to be assimilated.

Looked at abstractly, the process by which new elements are incorporated and old ones eliminated may be described as a kind of social metabolism, and the rate at which it proceeds can be measured. Now, the rate at which metabolism takes place, like the amount of general movement and mobility, which I shall consider later, is

---

[10] Willcox, Walter F. *Proceedings of the American Sociological Society*, Vol. XX, p. 97. This and other papers on related topics are republished in *The Urban Community*, Ernest W. Burgess, Editor. *See, also*, the bibliography in Park, Robert E., and Burgess, Ernest W., *The City*, pp. 165-166.

[11] Malthus, T. R. *An Essay on the Principle of Population*, 2d ed., London, 1803. Carr-Saunders, A. M. *The Population Problem: A Study in Human Evolution*. Oxford, 1922.

an index and measure of the intensity of the social process.[12] In the great cities to which the tide of immigration, particularly in these later years, so irresistibly tends, great and revolutionary changes, not only in the form but in the content of our social life, are evidently taking place. In the little villages of retired farmers, which have become a feature of rural life in America, particularly in the Middle West, there is, in spite of all the changes that the automobile has introduced, very little going on.

These changes in the social metabolism register themselves not merely in the figures that show the actual increase and overturn in population, but in the population pyramid, as well. A population which has grown by immigration, mainly, is represented by a very different sort of pyramid than one which owes its increase to the sheer excess of births over deaths, and this irrespective of increases in actual numbers. Similarly, the characteristic differences in urban and rural communities are reflected in the form of their respective population pyramids. But the most striking differences in the composition and in the overturn of populations are shown on the pyramids obtained from a study of the age classes and sex groups in different natural areas of great cities.

The fact that these divergencies and contrasts exist is one striking evidence of the rôle which cities play in modern life. They bring together, to be sure, the ends of the earth, all the breeds and types and classes; but having brought them together, the cities sift and sort and redistribute their ill-assorted populations into new groups and classes, according to new and unexpected patterns. The explanation is that competition, the sheer struggle for existence, finally compels each individual to seek and find the task that he can best perform, and the ever-widening division of labor multiplies his opportunities to find a vocation for which he is suited. This sifting-sorting process undermines old associations, takes individuals out of their inherited and racial groups, breaks up families; loosens all ties, in fact. And this is part of, or at least an incident and by-product of, the process of social metabolism.

---

[12] We are very much concerned in the social as in all other sciences about indices. It is only through indices that we can establish units and apply quantitative methods to our descriptions of things. To be sure, it sometimes happens that sociologists, like the psychologists with their intelligence tests, do not know just what they are measuring. Nevertheless, it is possible in this way to give precision to our comparisons of one object with another, even if we do not quite know what the things we are measuring measure.

GRADIENT OF POPULATION, BY AGE AND SEX

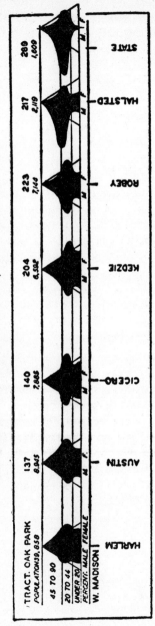

The use of the population pyramid as an index of movements and changes of population seems to have been made in the first instance by Italian students of population. (See *Annali di Statistica*, Series 2a, Vol. I, Roma, 1878.) One of the first writers to discuss and develop the theoretical implications of the population pyramid was Levasseur. (*See* Levasseur, Émile, *La Population Française*, Vol. II, Chap. XV, Paris, 1891.) Levasseur points out that there is a definite functional relation between age and sex groups; such that, given a certain distribution of age groups in any population we might expect a correlative distribution of the sexes. The possibilities and limitations of the population pyramid as an index to social conditions in natural areas has been worked out practically and theoretically in a paper now in preparation by Charles Newcomb, instructor in sociology at the Young Men's Christian Association College, Chicago.

The population pyramid, in so far as it exhibits the deviations of age classes and sex groups, has proved a useful device of social exploration. In exhibiting the anomalies and deviations from the normal distribution in the urban population, it becomes a measure of change, as well as an index to problems of the urban community. For in a society in which a stable equilibrium has been achieved, there are, generally speaking, neither poverty, crime, nor vice—no problems and no progress. For social problems, like diseases, arise in the efforts of the individual and the organism to adjust themselves to a changing environment.[13]

This sorting and segregating of the communal population, putting individuals into new locations and into new occupations—of which the loosening of family ties and the breaking of local associations is an incident—is roughly correlated, though not identical with what we have called social metabolism. When populations are increasing rapidly, either by immigration or by the excess of births over deaths, the movement and segregation of its component individuals proceeds at a more rapid pace. The amount of change that inevitably takes place in a growing community is, moreover, multiplied and intensified by the invention of new mechanical devices for the production of goods, by new facilities for transportation and communication, and by the incidental extension of the division of labor.[14]

In recent years, for example, electrical transportation has, among other things, put travel underground; steel construction has made skyscrapers possible; passenger elevators have made them practicable. These, together with the telegraph and the telephone, which have immensely extended the radius of effective organization and control, have probably contributed much toward the transforming of conditions of collective and corporate life.

These observations are based largely upon recent studies of the character and the consequences of the rapid growth of cities. They may be regarded, however, as specific illustrations of the operation

---

[13] The suggestion that disease may be regarded as an incident of biological adjustment is supported by pathological observations (*Evolution and Disease*, J. Bland-Sutton, London, 1895, the Contemporary Science Series), and by facts noted by Carr-Saunders (*The Population Problem*, Oxford, 1922, pp. 156-57), showing that diseases, if they have not originated, have at any rate multiplied with the evolution of civilization.

[14] *See* "The Growth of the City," Chap. II, *The City*. Park, Robert E., and Burgess, E. W. Chicago, 1925.

of a more general principle, long recognized by students of civilization and social life, the principle that movement and migration are not merely an incident but a cause of almost every form of social change. Teggart quotes Waitz, the German anthropolgist, to the effect that "Where we see people, of whatsoever degree of civilization, not living in contact and reciprocal action with others, we shall generally find a certain stagnation, a mental inertness, and a want of activity which render any change of social and political condition next to impossible." The obvious illustration to which Waitz makes reference is China. China has been the classic example of what Teggart calls "the processes which are manifested in fixity, persistence, stagnation, and conventionality." [15] The explanation, in this instance, is not any inherent lack of acumen or of ingenuity in the Chinese mind, but simply the absence of any intrusive factors— commerce, migration, war—capable of interrupting the processes of cultural fixation and crystallization, and so "freeing the individual judgment from the restraint of conventional modes of thought."

From the point of view of sociological research, two observations with reference to this general theory of social change suggest themselves:

1. If it is true that the processes which we can study intensively and at first hand in the city are at all comparable with those larger secular changes which the historian, from his wider horizon, has observed, then it is possible—using the urban community as a unit of investigation—not merely to report but to investigate the processes of civilization.

2. If movement, migration, and commerce are so immediately associated with social changes as has been suggested, then mobility may be taken as an index of social change, and the intensity of the social processes, through which these changes are effected, can be made the subject of quantitative investigation.

III. MOBILITY AND LAND VALUES

All the movements, migrations, and changes of location that take place within the community, or in any way affect the routine of communal life, are included under the concept of mobility. Sorokin has extended the term to include changes in the occupational status between the first and the second generations. He has sought, in

---

[15] Teggart, *Theory of History*, p. 189.

other words, to determine statistically to what extent children do or do not follow the vocations of their parents. He distinguishes, therefore, between horizontal and vertical mobility. Vertical mobility he applies to changes in occupational status; horizontal mobility, on the other hand, is limited to changes of location.[16]

This extension of the concept mobility to include changes in status is quite in accord with the original intention of the term, as it has been used by sociologists, at least. Spatial movement and occupational mobility are sociologically significant mainly and on the whole only so far as they serve as indices for measuring the "contacts," i.e., the shocks, clashes, and the incidental interruptions and breakdowns of customary modes of thought and action which these new personal encounters inevitably produce. Changes in vocational status are, however, merely one of many ways in which the social ritual and routine, which otherwise would be perpetuated by the sheer "weight of authority, superstition, and public opinion," are interrupted and the energies of individuals released for new enterprises and adventures. The importance of these changes in status, from the point of view of research, is that they are capable of statement in quantitative terms.

It is, naturally, in the great cities, with their world-wide commerce and their vast cosmopolitan populations, where the movements of population are greatest and the incidental clashes of personalities and cultures are most intense, that social changes are most rapid. If cities have always been the centers of civilization and intellectual life, it is partly because they are the inevitable meeting places of strangers and the centers of news. The stir, the bustle, and the vivacity of city life are but the reflections of that intenser social life, of which we have sought to make an abstraction and to measure in terms of mobility.

But the movements and migrations of populations are many and various. Not all the changes of location of the urban populations are due to social metabolism and growth. In measuring the growth of cities, too, we have not always taken account of the movements outward, which tend to balance the movement inward. In the great cities, as in the country as a whole, migration statistics show that immigration is largely balanced by emigration. It is estimated that the population in one particular region of Chicago, inhabited mainly

---

[16] Sorokin, Pitirim. *Social Mobility*. New York, 1927.

by casual laborers, fluctuates in the course of a year between 30,000 and 75,000.[17]

Statistics such as exist in Europe of the transient dwellers in cities are not available for the United States. We are just beginning now to reckon with the seasonal and cyclical movements of our increasingly nomadic populations, with the annual movements back and forth across the ocean of immigrant labor, with the seasonal movements north and south, east and west, our throngs of tourists, casual and seasonal laborers, automobile tramps, and with the enormous increase in our hotel populations.[18]

In addition to these, there are the semi-annual movements, spring and fall, of our apartment house dwellers, and the daily tide which pours into the centers of our great cities every morning and back to the peripheries every evening. These movements are so intimately bound up with every aspect of our commercial life, and are to such a degree symptomatic of the deeper and more obscure changes in our political and cultural life, that it is as if we had our hand upon the pulse of the community.

There is, of course, more than one way in which mobility may be measured and interpreted. As a matter of fact, no wholly satisfactory units or formulæ for describing these more complex population movements in quantitative terms have been as yet devised. It is evident that mobility, measured in terms of change of residence, within the city, has a quite different significance from mobility as exhibited in the daily ebb and flow of the population to and from the business centers. McKenzie has been disposed to distinguish recurrent and cyclical movements of this kind from migration, which involves a change of residence, by the term "fluidity." [19]

This seems, however, a needless multiplication of words, since it is apparent that mobility, if defined as a "change of location or position," is relative to the term position. What one regards as position determines the unit in which mobility is reckoned. When position is defined in terms of residence these movements like the daily movements to and from the center of the city, which for certain purposes are important, are not taken into the reckoning.

---

[17] Anderson, Nels. *The Hobo: The Sociology of the Homeless Man.* Chicago, 1923.

[18] Hayner, Norman S. *The Hotel: The Sociology of Hotel Life.* (University of Chicago Ph.D. thesis, 1923.)

[19] McKenzie, R. D. "The Scope of Human Ecology," *Proceedings of the American Sociological Society,* Vol. XX, 1925.

It is an interesting fact, in this connection, that land values seem to be rather definitely correlated with population movements and with mobility generally.[20] It hardly seems necessary to say that land values rise with the movement and increase of population. What is not so obvious is the fact that increase in land values in any section of the community serves to bring about, in turn, a redistribution of population in the community as a whole. Cities, particularly since the introduction of new forms of transportation and of locomotion —the electric tram-car, for example, and the automobile—have grown rapidly by territorial expansion. The appearance of a new suburb on the outskirts of the city does not, however, decrease the pressure on the central business area. Quite the contrary. Suburbs spring up along the lines of local transportation. Any addition to the population within the so-called commuting area means that more people travel every day to the business center, to the city proper, for trade, for recreation, and for all the purposes of communal life. The addition of population at the periphery increases land values at the center, and the pressure of land values at the center radiates over the whole city. One effect is to create, just outside the limits of the central business section, an "area of transition," as Burgess has called it; in other words, a slum.[21]

The encroachment of the slum on the residential areas tends to produce, however, a second area of transition, the so-called "rooming house" area. The rooming house area is almost invariably what is or was residential territory which, because of impending changes, has been abandoned by its original owners to the temporary uses of transients. Out beyond the limits of the rooming houses, with increasing land values, apartment houses replace individual dwellings, the height of the apartment building being determined by the value of the land. On the outer limits of the inner city, bordering upon the suburban area, single dwellings, duplex apartments, and bungalows, the last refuge of the traditional American home, still hold their own.

It thus appears that land values, which are themselves in large measure a product of population aggregates, operate in the long run to give this aggregate, within the limits of the community, an or-

---

[20] MacGill, Helen Gregory. *Land Values: An Ecological Factor in a Community in South Chicago.* (University of Chicago M.A. thesis, 1927).

[21] *See* Burgess, E. W., "The Growth of the City," in Park and Burgess, *The City.* Chicago, the University of Chicago Press, 1927.

derly distribution and a characteristic pattern. Under the pressure of land values at the center, cities tend to assume the form of a series of concentric circles, each of which circumscribes an area of decreasing mobility and descending land values. If the highest land values are in the retail shopping area, they will usually be located at the point where, in the course of twenty-four hours, the largest number of people meet and pass.

If the assumptions upon which we have been proceeding were wholly valid, one would expect to find land values descending from a high point at the center of the city by regular gradients to the periphery. But the thing is not quite so simple as that, partly because the incidence of geographical location and of transportation intervenes to modify and complicate the pattern which the pressure of land values alone might otherwise impose, and partly because the distribution of industry and commerce is effected by forces relatively independent of those which determine the location of residential and retail business centers.

In the distribution of industry and commerce, as in the distribution of population, the primary tendency is to concentrate everything—population, public institutions, industry, and commerce—around a central market. But as land values increase, population moves out steadily toward the periphery. This centrifugal movement of population, which is exhibited best in London, has been studied in America mainly by the telephone companies to enable them to predict for some considerable period in advance the future use and locations of telephone lines and stations.

The ultimate effect of the centrifugal movement is to create an outer circle of satellite cities, more or less independent, but still dominated by the metropolis. The tendency to concentrate retail trade in the central shopping district, represented by the growth of department stores, eventually is modified by centripetal tendencies due to high rents and cost of transportation. But while shops in which trade is carried on move out, the control of business remains at the center. The chain store, with its distributing units dispersed but its control centrally located, is the type of organization that results.

The centrifugal movement in modern cities is very great, and increases as the city extends its domination through the organization of banking and credit over wider areas. Great cities are constantly throwing off and expelling the industries which they have created.

But trade and industry migrate from the metropolis and from its central business district only as they become standardized, and for that reason subject to control at a distance. Control of industry and of commerce, on the other hand, tends to concentrate in the central banking city and in the central banking center, because these are the centers of communication and of credit. Credit is based finally upon information, and credit and banking institutions must be close to the news.[22]

From what has been said, it is apparent that land values contribute something like a third dimension to our human geography. Each of us, every individual member of the community, and every institution, occupies a position with reference to other individuals, and with reference to the institution of the community, which can be described in distance measured in terms of space or time. But we also occupy a position which is determined by the value of the space we occupy and by the rent we pay. Rent maps have become indispensable to so-called market annalists and to professional advertisers. They are indications of social status, buying power, and general commercial credit. Land value maps thus become, also, in a rough way, an index to cultural life of the community. They serve to delimitate, so to speak, the cultural contour of the community. In any case, land values offer a new device by which we may characterize the ecological organization of the community, the social environment, and the habitat of civilized man.

---

[22] The exercise of this managerial function of coördinaion and control is at first glance singularly independent of transportation. It does not require the transfer of huge quantities of materials. It deals almost exclusively with information. What is all-important is transporation of intelligence. The mail, the cable, the telegraph, and the telephone bring in its raw material and carry out its finished product. Internally easy contact of man with man is essential. The telephone is prodigally used, of course, but the personal conference remains, after all, the method by which most of the important work is done. Conferences with corporation officers, with bankers, with lawyers and accountants, with partners, with fellow directors, fill the day. The work is facilitated when the time of the men whose time is most valuable is conserved. The district must be conveniently accessible and must be at the heart of the system of communication. It must be arranged so as to give the greatest possible ease of contact among men whose presence is desired in arriving at decisions. The financial district is in effect one big structure; the streets, practically cleared of all except pedestrian traffic, are little more than corridors and airshafts. The corner of Wall and Broad on a busy morning is much more quiet than many a suburban business corner. The geometrical proposition that the contents of two spheres are to each other as the cubes of their diameters has sent skyscrapers up into the air. This was the economical way to produce accessi-

The making of a land value map which will exhibit graphically the extraordinary variations in land values within the limits of the urban community is one of the technical problems of methodology with which students of human ecology have recently begun to experiment. For the purposes of such a map, geographical levels are disregarded, and, in place of these, land values are represented either by contour lines drawn upon a flat surface or by plastic models. By a recently invented device known as the "Wenschow process" it is

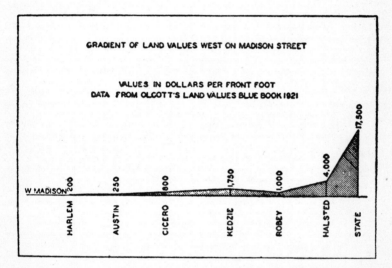

GRADIENT OF LAND VALUES WEST ON MADISON STREET

VALUES IN DOLLARS PER FRONT FOOT
DATA FROM OLCOTT'S LAND VALUES BLUE BOOK 1921

now possible to multiply mechanically plastic models which were formerly produced in single examples by handicraft.

From recent studies in Chicago it appears that while land values tend, as might be expected, to fall away gradually and regularly from the center, the symmetry of this pattern is broken at the thoroughfares which radiate from the center of the city. These radial lines, which are occupied by business, mostly retail shops, rise like ridges above the intervening territory occupied by residences. As they approach the center of the city these ridges mount slowly at first, and then rapidly, toward a central dome of high land values. In profile, land values on one of these radial streets look something like the chart. "Gradient of Land Values on Madison Avenue."

bility in the center.—Robert Murray Haig, "Toward an Understanding of the Metropolis," *The Quarterly Journal of Economics*, Vol. XL, May, 1926, p. 427.

The land value map of Chicago may be represented schemati-
cally as shown on the accompanying chart. In this, "C" indicates
the center of the city, where land values are highest; "A B" represents the line of highest land values along the lake front, and lines
"D, E, and F" the streets radiating from the center toward the west,

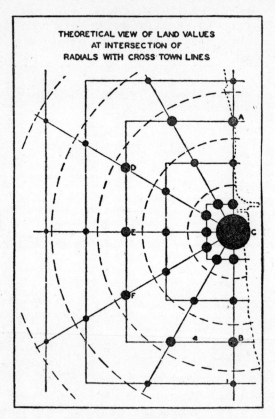

THEORETICAL VIEW OF LAND VALUES
AT INTERSECTION OF
RADIALS WITH CROSS TOWN LINES

northwest, and southwest. These radial lines are intersected by diago-
nals running west, north, and south. At the point of intersection
new business centers tend to spring up, and in these centers land
values rise, and, in general, these subcenters exhibit all the characteristics of the original and central business area at the lake front.

Of all the facts that can be expressed geographically, land values,
for the sociologist, are probably the most important. They are important because they offer a relatively accurate index to the forces
that are determining the occupational and cultural organization of

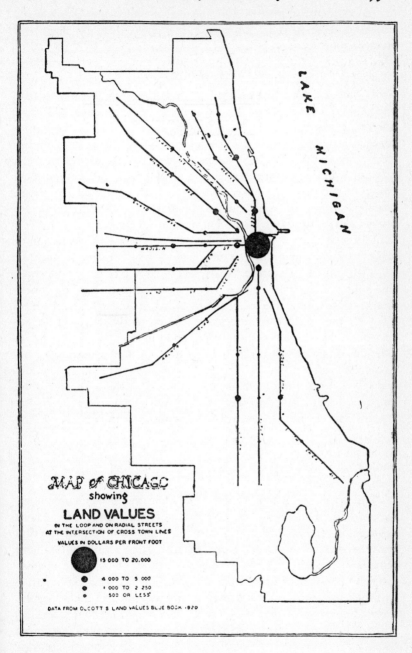

MAP of CHICAGO
showing
LAND VALUES
IN THE LOOP AND ON RADIAL STREETS
AT THE INTERSECTION OF CROSS TOWN LINES

VALUES IN DOLLARS PER FRONT FOOT

15 000 TO 20.000

4 000 TO 5 000

1 000 TO 2 250

500 OR LESS

DATA FROM OLCOTT'S LAND VALUES BLUE BOOK 1920

the community, and because by the aid of land values it is possible to express in numerical and quantitative terms so much that is socially significant.

IV. FRAMES OF REFERENCE

The urban community turns out, upon closer scrutiny, to be a mosaic of minor communities, many of them strikingly different one from another, but all more or less typical. Every city has its central business district; the focal point of the whole urban complex. Every city, every great city, has its more or less exclusive residential areas or suburbs; its areas of light and of heavy industry, satellite cities, and casual labor mart, where men are recruited for rough work on distant frontiers, in the mines and in the forests, in the building of railways or in the borings and excavations for the vast structures of our modern cities. Every American city has its slums; its ghettos; its immigrant colonies, regions which maintain more or less alien and exotic culture. Nearly every large city has its bohemias and hobohemias, where life is freer, more adventurous and lonely than it is elsewhere. These are the so-called *natural areas* of the city. They are the products of forces that are constantly at work to effect an orderly distribution of populations and functions within the urban complex. They are "natural" because they are not planned, and because the order that they display is not the result of design, but rather a manifestation of tendencies inherent in the urban situation; tendencies that city plans seek—though not always successfully—to control and correct. In short, the structure of the city, as we find it, is clearly just as much the product of the struggle and efforts of its people to live and work together collectively as are its local customs, traditions, social ritual, laws, public opinion, and the prevailing moral order.

The structure which recent studies of the urban community have disclosed is, moreover, one that is characteristic of cities; it exhibits, in other words, a pattern that can be described conceptually. Urban areas are not mere "events"; they are things, and the regions of one city are comparable with those of another.

Now, the fact of primary importance here is that social statistics —births and deaths, marriage and divorce, suicide and crime—assume a new significance when they are collected and distributed in such ways as to characterize these natural areas. An area is characterized by (1) the numbers and racial composition of the population that occupies it; (2) by the conditions under which they live; and (3) by the habits, customs, and behavior generally which they exhibit. In short, the place, the people, and the conditions under which they live are here conceived as a complex, the elements of which are more or less completely bound together, albeit in ways which as yet are not clearly defined. It is assumed, in short, partly as a result of selection and segregation, and partly in view of the contagious character of cultural patterns, that people living in natural areas of the same general type and subject to the same social conditions will display, on the whole, the same characteristics.

Investigations have shown that this assumption is so far true as to justify its use as a working hypothesis. In any case, it appears that when natural areas, rather than formal and administrative districts, are made the basis for statistical enquiries, the different regions display unexpected and significant divergences; divergences which were concealed when the statistics were distributed over areas not naturally defined. There are areas in the city of Chicago, as Mowrer's studies in family disorganization have shown, in which there are no divorces at all; and there are areas in which for the years studied the divorce rate was higher than in any state in the Union except that Mecca of divorce seekers, Nevada. The distribution of statistics on divorce and desertion shows, incidentally, that divorce is a luxury which most of the population cannot afford, and that desertion is the poor man's substitute for divorce.[23]

Recent studies of suicide seem to show that there is inverse correlation between crimes of violence and suicide—suicide being a form of violence directed not against others, but against oneself. Germans and Japanese, who exhibit everywhere a relatively low crime rate, contribute a relatively larger proportion to the annual quota of suicides. Negroes, on the other hand, and Irish, who register high in crimes of violence, are seldom guilty of suicide.[24] The region which Nels Anderson, in his account of the hobo, describes as "Hobohemia," exhibits an extraordinary number of deaths from alcoholism, which, incidentally, is, like suicide, a mode of self-destruction. On the other hand, Bohemia, the region of youth and disenchantment, exhibits a marked excess in suicide.

[23] Mowrer, Ernest R., Ph.D. *Family Disorganization*, p. 12. Chicago: The University of Chicago Press, 1927.
[24] Shonle, Ruth. *Suicide: A Study of Personal Disorganization*. (University of Chicago Ph.D. thesis, 1926.)

The natural areas of the city, it appears from what has been said, may be made to serve an important methodological function. They constitute, taken together, what Hobson has described as "a frame of reference," a conceptual order within which statistical facts gain a new and a more general significance. They not only tell us what the facts are in regard to conditions in any given region, but in so far as they characterize an area that is natural and typical, they establish a working hypothesis in regard to other areas of the same kind.[25]

It is evident that the areas of an urban community can be characterized, in the manner indicated, to an unlimited extent. Perhaps, not all but most facts that can be stated statistically, once they have been plotted in this conceptual scheme,—this ecological frame of reference,—can be made the basis of general statements which may be eventually reduced to abstract formulæ and scientific generalizations.

The possibility of drawing inferences from what has been observed and described in London, as to what we might expect in New York or Chicago, it should be said, rests on the assumption that the same forces create everywhere essentially the same conditions. In practice it might turn out that this expectation would not be, or would seem not to be, justified by the facts. It could at least be verified, and that is the main point. Should it turn out that the expectations in regard to London, based upon studies in New York and Chicago, were not justified by the facts, this would at least raise the question as to how far the forces that made London what it is were different from those that made Chicago and New York. And this would lead, in turn, to a more thoroughgoing and a more accurate analysis of the actual forces at work in both instances.

Thus the result of every new specific enquiry should reaffirm or redefine, qualify or extend, the hypothesis upon which the original enquiry was based. The results should not merely increase our fund of information, but enable us to reduce our observations to general formulæ and quantitative statements true for all cases of the same kind. The possibility of general deduction rests, in the present case, upon the validity of the conception of the natural area. The ecological organization of the community becomes a frame of reference only when, like the natural areas of which it is composed,

[25] Hobson, Ernest W. *The Realm of Nature.* Cambridge University Press, 1922.

it can itself be regarded as the product of factors that are general and typical. Knowledge becomes systematic and general when one is able to make statements in regard to things, and not merely describe events.[26] It is by means of such a frame of reference as I have here described that it is possible to make the transition from concrete fact to systematic and conceptual knowledge.

V. HISTORY

The natural areas into which the urban community—and every other type of community, in fact—resolves itself are, at least in the first instance, the products of a sifting and sorting process which we may call segregation. Every change in the conditions of social life manifests itself first and most obviously in an intensified mobility and in movements which terminate in segregation. This segregation determines the physical patterns which the changing community successively assumes. And this physical form, in turn, effects modification in the cultural organization of the community.

Population movements are usually initiated by economic changes, and a new equilibrium is achieved only when a more efficient economy has been established. Society, however, is something more than an economy, and human nature is always animated by motives that are personal and social as well as economic. While the community may be characterized, in one of its aspects, as a division of labor and a form of competitive coöperation, it is characterized, on the other hand, by consensus and a moral order. Within this moral order individuals assume the character of persons conscious of themselves and of their rôle in the community. One of the most urgent and persistent of human motives is that which impels each one of us to maintain, to defend, and, if possible, to improve his status. Status, however, is a matter of consensus. It is determined in any single case largely by the extent to which the individual man is able to participate in the common purposes of the community, conform to its standards, submit to its discipline or, through the force of personal prestige and influence, impose his own purposes upon his fellows.

In a complex society like our own the individual becomes a member of a number of different societies and social groups, in each of which he has a different status and plays a different rôle. Migra-

---

[26] Whitehead, Alfred North. *An Enquiry Concerning the Principles of Natural Knowledge.* Part 4, The Data of Science. Cambridge, England, 1919.

tion, movement, and changes in economic conditions break up existing forms of social order and undermine status. New means of locomotion, like the automobile, for example, have already profoundly changed the conditions and the character of modern life. The automobile has been charged with the responsibility for new forms of crime and new types of criminals. The cinema and the newspaper have brought about striking changes in our manners and mores. It is not possible even to guess to what extent the radio and the aeroplane have complicated and ultimately will change our international relations. New contacts compel new adjustments, create new forms of social intercourse, and extend to larger numbers the possibility and the necessity of participation in the common life. It has been the task of history to preserve the records of this common life, to interpret and make intelligible the common cultural tradition. It has been the function of education to transmit it and so preserve the historical continuity of society and social life.[27]

Ethnology and anthropology, which in the origins, at any rate, are historical sciences, have been interested hitherto mainly in the study of the cultural forms and artifacts of primitive societies or the cultural remains of societies that no longer exist. But cultural remains, folklore, cultural forms, and social organization, interesting as they may be in themselves, do not offer an adequate account of any society or social order until we have discovered what they mean. We want to know how the tools were used; what were the sentiments and attitudes with which they were regarded by the peoples who used them. Institutions still present their ancient and external forms after they have ceased to serve the purposes for which they were originally created. Religious forms and ceremonies which at one time were the expression of a living faith and a source of comfort and inspiration to those who practiced them, become, with time, merely venerable but unintelligible vestiges. Ritual forms that were once symbolic and expressive degenerate into mere magical formulæ. It is characteristic of the social sciences, including sociology, that they want to know not merely that things exist or that they have existed, but what they meant to the people of whose culture they were a part.

Sociology, as distinguished here from social anthropology, has been interested mainly in social problems, so-called, i.e., poverty,

---

[27] Dewey, John. *Democracy and Education.* New York, 1923.

vice, crime, personal and family disorganization, the abuses of political power, and the efforts to reform them. The attempt to understand these problems has led, however, to more and more disinterested investigation of the forms of contemporary life; its institutions and its cultures. Incidentally, sociologists have discovered that every natural area is, or tends to become, in the natural course of events, a cultural area. Every natural area has, or tends to have, *its* own peculiar traditions, customs, conventions, standards of decency and propriety, and, if not a language of its own, at least a *universe of discourse*, in which words and acts have a meaning which is appreciably different for each local community. It is not difficult to recognize this fact in the case of immigrant communities which still preserve more or less intact the folkways of their home countries. It is not so easy to recognize that this is true in those cosmopolitan regions of the city where a miscellaneous and transient population mingles in a relatively unrestrained promiscuity. But in these cases the very freedom and the absence of convention is itself, if not a convention, at least an open secret. Even in regions where custom no longer reinforces conscience, public opinion and fashion exercise a powerful external control.[28]

In studying a community, or any natural area, from the point of view of its culture, sociology employs the same methods as cultural anthropology or history. It writes the history, as far as that is possible, of the particular community or area that it proposes to investigate.[29]

The local newspapers are sources of information in regard to local traditions, sentiment, and opinion. The names and personal histories of local characters are often worth recording. Not what happened, but what is remembered, is significant. Local institutions, like works of art and literature, are symbolic expressions of the common life. Like art and literature, they have extension and form, but at the same time they have a fourth dimension, namely, meaning. This meaning is not immediately accessible to us. We get the meaning of social institutions as we get the sense of words, by observing the ways in which they are used; by investigating the oc-

---

[28] Tarde, Gabriel. *Les lois de l'imitation; étude sociologique.* Second edition. Chap. VIII, pp. 267-396. Paris, 1895.

[29] In connection with local community studies which have been in progress for some years at the University of Chicago, Miss Vivien M. Palmer is now writing the history of some 80 local communities within the city limits of Chicago.

casions and incidents of their origin and growth, and by taking account of whatever is unusual or unique in their history. Sociology, it is true, like every natural science, classifies its objects, and in order to define them conceptually and make of them abstractions in regard to which it can draw general conclusions, it is necessary, eventually, to disregard what is unique and unclassifiable about them. But sociology must have its objects before it can classify them.

What is a social object? It is an artifact; something made; or a ceremony, custom, ritual, words; anything which, like a word, has meaning and is not just what it seems. A physical object becomes a social object only when we know its use, its function; its meaning; its different meanings for different persons. Consider such an object as that familiar Christian symbol, the cross, or better, perhaps, the crucifix; what different meanings it has had, and still has, for devout Christians and orthodox Jews. History alone can, it would seem, make these different meanings intelligible to us. Nevertheless, its meanings are an essential part of the thing. Just because it has been a *record of events* rather than a *description of things*, history has given sociology much, if not most, of its subject matter. Something like history—the history of contemporary life—must, it would seem, continue to perform that function.

VI. LIFE HISTORIES

In the study of contemporary life the sociologist has one point of attack and one device for exploration of his subject which is not to the same extent available to the historian nor the anthropologist.[30] He can interview the individuals who have participated in and are themselves a part of the social order he is seeking to investigate. He can, by means of interviews or by the use of intimate personal documents, build up what is called, technically, life histories.

The relation of the individual to the society in which he lives is probably much more real and intimate than has hitherto been assumed, even by those who have been the first to direct attention

---

[30] The difficulties of the anthropologist in studying primitive peoples are not merely the ordinary difficulties of language. A special difficulty is due to the fact that the primitive man is not sophisticated and articulate, and he has no words for the subtile meaning of things—things that are to such an extent taken for granted that he does not speak of them except, perhaps, in symbolic and expressive language.—See the paper by Bronislaw Malinowski in *The Meaning of Meaning,* by C. K. Ogden and I. A. Richards.

Sect on
develops 9
norm order
w Strategy —
Intelligence

to it.[31] It is inevitable that people who live together, even on the most casual terms, should eventually come into possession of a common stock of memories, a tradition; that they should acquire some common standard of decency, some accepted forms of intercourse, etiquette, manners, and social ritual, even when the deeper motives and interests of life remain relatively untouched. It is just as inevitable that continued intercourse should reduce personal habits to conventional forms, and that these should assume, in time, the character of binding social customs.

In such a world the individual is born and lives. The customs of the community become his habits. In the ordinary course of events he accepts the rôle to which society assigns him, and seeks, at least outwardly, to conform to it. He does this for various reasons; among others, because he wants recognition, respect, status. Independence of action beyond certain prescribed limitations is not expected of him, and as long as he conforms, he is likely to remain naïve; unconcerned about himself, and unconscious of his conduct.

It is by non-conformity, nevertheless, that the individual develops his personality and society ceases to be a mere mass of inert tradition. He may distinguish himself and become ambitious. He may fail; he may cheat; he may do the unpardonable thing and suffer the pangs of remorse. In any case, as a result and to the extent of his collision with the existing social order he is likely to become acutely conscious of himself. The ultimate effect of this is to create that inevitable personal reserve which constitutes his private life. This reserve, which, by the way, little children do not possess, assumes in time, and under certain circumstances, the character of something sacred and terrifying. The individual himself conceives it as something wholly, or almost wholly, inaccessible to other minds. Society is composed of such self-conscious personalities, and these brooding, subjective, inscrutable egos are apparently just as much a product of personal association as are the traditions, customs, and objective forms of social life over against which, in their inaccessible privacies, they set themselves as a contrast effect.

It appears, then, that habit and custom, personality and culture, the person and society, somehow are different aspects of the same thing. Personality has been described as the subjective and individual aspect of culture, and culture as the objective, generic or general

---

[31] Cooley, Charles Horton. *Human Nature and the Social Order*. New York, Charles Scribner's Sons, 1902.

aspect of personality. But the relation between the cultural life of the community and the personal life of the individuals who compose it is more real and dynamic than this statement suggests. The intimate verbal and documentary records upon which such life histories are based serve to lay bare the interaction between this private life, of which the individual is usually so intensely conscious, and the more objective aspects of his personality; namely, the customs and mores of his set, society or social group, of which he is usually unconscious—at least until he finds himself in conflict with them.

This conflict, incidentally, is also likely to have its internal and subjective, as well as its external and objective, aspects. In other words, the individual becomes a problem to himself as well as to society. In the first instance the conflict assumes, in general, the character of a moral struggle. In the other it may take the form of a cultural and, eventually, of a political conflict. The struggle to enforce the prohibition law is a case in point. Migration, since it brings together peoples with different cultural heritages, inevitably provokes cultural conflicts, first between the native and the alien stocks, and then, particularly since the second generation takes over the native culture more rapidly than the first, between the first and the second generation immigrants.

Life histories such as the immigrant biographies, of which so many have been published in recent years, illuminate this struggle and make intelligible the character of the cultural process involved.

Life histories, as sociologists have conceived of them, are not, however, autobiographies in the ordinary sense of the word. They have rather the character of confessions, intimate personal documents intended to record not so much external events as to reveal sentiments and attitudes. Of the attitudes which life histories reveal, the most important for the sociologist are those of which the individual is, or was, until his attention was called to them, quite unconscious. Men know themselves as they know and are known by other men about them. They are keen for what is unique and different, but the things in which one man seems like another do not interest them. The individual's opinions, for example, of which he is always so keenly conscious, are usually the least important of his personal attitudes. It is things that people take for granted which reveal at once the person and the society in which he lives. The naïve behavior of the individual is therefore an unfailing index of the society of which he is a member.

It is only recently that sociologists have undertaken to study society—the family, the local community, boys' gangs, political parties, the public, the public opinion—in the private lives and experiences of its individual components. Thomas and Znaniecki were the first to attempt the thing in an impressive way. They collected 15,000 personal letters interchanged between Polish peasants in this country and Poland.[32] They published in full the autobiography of an anonymous Polish adventurer, and upon this and other material of the same sort they were able to make an elaborate analysis of contemporary Polish peasant culture in Europe, and of the consequences to the Polish immigrant of the breakdown of this culture under the influence of an urban environment in this country.[33]

A little later Maurice T. Price published a volume entitled *Christian Missions and Oriental Civilizations*, based very largely upon the

---

[32] Thomas, W. I., and Znaniecki, Florian. *The Polish Peasant in Europe and America*, in five volumes. Boston, 1918.

[33] In an introduction to Volume III of *The Polish Peasant*, which contains what the authors describe as "the life record of an immigrant," Thomas and Znaniecki have made an interesting statement in regard to the nature and value of documents of this kind. Among other things, they say:

"We are safe in saying that personal life-records, as complete as possible, constitute the *perfect* type of sociological material, and that if social science has to use other materials at all it is only because of the practical difficulty of obtaining at the moment a sufficient number of such records to cover the totality of sociological problems, and of the enormous amount of work demanded for an adequate analysis of all the personal materials necessary to characterize the life of a social group.

"Indeed it is clear that even for the characterization of single social data—attitudes and values—personal life-records give us the most exact approach. An attitude as manifested in an isolated act is always subject to misinterpretation, but this danger diminishes in the very measure of our ability to connect this act with past acts of the same individual. A social institution can be fully understood only if we do not limit ourselves to the abstract study of tis formal organization, but do analyze the way in which it appears in the personal experience of various members of the group and follow the influence which it has upon their lives. And the superiority of life-records over every other kind of material for the purposes of sociological analysis appears with particular force when we pass from the characterization of single data to the determination of facts, for there is no safer and more efficient way of finding among the innumerable antecedents of a social happening the real causes of this happening than to analyze the past of the individuals through whose agency this happening occurred. The development of sociological investigation during the past fifteen or twenty years, particularly the growing emphasis which, under the pressure of practical needs, is being put upon special and actual empirical problems as opposed to the general speculations of the preceding period, leads to the growing realization that we must collect more complete sociological documents than we possess."

personal records made by missionaries of their own work in the Orient.[34] Still later, Charles S. Johnson contributed to the Survey of Race Relations in Chicago, made under the direction of a state commission, a study of the attitudes of the American public toward the Negro.[35] This, like other studies mentioned, was based largely upon personal records and the interpretation of documents.

If it is true that we must explore the personal experiences of individuals to find the origins and meaning of our cultural forms, it is equally true that the actions of the individual can be understood and explained only by considering them in the social and cultural context in which they occurred. Sociology has always been disposed to emphasize "environment" as a determining factor in human behavior, and many, if not most, of the reforms of recent years, improvement of homes, the laying out of playgrounds and the general improvement of the physical conditions of our cities have had the support of some sort of environmental theory of social causation. Attempts have been made, for example, to justify the erection of playgrounds on the theory that they reduced juvenile delinquency. If delinquency meanwhile increased, an explanation was likely to be found in the increasing popularity of the motion picture theater, and of the dance hall. Recently more detailed and specific studies have given us a clearer conception of the social environment and its relation to crime and vice.

At the meeting of the American Sociological Society in December, 1926, Clifford R. Shaw, of The Institute for Juvenile Research, made a report upon some studies of juvenile delinquency in which he had made use of what we have called life history material.[36] These detailed investigations, based upon interviews with delinquent boys, with members of the boys' families, and with neighbors, revealed, almost for the first time, the sort of world in which delinquent boys actually live.

Thrasher, in his study of the gang, which is likewise based upon personal interviews and intimate documents, had already given us a lively picture of what he called "gangland." [37] But the materials upon which Shaw's study was based were elicited in what amounted

---

[34] Price, Maurice T. *Christian Missions and Oriental Civilizations*. A Study in Culture Contacts. Shanghai, China, 1924.

[35] *The Negro in Chicago: A Study of Race Relations and a Race Riot*. By the Chicago Commission on Race Relations. Chicago, 1922.

[36] *Proceedings of The American Sociological Society*, Vol. XXI, pp. 149-57.

[37] Thrasher, Frederic M. *The Gang*. Chicago, 1927.

to an informal trial, in which the members of the family were the accusers and the delinquent boy the accused, the investigator acting in the rôle of the court. As a matter of fact, the procedure in getting the materials for case histories of this sort is not unlike the more formal proceeding of the French criminal courts, where the accuser and the accused are brought face to face and invited to substantiate, by question and answer, each his own side of the case. Under circumstances such as these, in which all the actors are actively engaged, not only the language but the accents and gestures of the participants are significant, and, as far as possible, made a part of the record.

The difference in the procedure begins after the informal court has adjourned and the record is completed. Since inquiry thus instituted is not a judicial proceeding and the "family interview" is not evidence but merely a record of behavior, it is not made the basis of a legal proceeding, but, together with the mental tests and psychiatric record, furnishes a basis of a social diagnosis. Since such a diagnosis may involve, and frequently does, not merely the delinquent child but the delinquent's family, the neighborhood and the play group, the subsequent procedure is often rather formidable. Frequently, however, the delinquency is due, and this is particularly true in the case of immigrants, to a failure on the part of parents to understand the kind of world in which the child is living. Sometimes the difficulty is not in the family but in the neighborhood. It is not easy for a family to maintain discipline over its members in a "mixed" community. When there is no support in the neighborhood for the standards and mores that the family seeks to maintain, family discipline almost invariably breaks down.

A report made at the meeting of the American Sociological Society in 1926 by Ernest W. Burgess [38] showed, among other things, that the delinquency rate reached its highest point, 443 per 1000, in the slum, and declined to 54 in the rooming house area; and from that point it continued to decline in a regular curve until, at the sixth and seventh mile from the "loop," where home ownership is high and the community relatively homogeneous and stable, it reached zero. These figures, which show how variously different cultural areas of the city are characterized by the incidence of ju-

---

[38] Burgess, Ernest W., "The Determination of Gradients in the Growth of the City," *Proceedings of The American Sociological Society*, Vol. XXI, pp. 178-84.

venile delinquency, become all the more intelligible and all the more significant when they are considered in the light of Shaw's more intensive and intimate studies of the individual cases. In this way the life history and the statistical studies supplement one another.

Life histories, where it is possible to secure them, are almost always interesting, because they nearly always illuminate some aspect of social and moral life which we may have known hitherto only indirectly, through the medium of statistics or formal statements. In the one case we are like a man in the dark looking at the outside of the house and trying to guess what is going on within. In the other, we are like a man who opens the door and walks in, and has visible before him what previously he had merely guessed at. The difficulty is that personal histories are voluminous, and in the interest of economy we must eventually reduce them to more or less formal types. However, no wholly satisfactory scheme of classification of personality types has yet been suggested, though much has been written and many experiments made. A sociological scheme for the classification of personality types must be based upon life histories, but with the exception of the three types mentioned by Thomas and Znaniecki—the philistine, the bohemian, and the creative man (the genius)—no such classification exists.

If, now, one asks, What facts in the personal history of an individual are for most or all purposes genuinely significant, it seems to me that we are bound to say that the most important fact about any person is this: What is it that habitually engages his attention? What are the subjects of his dreams and reveries? And what is the rôle in which he conceives himself? What his acts have been and what his habits are, we can know. In addition to these facts of his history, it is important to know, however, his incompleted acts: what he hopes; what he dreams; what his vagrant impulses, "temptations," are.

In the study of the family we are interested in knowing whether the traditions of the parents carry over to the children, and whether the plans and hopes of one generation are transmitted to and fulfilled by the second. If this does not happen, we may be said already to have family disorganization, for the family is a bearer of tradition, and in carrying on this tradition the family is engaged in a collective act. It is by such collective acts and by such handing on of the incompleted act of one generation in one individual to another that culture not only comes into existence, but is kept alive.

But just as the most important fact about the individual person is his hopes and dreams, so the most important fact about a nation or a people is its literature. Do our writers and social prophets look forward or backward? Are they critical and querulous merely? What dreams are they inspiring in us? What future actions are they inspiring? The most significant thing about the Negro since his emancipation, to cite a conspicuous instance, is, it seems to me, the rise of a Negro literature. So, likewise, the most significant recent incident in the life of the Jew is Zionism; in the life of Asia, Chinese nationalism. This phenomenon can also be studied systematically, but that is another and a different story, and it involves another and a different technique.

CHAPTER 16

NEWSPAPER CIRCULATION AND METROPOLITAN REGIONS[1]

AS ANALYSIS will show, many characteristics of newspaper circulation lend themselves to consideration when one is concerned with the general topic of the metropolitan community and regionalism. The newspaper is largely dependent on city populations for its sale, and there is consequently a high degree of correlation between circulation and urban concentration. Newspapers in America are characteristically local and are not distributed nationally, as are magazines of general literature and journals of opinion. Hence, with two or three exceptions,[2] their circulations are confined to the city and the tributary area in which they are published. This is due in part to the early settlement of the country in a number of isolated regions.

Reprinted by permission of the publisher from R. D. McKenzie, *The Metropolitan Community*, (New York: McGraw-Hill Book Co., 1933), pp. 98-110.

[1] Prepared by R. E. Park and Charles Newcomb, University of Chicago.

[2] Exceptions are the *United States Daily*, published in Washington, D. C., the *Christian Science Monitor*, Boston, and the *New York Times*. Papers which achieve a national distribution are ordinarily those that appeal to a particular class. The tendency of the American papers has been to assume a form that would appeal to all classes within a relatively limited territory. This has been achieved in part by describing current events in such a way as to emphasize their human interest, giving to news something of the symbolic character of literature. The same result has been accomplished by departmentalizing the news in such a way that there will be something for every class of readers.

More generally, however, the explanation lies in the establishment of the penny newspaper in 1833, with its emphasis on local news rather than on opinion and foreign news. This development is distinctly American and is quite removed from the European pattern even today.

NEWS AS A COMMODITY

The newspaper in America has gradually assumed the character of a commodity, that is, something to be sold and distributed. Similar though the newspaper is to other commodities, there are a number of special considerations operating to determine and limit the extent of its circulation. Time is an essential element of news, and any record of events, in order to preserve its character as news, must be distributed as quickly as possible.

The necessity for the rapid collection and distribution of the news is not, however, the only factor that determines the place of publication and the distribution of newspapers. If time is an essential element of news, so, in less direct and positive way, is distance, for news is always, in the last analysis, local in character, since it is not everything that happens but only those things that happen in the particular world in which we are oriented, which have for each of us the specific character of news. Events that happened far away and long ago may have human interest but they are not news.

Another less obvious factor in limiting and localizing the distribution of news and newspapers has been the increasing importance in newspaper budgets of the income derived from advertising. Since 60 to 75 per cent of the total revenue of daily papers at present is from advertising, and since a very considerable part of that is paid by local advertisers—department stores, for example—newspaper publishers have come to recognize the fact that circulation which is distributed outside and beyond the limits of the local trading area is of very doubtful value. Since both newspaper publishers and advertisers have come to recognize, also, that what the advertiser buys from the newspaper is not advertising space, merely, but circulation, and that circulation is valuable only when it puts the dealer in touch with a potential buyer, the distribution of circulation has assumed an increasing importance in determining the value of what is, after all, the most important commodity which the newspaper publisher has to sell, namely, circulation.

Perhaps, then, it may be said that no one thing has been more influential in giving to the American newspaper the distinctive character it has acquired, in the last hundred years, than the gradual discovery by newspaper publishers and editors of the nature, the function, and the commercial value of news.

CIRCULATION AND THE TRADE AREA

The similarity of the newspaper to other articles of commerce together with its advertising function makes for distribution of newspapers, like other commodities, from local centers of trade, and the limits within which they circulate tend to coincide with the trade area. It is the purpose of this section to examine the pattern of circulation of one group of metropolitan papers and to note how, through competition with the local papers of the region, the various types of trade areas are revealed. Before proceeding with the analysis, it is desirable to consider two or three general points.

Limitations on Extent of Distribution.—The size of the trading area within which any paper will circulate is determined primarily by two factors: (1) the size of the town, city, or metropolitan center in which it is published; and (2) the proximity of other competing centers of publication.

Thus Boston papers circulate widely over the whole of New England, while the circulation limits of competing centers such as Philadelphia, Baltimore, and New York are definitely restricted by their proximity to each other. And yet the very size of New York City assures her papers a wide circulation even in these adjacent competing centers, and, conversely, the relatively small sizes of Philadelphia, Boston, and Baltimore operate to restrict the circulation of their papers in New York.

Another example is found in the Minneapolis-St. Paul papers, where the circulation area to the northwest is limited only by factors of time and space, while to the south and east it is narrowed by competition with Chicago papers.

Metropolitan and Local Papers.—Similar influences are dominant in determining the areas of circulation of metropolitan and local newspapers within a given region. Metropolitan papers are defined as those published in the central city, and local papers as those published in the metropolitan region but outside the corporate limits of the central city; that is, in the suburban towns, the so-called "satellite cities," and in that greater region outside the immediate influence of the metropolis, but still more or less dependent upon it, which may be described as the metropolitan hinterland.

Now, while it is true that metropolitan papers circulate in the surrounding satellite centers in competition with local papers, the converse situation is rarely found to exist. New York City papers circulate widely throughout the adjacent territory, but Connecticut and New Jersey papers do not circulate in New York. Similarly, Chicago papers circulate in Gary, Indiana, but Gary papers do not circulate in Chicago, although they do compete with Chicago papers in territory suburban to Gary. The extent to which a metropolitan paper circulates outside its corporate limits in competition with a locally published paper may be taken as an index of its dominance in that area. Conversely, the number of copies published and circulated by a local paper, in competition with a metropolitan paper, is an index of the degree of its economic and cultural independence.

Occasionally it is found that a local paper is published within the limits of a larger city. Such newspapers are limited in their circulation to the particular quarter of the city or the particular element of the population for which they are published. Such, for example, are the foreign-language papers. There are, besides, a number of local urban community papers published weekly for the purpose of advertising the local merchants in different quarters of the metropolis. South Chicago has published for some years a daily paper of its own, the *Calumet*.

It is, however, difficult to maintain a daily newspaper in competition with the more important metropolitan dailies within 50 miles of a metropolis and the difficulty increases as the means of interurban transportation and communication tend to integrate the metropolis with its suburban territory.

Organic Nature of the Trade Area.—The correlation of newspaper circulation and the limits of the trade area resolves itself into two problems: (1) the metropolitan daily in the local trade area; and (2) the circulation and the outside limits of the trade area. The first problem is most clearly indicated when the circulations of the daily papers published in the Chicago area are plotted on a map. The spatial pattern of distribution at once reveals the organic relation of the functional units. This pattern shows the whole region as a complex of local trading centers, which are also local publishing centers, each encircled by an area in which its circulation dominates.

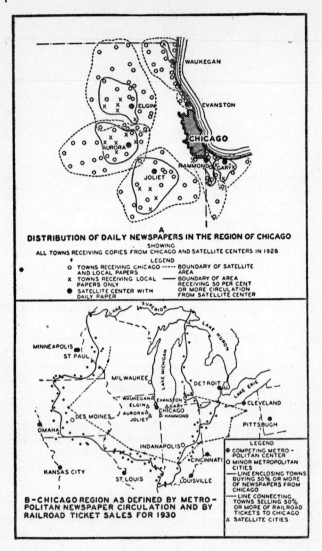

The Chicago region as defined by newspaper circulation and by railroad ticket sales, 1930.

The total circulation consumed by each small town is supplied by both the metropolis and the local trade center, and the ratio supplied by each depends mainly on the distance of the town from its local trade center. That is, the proportion of circulation from the local publishing center declines for each town as its distance from the center increases, and conversely the proportion of circulation from the metropolitan center increases. The solid lines in Figure 5 encircling the local publishing center show the distance at which the circulations of local and metropolitan papers are substantially equal.

The outer limits of the circulation of the local papers, shown by the dotted line, will indicate the limits of the local trade area. The ratio between the circulation of the metropolitan and the local papers in the local center is an index of the degree to which the local trading center is integrated with and dominated by the metropolitan.

Varying Degrees of Interdependence.—Figure 5 shows that there are seven satellite cities within 40 miles of Chicago circulating daily newspapers of their own in competition with papers from the metropolitan center. Among the satellite cities themselves and their own local areas, there are wide differences in the extent of domination by Chicago newspapers. Table 41 gives the proportion of the circula-

CIRCULATION OF ALL CHICAGO PAPERS IN SATELLITE CENTERS AND
TOTAL CITY CIRCULATION OF SATELLITE PAPER IN CENTER WHERE IT IS
PUBLISHED, 1928 [a]

City	Miles from Chicago (Loop)	Total city circulation of satellite paper	Total circulation of Chicago paper	Percentage Chicago paper
Evanston, Ill.........	12	6,522	26,731	80.5
Waukegan, Ill.......	39	8,131	11,503	58.5
Gary, Ind...........	31	16,647	16,760	50.1
Elgin, Ill...........	38	10,235	8,658	46.0
Joliet, Ill...........	38	14,939	12,283	45.0
Hammond, Ind.......	19	17,970	14,491	42.0
Aurora, Ill..........	38	12,435	8,426	40.0
Total.............	..	86,879	98,852	53.2

[a] Robert E. Park, "Urbanization as Measured by Newspaper Circulation," *American Journal of Sociology*, Vol. XXXV, No. 1, July, 1929, p. 67.

tion of Chicago papers within each of the satellite centers. The variation in these proportions leads one to suspect the operation of individual factors of a local nature and may perhaps be taken as an index of the degree of interdependence between the central city and the different parts of the metropolitan region. Six of these cities are about equidistant from Chicago and have approximately the same commuting time to that city, from an hour to an hour and a half. Yet they are widely different in character and the differences are reflected in newspaper circulation. Chicago papers compete with local publications most successfully in Evanston. Evanston, however, is a residential suburb not differing except in size from some of the residential areas of Chicago and from a series of other suburbs located along the line of rapid transit connecting Chicago and Milwaukee. Waukegan, with the next largest proportion of papers coming from Chicago, is also a residential community, but lying at a greater distance from the metropolitan center and hence enjoying a life apart from that of the larger city.

The other five cities, however, appear less important as residential areas for persons employed in Chicago. Instead, a greater proportion of their inhabitants are engaged in local industries and commercial enterprises. Quite naturally they are less integrated with the central city, and, in fact, become centers of their own suburban territory. The immediate result is that where there is not a large volume of daily commutation traffic between the small city and Chicago, the circulation of papers from the latter city drops off in proportion to local paper circulation. The daily commuter from Aurora is likely to buy a Chicago paper on the way into the city in the morning and another in the evening on the way out, but the noncommuter who does not have daily contact with the large city ordinarily buys the newspaper published in the smaller center where he lives and trades. It is also noted that only in the areas surrounding the industrial satellites do there appear communities taking no papers at all from the metropolitan center.

Further examination of Figure 5 reveals an open space between the city limits of Chicago and the first towns taking any daily newspapers from the satellite centers. This area is filled with an almost contiguous mass of communities such as Des Plaines, Melrose Park, Maywood, Oak Park, Cicero, and Blue Island. These communities are densely populated and are entirely dependent on Chicago for their daily papers. Nearly all of the interests of the people in these suburbs are centered in Chicago, and hence it is to be expected that Chicago papers would circulate to the exclusion of those from the smaller outlying cities. In the crescent-shaped area beyond this open space, 71 per cent of the papers are from Chicago; and in those communities outside the immediate local trade areas, 80 per cent of the papers are from Chicago. Thus Chicago supplies the bulk of all circulation within 50 miles of its center at State and Madison streets, even including the local publishing centers. It should be noted that although each local publishing center has its trade area, dominated by its own circulation, these towns consume a relatively small proportion of the circulation consumed in the area generally. This is due to the fact that these towns are smaller and are relatively less important than the ones on the outer rim of the satellite trade area. Their lesser importance and size are determined by their relation to the satellite even as the satellites are circumscribed, compared with cities of comparable populations that lie beyond 100 miles from the metropolis, by their proximity to Chicago. In other words, the satellite centers tend to limit the competition and relative independence of their small subsidiary towns in about the same way that the metropolis tends to limit the competition between satellites. As supplementary forms of communication and transportation develop in the metropolitan area to a point where the system is completely flexible, we should expect the importance of the satellite to diminish even more.

The conventional form which the Chicago suburban area assumes suggests that in similar situations, where populations, industries, and institutions are making similar demands upon the territory they occupy, one might expect to find a pattern of territorial distribution not identical but at least comparable with the one here presented. Further investigation will be necessary to determine how far this general hypothesis is in accordance with the facts, but if, and so far as, it turns out to be true, it will be due to the fact that in the gradual accommodation of competing interests within a limited territory, something approaching the highest possible use of space available has been more or less completely achieved. The existing distribution of newspaper circulation in the metropolitan region, since it seems to have arisen in response to the same forces which have brought about the existing territorial distribution of social and economical function, is an index of the existing social and economic organization of the region.

The Outer Limits of the Trade Area.—Beyond the satellite communities surrounding the city, Chicago papers circulate in competition with those of other metropolitan centers. It is of considerable interest to determine the outer line of dominance of Chicago newspaper circulation, for just as within the 40-mile commuting zone, traffic and newspaper circulation were correlated, so in the outer zone there seems to be a considerable interdependence between circulation and the wholesale-trade area. In recognition of the fact that the local dealer is largely influenced by convenience in his buying, the *Chicago Tribune* in 1930 made a survey of passenger traffic to discover the points on 11 railway lines out of Chicago where the traffic divided, 50 per cent moving toward and 50 per cent away from the metropolis. The points determined are connected by the broken line in Figure 5. The marked similarity between the ebb and flow of traffic and newspaper circulation is seen by comparing the broken line with the solid line which connects the outermost cities taking 50 per cent or more of their metropolitan newspapers from Chicago as opposed to competing centers. It thus appears that there is a gradient character to newspaper circulation and to traffic and trade as well, and that the extent of the areas of dominance are very nearly coterminous. Hence the distribution of newspaper circulation might be useful in attempting to delimit the region of metropolitan influence.

METROPOLITAN REGIONS DETERMINED BY NEWSPAPER CIRCULATION

Communication is fundamental to the existence of every form and type of society, and one form of communication, namely, the newspaper, has been found to circulate over the natural areas within which society is organized. Thus it may not seem unreasonable that the newspaper should be used as an index in outlining a number of metropolitan regions of the United States. This was done with the result shown in Figure 6.

Procedure.—The procedure adopted in outlining these regions was that employed in locating the outlying boundary of the Chicago region, namely, the selection of a number of large cities and the plotting of the circulation of certain newspapers published in these cities. When this had been done, it was found that the limits of each of the regions so defined were coterminous with those of adjoining regions, and that the whole country had been divided into a number of cultural and economic provinces, each with a single dominant city, the center and focus of a population and a territory more or less completely integrated with it.

While it was generally assumed that a city was to be regarded as metropolitan when its papers circulated over a considerable area in competition with the local papers published in the area, the pro-

cedure of selecting the cities was simplified by taking the Federal
Reserve cities since they had already been selected to perform one
type of regional service. To these cities, Milwaukee, Sioux City,

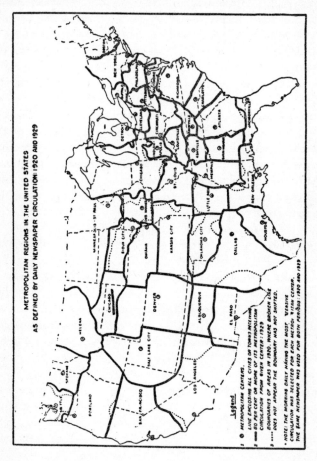

METROPOLITAN REGIONS IN THE UNITED STATES
AS DEFINED BY DAILY NEWSPAPER CIRCULATION: 1920 AND 1929

Des Moines, Albuquerque, Charlotte, and Louisville were later
added.

One morning newspaper in each city was selected for the analysis, since these possess wider geographic circulation than do papers
published in the afternoon.[3] The statistics were taken from the rec-

[3] The morning papers selected were *Atlanta Constitution, Baltimore Sun,
Birmingham Age-Herald, Buffalo Courier-Express, Boston Globe, Chicago
Tribune, Cincinnati Enquirer, Cleveland Plain Dealer, Dallas News, Denver*

ords of the Audit Bureau of Circulation which show the distribution of member papers in all towns where at least 25 copies are circulated.[4]

In each of the 41 regions, the total morning circulation was compared with similar circulations of competing metropolitan centers in towns which took copies of newspapers from more than one center. This procedure made it possible to draw a line around nearly all towns taking more than 50 per cent of their metropolitan circulation from each of the several centers. For Chicago, the boundary so determined circumscribes a region with an average radius of about 200 miles. In order to compare the distribution of circulation for each city, it was necessary to take account of the distribution in from three to eight adjacent cities. The circulation of Chicago papers was compared with that of newspapers published in eight other cities, Milwaukee, Minneapolis, Des Moines, Kansas City, St. Louis, Louisville, Indianapolis, and Detroit. Some 2,500 towns and cities receive papers from more than one of the 41 metropolitan centers. In the course of analysis, individual maps were made for each of the 41 centers, showing the area in which their circulation dominated the combined circulation of the centers in competition. These maps were later transferred to the single map shown in Figure 6.

Difficulties and Anomalies in Outlining Regions.—The attempt to delimit the metropolitan region systematically gave rise to certain difficulties and disclosed some anomalies. An account of some of these situations is useful in revealing how certain conditions operate in determining regional boundaries.

Overlapping Territory.—In some cases, it happened that the town or territory whose position was to be determined was located where the circulations of two or more metropolitan papers overlapped. According to the procedure adopted, the city of Walla

---

Rocky Mountain News, Des Moines Register, Detroit Free Press, El Paso Times, Helena Independent, Houston Post, Indianapolis Star, Jacksonville Florida Times-Union, Kansas City Times, Little Rock Arkansas Gazette, Los Angeles Times, Memphis Commercial Appeal, Milwaukee Sentinel, Minneapolis Tribune, Nashville Tennesseean, New Orleans Times Picayune, New York Times, Oklahoma City Oklahoman, Omaha Bee News, Philadelphia Inquirer, Pittsburgh Post-Gazette, Portland Oregonian, Richmond Times-Dispatch, Salt Lake City Tribune, St. Louis Globe-Democrat, San Francisco Chronicle, Seattle Post Intelligencer, Sioux City Journal, Spokane Spokesman-Review, Charlotte Observer, Albuquerque Journal, Louisville Courier-Journal.

[4] The newspaper statistics compiled by the Bureau of the Census do not show the distribution of circulation.

Walla, Washington, is dominated by no one of the three neighboring centers for not one of them sends 50 per cent of all the outside papers circulated in the city. Spokane, Portland, and Seattle all send daily papers, but those of Spokane, greatest in number, are but 43 per cent of the total.

Excluded Territory.—Contrasted to the situation described above there were found areas which, according to the procedure adopted, seemed to be outside the region dominated by any of the neighboring centers. Thus, in certain mountain areas, as in northern Wyoming and again in southeastern Montana, papers from the nearest cities, Denver, Omaha, and Helena, did not circulate. When the lists for the Chicago papers were examined, it was found that this section, together with the Black Hills area of South Dakota, was apparently *Chicago Tribune* territory, which suggests that this territory is more closely tied up with Chicago than with any of the adjacent metropolitan regions. For this and other reasons, it seems that this territory is a remnant of the old frontier served by the mail-order system.

Enclaves.—Among the 41 cities used in this study three—Milwaukee, Des Moines, and Indianapolis—present certain interesting anomalies. An examination of the distribution of Chicago papers in Milwaukee territory, for example, reveals the fact that there is no such sharp dividing line separating Milwaukee from Chicago as that which marks the boundary between Chicago and St. Louis or between Chicago and Detroit.

There are approximately 75 towns and cities that receive 25 or more papers from both St. Louis and Chicago. These cities are all located on the border that divides the region of Chicago from that of St. Louis. Outside of these border cities, Chicago papers do not circulate in Missouri, except in two metropolitan cities, St. Louis and Kansas City.

This is not true either of Milwaukee, Des Moines, or Indianapolis. Chicago papers circulate everywhere in the states of Wisconsin, Iowa, and Indiana in competition with Milwaukee, Des Moines, and Indianapolis papers.

Nearly every town in the region outside of Illinois takes papers from both the local large city, that is, Milwaukee, Des Moines, or Indianapolis, and the distant metropolitan city, that is, Chicago. In the case of the Des Moines region, some 150 towns take papers from both Des Moines and Chicago, and although a line of dominance can be drawn between Des Moines and Chicago, still the Chicago papers circulate beyond Des Moines into the western part of Iowa.

These cities, dominant in their own more limited areas, are nevertheless surrounded by territory in which the circulation of Chicago papers is greater than theirs. They are, so to speak, enclaves in the larger metropolitan region, so that their position with respect to Chicago is not unlike that of other local and regional cities outside the commuting area of Chicago.

SUCCESSION, AN ECOLOGICAL CONCEPT

THE term "succession" seems to have first gained currency and definition as a result of its use in the writings of the plant ecologists. It has not the same wide application in animal ecology, and where it has been used elsewhere, as it has by sociological writers, it seems to be a useful word but without as yet any very precise connotation. It has been used, for example, in describing the intra-mural movements and shiftings of population incident to the growth of the city and of its various "natural areas."

It has been observed, for one thing, that immigrant peoples ordinarily settle first in or near the centers of cities, in the so-called areas of transition. From there they are likely to move by stages (perhaps one might better say, by leaps and bounds) from an area of first to areas of second and third settlement, generally in the direction of the periphery of the city and eventually into the suburban area—in any case, from a less to a more stable section of the metropolitan region. To these movements, seeing in them the effects of natural tendencies in the life of the urban community, students have applied the term "succession."

In this same sense the term has been applied to the successive waves by which the frontier in America advanced from the Atlantic seaboard westward across the plains to the Pacific coast, each advance marked by a different type of culture and by a different occupational and personality type.

Reprinted by permission of the publisher from *American Sociological Review*, I (April, 1936), pp. 171-79.

First arrivals were the explorers, trappers, Indian traders, ar prospectors, with a sprinkling of outlaws. In the next line of advanc were land seekers, squatters and frontier farmers bent on establisl ing the first frontier settlements. They were followed finally by swarm of restless enterprising adventurers of all sorts, among the representatives of a frontier *intelligentsia*—the men who eventuall became the lawyers, politicians, and newspaper men of the boomir settlements.[1]

A similar "territorial succession" may be said to have marked tl expansion of European population and European culture during tl period of four hundred years in which European commerce h made its conquest of the world.[2]

In a study of Lowell, made by George F. Kenngott and pul lished in 1912, the most striking feature of the study was the succe sion of immigrant invasions which in the course of the city's histor i.e., from about 1830 to about 1912, the steady demand for labor i the woolen mills had brought to it. This was a study in populatio succession, though not so designated. It was also a study in progre sive cultural change—a progress, however, that was mostly for tl worse.[3]

Although the term succession, as originally employed by sociolc gists, would seem to be more appropriately applied to movements c population and to such incidental social and cultural changes a these movements involve, there seems to be no sound reason wh the same term should not be used to describe any orderly and i reversible series of events, provided they are to such an extent co related with other less obvious and more fundamental social chang that they may be used as indices of these changes.

Thus a series of fundamental inventions like the alphabet, tl printing press, the newspaper, and the radio may be said to const tute a succession. At any rate, each may be said to mark an epoch i the history of communication, and in doing this each new inventio characterizes the culture of which it is a part and defines its place i the historical succession. In the same sense we may speak of tl waterwheel as in the same line of succession as the steam engine an

---

[1] Rupert B. Vance, "Frontier: Geographical and Social Aspect," *Ency. Soc. Scis.*

[2] E. B. Reuter, *Race and Culture Contacts*, Chap. V.

[3] George F. Kenngott, *The Record of a City: A Social Survey of Lowel Massachusetts*, N. Y., 1912.

the electric motor, each marking a phase in the evolution of the machine age. Manifestly such a series of events represents something more than a mere temporal sequence. It represents rather an irreversible series in which each succeeding event is more or less completely determined by the one that preceded it.

In a recent paper by Edgar T. Thompson on the plantation as an institution of the frontier, the author refers to the fact that a typical plantation society ordinarily passes through a cycle of change, the plantation cycle, and to this he applies the term succession. Thereupon he proceeds to describe in detail the irreversible stages in the natural history of the plantation community.[4]

In a recent study of the "granger movements" in the United States, Thomas C. McCormick pointed out that the different individual movements seemed to be merely the periodic outbreaks of a disease that was endemic in the country, so that the different movements might well be conceived as the recurrent manifestations, the periodic risings and subsidings, of discontents that had their source and origin in a kind of permanent malaise that could be relieved but never quite cured.[5]

Among other things interesting from the point of view of succession which this study showed were: (1) each succeeding rural movement was under way and rising before the one preceding it had wholly subsided: (2) although each wave of utopianism was incontinently followed by a corresponding period of depression and disillusionment, there was, nevertheless, evidence with each recurring wave of a growing realism in the attitudes of the leaders at least. This was manifest in the character of the programs and in the methods for putting them into effect. This is an instance of succession in the psychic or subjective aspect of social change.

A more obvious and impressive example of succession, in the very elementary sense in which this term is here used, is the procession of peoples that have invaded and settled South Africa. First came the Bushmen; they were hunters who have left in caves in the mountains, as records of their presence, interesting rock pictures. The Hottentots followed. They were hunters, to be sure, but herdsmen also, and they had a great deal of trouble with the Bushmen

---

[4] Edgar T. Thompson, "Population Expansion and Plantation System." *Amer. Jour. of Sociol.*, 41, 3 (Nov., 1931), pp. 314-326.

[5] Thomas C. McCormick, *The Rural Life Movement*, unpublished thesis, The University of Chicago.

who killed their cattle with poisoned arrows. So the Hottentots drove the Bushmen into the Kalahari desert. The Bantu were next. They were hunters and herdsmen but they were more. They cultivated the soil and raised Kaffir corn.

Later still came the Boers, particularly the *voortrekkers,* who settled the Transvaal and the Orange Free State, conquered and enslaved the natives, settled on the land, raised large families, and lived on their wide acres in patriarchal style. Although they were descendants, for the most part, of the earlier Dutch immigrants, with a sprinkling of Huguenots and other Europeans, they had become, as a result of their isolation and their long association with the country, an indigenous folk, having their own language, their own customs and culture.

Then, finally, came the English. They were a sophisticated city folk, and they came in force only after diamonds were discovered in Orange Free State in 1867 and gold was discovered in the Transvaal in 1884. They built Johannesburg, a cosmopolitan city—a world city, in fact, like Calcutta, and Shanghai, and London. In this way they drew South Africa out of its isolation into the current of international trade and the new world civilization.

What makes this instance of succession ecologically interesting is the fact that it illustrates a principle familiar to ethnologists: the principle, namely, that the more primitive the culture of a people the larger the territory needed, in proportion to its numbers, to support its population. A corollary of this is the principle that the land eventually goes to the race or people that can get the most out of it. This, on the other hand, is merely another version of the rule of agricultural economics, which declares that the best lands eventually go to the best farmers.

The thing that makes the settlement of South Africa relevant and significant, as an example of succession, is the fact that it seems to represent not a casual sequence of events but the consequences of an inexorable historical process.

It is evident that in the conception of succession, as here defined and illustrated, there is implicit a more fundamental notion of social change and of society which is nowhere explicitly set forth.

Generally speaking, succession, as the term is used by ecologists, seems to be identical with a notion of social change suggested by Walter Bagehot's phrase, "the cake of custom," in his volume *Phys-*

ics and Politics; a conception which has been further elaborated by Frederick Jackson Teggart in his *Theory of History.*[6]

Teggart's is what I have described as the catastrophic theory of history; the theory that each succeeding social order has its origin in the conditions created by the earlier; that society is continually reborn, but that now and then a new and fundamentally different society emerges. In that case, it emerges suddenly and abruptly with the accumulation of minor changes in the course of a long-term trend.

The changes here referred to, have taken place upon the cultural, rather than the biotic level. Nevertheless, they seem to be identical in form, at least, with the kind of change that plant and animal ecologists have called succession, the nature of which is elaborately set forth by F. C. Clements.[7]

On the other hand, the conception of social relations and society on which this account of succession is based is that suggested by J. Arthur Thomson's description of "the web of life" as "a system of inter-related lives." This is a notion that had its origin in a long series of observations and reflections like those from which Darwin arrived at his theory of the origin of the species. It is this concept of a symbiotic society based on physiological correlation rather than culture which has been adopted and elaborated in writings of the plant and animal ecologists.

Perhaps I can make clear the connection of these conceptions of society and social change with the ecological conception of succession if I state briefly certain points of evolutionary and ecological theory. In brief, then, the argument is this:

Man is involved, with all the hosts of other living creatures, in what Darwin calls "the web of life." In certain places and under certain conditions this interdependence of the species, to which Darwin's expression "the web of life" refers, assumes a relatively permanent, structural character. This is true of the so-called plant and animal communities.

The same biotic interdependence of individuals and species, which has been observed and studied in plant and animal communities,

---

[6] Walter Bagehot, *Physics and Politics; or Thoughts on the Application of the Principles of "Natural Selection" and "Inheritance" to Political Society,* N. Y., 1873; and Frederick Jackson Teggart, *Theory of History.*

[7] F. C. Clements, *Plant Succession,* Washington, D.C., Carnegie Institution, 1916.

seems to exist likewise on the human level, except for the fact that in human society competition and the struggle for existence are limited by custom, convention, and law. In short, human society is, or appears to be, organized on two levels, the biotic and the cultural.

We may distinguish between a society based on symbiosis, and one based on communication and consensus. As a matter of fact, however, the two are but different aspects of one society. The cultural superstructure rests on the basis of a symbiotic substructure, and the emergent energies that manifest themselves on the biotic level in movements and actions which are obvious enough reveal themselves on the higher, social level in more subtle and sublimated forms. The distinction and relation between the two levels of society, the biotic and the cultural, is, or seems to be, analogous to that between the somatic and psychic aspects of the individual organisms of which the society is composed.

Economic competition, as one meets it in human society, is the struggle for existence, as Darwin conceived it, modified and limited by custom and convention. In other respects, however, it is not different from competition as it exists in plant and animal communities.

Society, in the more inclusive sense in which ecologists have defined it, may be said to exist wherever competition has established some sort of order or war has established some sort of peace. It is the area within which an intrinsic and functional social order has succeeded one that was extrinsic and mechanical. This does not imply that the original relations of men were, as Hobbes described them, a war of each against all, a *bellum omnium contra omnes*, but rather that the function and effect of competition has been to bring about everywhere a division of labor which has diminished competition. In the same sense the function of war has been to achieve peace and order, and to create a social organization capable of maintaining it.

There is this difference, however, between a symbiotic and cultural society: namely, that the restraint in the case of symbiotic society (as for example in the plant community) is physical and external. In the case of cultural, i.e., human, society the restraints upon the individual are, so to speak, internal and moral, i.e., based on some sort of consensus.

A social organization on either the biotic or social level, so far as it involves the incorporation of individuals into a more intimate association, imposes limits, control, and direction upon these individual units. One may regard the plant and animal community as an association that is wholly anarchic and free. In that case, however, every form of association on the cultural level will involve a limitation of freedom of the individual.

The individual man, although he has more freedom in some places than in others—more freedom on the economic level than upon the political, more upon the political than the custom or moral level—never has in human society the same absolute freedom to compete with other individuals that plants and animals have.

Competition implies the existence of what J. Arthur Thomson describes as "the self-assertiveness and insurgence of the creature." The adaptations and accommodations which make society possible are for the individual organism or the individual species a partial or temporary solution of its struggles to survive.[8] But they limit freedom.

As the equilibrium we call society becomes relatively fixed in social structure, competition is increasingly diminished. Nevertheless, competition persists in human society and continues to manifest itself, as does the sexual instinct, in manifold indirect and insidious ways.

Every now and then something occurs, however, to disturb the biotic balance and the social equilibrium, thus tending to undermine the existing social order. It may be the advent of a new insect pest, like the boll weevil, or the arrival of a newly invented and perfected artifact, like the automobile. Under these circumstances, forces and tendencies formerly held in check are released, and a period of intense activity and rapid change ensues which then continues until the cycle is completed and a new biotic and social equilibrium is achieved.

Changes, when they are recurrent, so that they fall into a temporal or spatial series—particularly if the series is of such a sort that the effect of each succeeding increment of change reënforces or carries forward the effects of the preceding—constitute what is described in this paper as succession.

In view, however, of the complexity of social change and of the peculiar manner in which change in the social superstructure is involved in change in the biotic or symbiotic substructure, it seems desirable to include within the perspective and purview of the con-

---

[8] "The living creature is by its very nature insurgent and it finds itself encompassed by limitations and difficulties" (Thomson, *op. cit.*, p. 294).

cept, and of the studies of succession, every possible form of orderly change so far as it affects the interrelations of individuals in a community or the structure of the society of which these individual units are a part.

Conceived in this way succession will include studies of the form (morphology) and of the causes (etiology) of social change.

Sometimes the forms of social change are such, as in the case of periodic "psychic epidemics" or recurrent business booms, that their courses can be precisely described in a mathematical equation. In that case it may be possible to predict, with some accuracy, not merely the direction but the duration of change.

Studies of succession, however, seek less to predict the course of change than to make change intelligible, so that it can eventually be controlled by technical devices or political measures. For this reason studies of succession are concerned not only with the form which change takes but even more with the circumstances and events which precede, accompany, and follow change—in short, with its natural history.

The study of succession involves, it seems, not merely the life-cycle of individual types of institution and society, but eventually a study of processes by which new types of society are incubated and, eventually, by which a new social order emerges from the lap of the old.

The problems with which plant and animal ecology have traditionally been concerned are fundamentally population problems. Society, from the ecological point of view is, like the natural as opposed to the institutional family, a symbiotic rather than a social unit. It is a population settled and limited to its habitat. The ties that unite its individual units are those of a free and natural economy, based on a natural division of labor. Such a society is territorially organized, and the ties which hold it together are physical and vital rather than customary and moral. It is, of course, not assumed that this is all of society, but it is one aspect of it.

The changes in which ecology is interested, it follows, are primarily physical and vital. They are the movements of population and of artifacts (commodities), changes in location and in occupation—any sort of change, in fact, which affects an existing division of labor or the relation of the population to the soil.

Human ecology, in approaching the study of society from the aspect presented by its biotic substructure, assumes that the origin of social change, if one could trace it to its source, would be found in the struggle for existence and in the growth, the migration, the mobility, and the territorial and occupational distribution of peoples which this struggle has brought about.

Ecology conceives society as fundamentally a territorial as well as a cultural organization. So far as this conception is valid, it assumes that most if not all cultural changes in society will be correlated with changes in its territorial organization, and every change in the territorial and occupational distribution of the population will effect changes in the existing cultures.

The evolution of society is, therefore, in one of its aspects, the evolution of a territorial organization. Thus, N. B. S. Gras, in his *Introduction to Economic History*, is able to tell the whole story of economic history by describing the evolution of the metropolitan economy as it has developed through a series of stages which include the village, the town, and the city, and which ends in the metropolitan economy.[9]

In a similar way, the present economic, political and cultural order in Europe has come into existence with the growth in population and the migration and the territorial expansion of Europe. This expansion has been made possible by a series of inventions which have, at different epochs in its history, revolutionized and transformed the prevailing methods of transportation and communication. They are:

(1) The perfecting of ocean-going ships with which, in the age of discovery, Europeans extended their knowledge of the world outside of Europe.

(2) The steamship, by means of which a great commercial highway has been established around the world and has made of the seas, with their seaport cities, the center of the world.

(3) The railways, by which the continental areas have been penetrated and their resources transported to the seaboard, where they have entered into world commerce.

(4) The automobile, which has suddenly further transformed continental areas by spreading out over the land networks of roads which permit rapid and unlimited transportation in every direction.

(5) Finally, there is the airplane, the possibilities of which we are now just beginning to explore.

These changes have literally plowed up the ancient landmarks,

---

[9] N. B. S. Gras, *An Introduction to Economic History*, N. Y., 1922.

undermined the influence of the traditional social order in every part of the world, and released immense social forces which are now seeking everywhere a new equilibrium.

It is from the point of view of these spatial and temporal changes in the interrelation of human beings that ecology seeks to investigate the processes and mechanisms of social and cultural change.

CHAPTER 18

HAWAII AND THE NATURAL HISTORY OF WORLD ECONOMY

LUDWIG FRIEDLÄNDER, in his fascinating history of the manners and customs of the Romans, devotes one delightful chapter to the rise, among the peoples of imperial Rome, of an interest in travel —what we would probably describe, in modern phraseology, as tourism.[1] It was after Rome had completed her conquest of the Roman world that travel became fashionable in the Empire. By that time the great highways which had made that conquest possible had almost ceased to resound to the tramp of Roman legions. Peace had come to the Empire, and, with the change of scene, merchants, missionaries and wandering priests, itinerant philosophers, traveling mountebanks, actors, jugglers, gladiators, as well as men of wealth and leisure, all moved by the same "Bohemian curiosity to experience life in its various kinds," began in ever increasing numbers to swell the rising tide of travel between the metropolis and the provinces.

This sophisticated interest in foreign travel, and in the peaceful adventures which travel afforded, is at once an indication of the security which the Empire guaranteed and an evidence of its ma-

Reprinted by permission of the publisher from Andrew W. Lind, *An Island Community: Ecological Succession in Hawaii*, (Chicago: University of Chicago Press, 1938), pp. ix-xvi, where it appeared as the "Introduction."

[1] *Darstellungen aus der Sittengeschichte Roms in der Zeit von August bis zum Ausgang der Antonine* (Leipzig, 1922).

turity. The interest in travel continued, but the Empire ceased to expand. The Roman world had come of age, but the processes in which its existence was involved persisted.

As war on the frontiers ceased, discipline within the Empire was relaxed, and the unity and order which it had imposed on its widely scattered dominions gradually dissolved. Under these circumstances the seat of conflict was transferred from the periphery to the center of the Empire, from the provinces to Rome, where, by this time, peoples from every region of the Roman world were living in a vast cosmopolitan confusion.

In time, in what seems to be a natural and inevitable sequence of events, the long peace came to an end. Under the impact of the barbarian invasions, the Empire declined and died, though its ghost, in the shape of the Holy Roman Empire, still haunted the imagination of Europe for a time. Ultimately, with the rise of nationalism, modern Europe emerged—emerged as a congeries of independent national states.

A somewhat similar cycle of events, but on a grander scale, has characterized the expansion of Europe during the four hundred years and more since Columbus landed at San Salvador and the age of exploration and discovery ushered in the modern world. Since that time European commerce has gone out to the ends of the earth and drawn together, within the limits of a world-wide economy, the most remote regions and the most primitive peoples.

At the present moment there is not, it seems, anywhere in the world, outside of Japan, a commercially important city in which European peoples and European culture are not exercising a dominant, if not a dominating, influence. One might add, also, that there is hardly any part of the world, except, perhaps, West Africa, where there is not now some sort of ferment and opposition; something calling itself either communism or nationalism, which is seeking to throw off this ascendancy, where it still exists, and to escape from the tutelage which it imposes.

During these four hundred years of European expansion almost everything that is peculiarly characteristic of European culture and the modern world has come into existence: steam power and electricity, mass production and advertising, the automobile and the radio, joint-stock companies and the capitalist system, each and all directly or indirectly the product of Europe's expanding economy. At the present moment, however, European ascendancy has manifestly come to a pause, and there is every indication that it has reached limits it is not soon, if ever, destined to transcend.

European commerce is not now expanding and has not been since the World War. Migration, in every part of the world, has almost entirely ceased. European political power in the world outside Europe is obviously waning. The British Empire seems to be in process of dissolution; the United States is withdrawing from the Philippines; Japan has taken over a major share of the "white man's burden" in Asia and the Pacific; and the great powers of Europe are involved, to an extent that they have not been since the colonial wars of the seventeenth and eighteenth centuries, in a bitter and dangerous contest for dominance—dominance not only in Europe but in that vaster and vaguer dominion of colonies, dependencies, and spheres of interest which the expansion of Europe has brought not merely into existence but, in the last half century, to something like maturity.

There are still regions with natural resources that have not yet been fully exploited. There are still peoples whose modes of life have not yet been rationalized and stereotyped under the influence of European science and European culture. But there is no reason to believe that either Europe or Europeans will continue to exercise in these regions and among these peoples the same undisputed authority in the future that they have in the past.

What the present trend and movement of the modern world suggest is, rather, that Europe's economic imperium and the modern world are destined to repeat the same cycle of events, or something comparable to it, which accompanied the rise and decline of the Roman Empire and the ancient world.

There are, it seems, in human affairs, as in all other processes that involve life and growth, such long-term trends as here described. In many cases they take, or seem destined to take if sufficiently prolonged, the form of a cycle which may and often does repeat itself. In other cases, these secular trends terminate in a new equilibrium, a new constellation of interacting forces, and a new social order. In that case, and in every case, as a matter of fact, the equilibrium achieved will only be temporary or partial, and the termination of one sequence invariably becomes the starting-point for a new and different one. For society is, like a plant or any other living thing, a moving rather than a stable equilibrium. Always it is involved in a process of becoming; always it exhibits something that corresponds to what is here called "succession," and "succession," as the ecologists have used the term, seems to include at once the processes of development and evolution.

It is notorious that Rome's dominance in the ancient world was based on a system of highways. The Roman roads constituted the backbone and the skeleton of the Roman Empire. In somewhat the same manner Europe's domination of the modern world rests upon a system of highways and connections less obvious and visible because they are for the most part seaways—seaways supplemented by airplanes, radio and telegraph, and other means of communication unknown to the ancient world. These serve the purposes of commerce but, incidentally, make the centers of public opinion and political power in one part of the world instantly responsive to changes that take place in every other.

Most of the important cities in the world today are located along the great ocean highway that connects London, New York, and San Francisco with Yokohama, Shanghai, Hongkong, Calcutta, Bombay, and the Mediterranean. This thoroughfare is now the Main Street of the world.

It is, perhaps, one of the symptoms of the maturity of the modern world, as it seems to have been of the ancient, that the highways along which Europe moved out to colonize and conquer the world are now so secure that they are thronged with travelers. It is significant, also, that, at the moment when Europe's political dominance in the world seems to be declining, travel continues, and the prestige of European science and culture is still in the ascendancy. Everywhere along the main routes of travel one encounters, with slight local diversities, the same mixed populations and the same cosmopolitan culture. Everywhere one pays tribute at a European bank, patronizes European shops, and lives in European hotels, where he eats European food and pays European prices.

A trip around the world on one of the seagoing hotels now in vogue is about as much of an adventure as riding on the top of a bus up Fifth Avenue, in New York, or taking a stroll on Michigan Avenue, in Chicago. The Main Street of the world and the cities that have grown up along it now constitute the world's central shopping district.

Everywhere, it seems, one meets the same people and the same problems, for everywhere one finds one's self in cities in which the modern world and the new cosmopolitan culture, based on the steamship, the automobile, the radio, and the cinema, are taking on form and substance in a new tradition and a new *Lebenstil*, to use a German expression for which there seems to be no adequate substitute in English.

This is, of course, merely the tourist's first impression. A more intimate acquaintance with life, as it exists off the well-worn trails of tourist travel, reveals the fact that behind its European façade there is in every one of these great port cities a seething mass of native life that is quite alien to the ordinary European traveler.

Honolulu is one of the minor cities on the great encircling highway which connects Europe and the United States with the rest of the world. The Hawaiian Islands, of which Honolulu is the metropolis, owe their present strategic position in the world-economy to the fact they are located at the crossroads of the Pacific. In this location they have been subjected to all the varied cultural and economic influences which have brought into existence whatever is most characteristic of modern life. The result is that in Hawaii, where all the peoples of the world have come together in an association more intimate than is possible in regions less insular and less isolated by surrounding seas, the processes of assimilation and acculturation, characteristic of port cities and metropolitan communities elsewhere, have been going on at a rate that has made the Islands the most notable instance of a melting-pot of the modern world. On the other hand, all these changes in the cultural life of the Islands have been associated with other, more obvious and perhaps fundamental changes on the economic level—changes due to external rather than to internal factors. At any rate, for this and other reasons, Hawaiian economic life has passed through a great many changes, not to say transfigurations, since Captain Cook cast anchor at Waimea off the Island of Kauai, January 18, 1778.

At that time the Hawaiians were still living in the Stone Age, although their passionate interest in iron, which led them to trade pigs for nails, was an indication that they were by no means unaware of the value of the metals. Hawaiian society was, at that time, a primitive feudalism, based on a subsistence economy with very little trade among the islands of the archipelago.

Since that time Hawaiian economy has well-nigh completed the whole cycle of the changes ordinarily associated with the evolution of the capitalistic system. Honolulu, which a hundred and fifty years ago was a mere frontier town, a supply station for whaling vessels, has since that time become the metropolitan administrative and banking center for a highly centralized industrial kingdom. Its economic organization has reached, or nearly so, a stage of development which Sombart, the historian of the capitalist system, calls *Hochkapitalismus*, or, as he translates it, "full capitalism."

Under the conditions of *Hochkapitalismus* the entrepreneur has been succeeded by the administrator, the salesman by the office man, as the dominating personality in commerce and industry. Under these circumstances stability and security have come to be more important than expansion and speculative profits. As Sombart puts it, industry has assumed the character of a public institution and as such has become more responsive to the claims of the society upon which that security rests. Changes such as these are the characteristic symptoms of an approaching maturity not merely in the capitalistic system but in the society of which that system is so essentially a part.

One evidence of this maturity in Hawaii is the very large amount of profits that have been reinvested in the local industry. This is indicated by the fact that a few years ago the sugar planters were expending something like $750,000 annually in agricultural research. Another evidence of maturity is the amount of money expended annually for institutions of social welfare of various sorts. Here, likewise, there is evidence of the same rational planning, the same disposition to apply scientific method to social as to industrial problems.

One interest that attaches to the story of Hawaii is the fact that it is typical. Its changes of fortune and outlook have been more sudden and complete than in other parts of the Pacific and the world, but they have in the main re-enacted at higher speed and in a briefer space of time the same economic and cultural changes which have everywhere accompanied the expansion of Europe and the rise of the modern world.

The author of this volume has chosen to connect and correlate, so far as that is practicable and possible, the economic and racial history of the Hawaiian Islands, with the story of the land. In doing this, he has made the succession of types of land utilization the signature and index of all other changes. The effect has been to give his account of events a character that is systematic rather than historical.

By making one series of events which is regarded as fundamental an index to every other series, he has sought to bring into clearer outline than would otherwise be possible the actual course of events in other related aspects of life. This has made it possible to describe historical changes in Hawaii in terms that make them comparable with similar changes in other parts of the world. The result is what we might very properly describe as a natural history—a natural history of a society, that is to say, the history of one community in terms that make it comparable with the history of another.

Comparison inevitably reveals the individual as an example of a class. Natural history is interested not merely in what actually happened at a time and place but also in the historic process by which things have come to be what they are or seem.

So far as the series of changes which have taken place in Hawaii since the Islands were rediscovered and brought within the limits of the new world-economy may be said to repeat what has taken place elsewhere during the period of European expansion, the history of the Hawaiian community may be regarded as a chapter in the history of the modern world. On the other hand, in so far as these changes are characteristic and typical of cultural changes elsewhere, the account here given of Hawaii's life-cycle may be regarded as a contribution to the natural history of civilization.

If this seems to be setting up a rather large claim for what is, after all, a realistic and unpretentious study of a local community, it is nevertheless true that local studies have significance for social science only when and in so far as they present, in some specific instance, facts that throw light on some other and eventually more general situation, as well as upon the problems that inhere in it.

If what one learns in one instance throws light on some other, so that one learns in one situation what to expect in another, that knowledge, if not scientific, has in it at least the possibility of becoming science. For scientific, as distinguished from intuitive, knowledge and mere common sense is knowledge that can be communicated and so added to the general fund of accredited fact and theory which represents science in the substantive rather than adjective sense of that term.

CHAPTER 19

SYMBIOSIS AND SOCIALI-ZATION: A FRAME OF REFER-ENCE FOR THE STUDY OF SOCIETY

I. HUMAN SOCIETY AND HUMAN ECOLOGY

HUMAN society everywhere presents itself to the disinterested observer in many, but particularly in two, divergent aspects. Society is obviously a collection of individuals living together, like plants and animals within the limits of a common habitat, and it is, of course, something more. It is, though perhaps not always, a collection of individuals capable of some sort of concerted and consistent action.

Viewed abstractly, as it appears, perhaps, to the geographer or to the demographer, who scrutinizes it with reference to numbers, density, and distribution of the individual units of which it is made up, any society may seem no more than an agglomeration of discrete individuals, no one of which is visibly related to, or dependent upon, any other.

Closer observation of this seemingly unco-ordinated aggregate is likely to disclose a more or less typical order and pattern in the territorial distribution of its component units. Furthermore, as numbers increase this pattern is likely to exhibit a typical succession of

Reprinted by permission of the publisher from the *American Journal of Sociology*, XLV, 1939, pp. 1-25.

changes. Such a settled and territorially organized society is ordinarily described as a community.

A more searching inquiry is likely to reveal the fact that this particular society, and others of the same type, so far from being, as the demographer might be disposed to conceive them, mere aggregates of statistical entities, are better described as constellations of interacting individuals, each individual unit strategically located with reference to its dependence upon every other, as well as upon the common habitat. One further item: the whole constellation will be in a state of more or less unstable equilibrium.

This condition of unstable equilibrium permits a community to preserve at once its functional unity and continuity—i.e., its identity in time and space—by the constant redistribution of its population with relatively minor readjustments of the functional relations of its individual units. In such a community the existing territorial order, as well as the functional relations of the individuals and of the groups of which the population is composed, will be measurably controlled by competition or, to use a more inclusive term, by what Darwin described as the "struggle for existence."

This, in brief and in substance, is the conception of human society as it appears from the point of view of human ecology. The main point is that the community so conceived is at once a territorial and a functional unit.

Described in this fashion, abstractly, and without reference to its other and more concrete characteristics, the human is not essentially different from the plant community. I should like to add, if the comment were not wholly irrelevant, that it is a comfort in these days of turmoil and strife to realize that society and human beings, when in repose, do retain and exhibit some of the dignity and serenity of plants.

There is another point of view from which one may look at society—a point of view from which it does not appear as a community, not at least as a mere agglomeration of relatively fixed and settled units, but as an association of individuals participating in a collective act. The most obvious illustration of such a unit, the family, preserves its identity and integrity not merely when it is settled but when it migrates. Communities can hardly be said to migrate. Other examples of collective entities that act are mobs, gangs, political parties, pressure groups, classes, castes, nationalities, and nations. Anything that migrates in mass—a swarm of bees, a pack of wolves, or a herd of cattle—is likely to exhibit some or all of the characteristics of such societies as are capable of collective action.

It seems that every possible form of association is or should be capable, under certain circumstances, of collective action. But there are types of communities, the individual members of which live in a condition of interdependence that is sometimes described as social, which are, nevertheless, quite incapable of collective action. With the extension of commercial intercourse to every natural region of the earth one may perhaps say that the whole world is living in a kind of symbiosis; but the world community is at present, at least, quite incapable of collective action.

Symbiosis is ordinarily defined as the living together of distinct and dissimilar species, especially when the relationship is mutually beneficial.[1] But Wheeler, in his notable volume on the social insects, says that social life—all social life—"may, indeed, be regarded merely as a special form of symbiosis."[2] Other writers would, perhaps, be disposed to regard every form of symbiotic relationship as in some sense and to some degree social. At any rate there are many forms of human association in which there is co-operation sufficient to maintain a common economy, but no communication and no consensus sufficient to insure anything like effective collective action.[3] Any association in which widely scattered individuals unconsciously compete and co-operate, or by exchange of goods and services constitute themselves an economic unit, may be described as an entity that is symbiotic rather than social; that is, in the restricted sense in which the term is used when we think of the family as the prototype of every other species of social group.

But there are forms of association in which human beings live upon society as predators or parasites upon a host; or they live together in a relation in which they perform, directly or indirectly, some obscure function of mutual benefit but of which neither they nor their symbionts are conscious. All these varied forms of association may be described as examples of symbiosis, but they are forms of association that are not social in the sense in which that term is

---

[1] See *An Ecological Glossary* (Norman, Okla.: University of Oklahoma Press, 1938), p. 268.

[2] William Morton Wheeler, *Social Life among the Insects* (New York: Harcourt, Brace & Co., 1923), p. 195.

[3] Robert E. Park, "Reflections on Communication and Culture," *American Journal of Sociology*, September, 1938, p. 192.

ordinarily applied to human relations, particularly such relations as are recognized by the custom and enforced by the expectation of the "customers."

One remembers the so-called "silent trade," of which we have some infrequent accounts in the history of European contacts with primitive peoples. Here there is contact—some sort of understanding but no custom. Was this form of association symbiotic or social? This is clearly a marginal case.[4] And then there are in India the "criminal tribes" and pariah peoples who live in a kind of symbiotic relation with other peoples of that country. And there are finally the occupational castes, where individuals and groups of individuals live and work together under the terms of some general understanding but do not eat together or marry. Castes are not species and they do, in spite of regulations forbidding it, interbreed. However caste relations may be regarded in some sense as symbiotic, since they bring peoples together in economic and industrial relations while they prohibit the intimacies and understandings which seem necessary to participation in single moral order—such an order as one expects to find in a society democratically organized.

It is quite possible for castes to live together, each performing a distinct function in the economy of which it is a part. But it is likely to be difficult, though not impossible, for castes to participate in a collective act, such as is involved in the formation of a national state. The government of India is likely, when and if it achieves its independence of England, to retain its imperial character, since it will continue to be a collection of ethnic and linguistic minorities. Nationalism and imperialism, also, for that matter, invariably assume the existence of a kind of solidarity which is ordinarily created in the process of acting collectively, but which involves active participation of all individual units in the common purpose.

There are, of course, a great many kinds of collective action; the most elementary and the most pervasive is undoubtedly mass migration. Bees swarm, birds migrate, and human beings rush madly hither and yon in search for some new El Dorado or in hope of achieving somewhere a new Utopia. Collective action of every sort requires some form of communication; only in this way is it possible to achieve and maintain a concert and a consistency in the movements of individual units that we ordinarily ascribe to an act, in contrast

---

[4] P. J. Hamilton Grierson, *The Silent Trade* (Edinburgh, 1903).

with the casual and undirected movements in which mere impulse finds expression.[5]

It is apparent that we are concerned here with different types of association brought about and maintained, in the main and on the whole, one by competition and the other by communication, or both. The one is symbiotic and takes the form, ordinarily, of a division of labor among competing organisms or groups of organisms. The other is social in the ordinary and more restricted use of that term and is based on communication and consensus, which implies a kind of solidarity based on participation in a common enterprise and involving the more or less complete subordination of individuals to the intent and purpose of the group as a whole.

The way in which competition and communication function, the one to bring about the further specialization and individuation of the individual and the other to bring about the integration and subordination of individuals to the interests of society, I have indicated in the paper on "Communication," cited above. What remains to be made clear is how these two types of organization, the symbiotic and the social, interact and combine to bring about the specific types of association—ecological, economic, political, or customary and cultural—which distinguish the institutions of society or the types of social organizations which constitute the subject matter of the several social sciences, ecology, economics, politics, and sociology.

Sociology, as ordinarily conceived, is primarily concerned with the nature and natural history of institutions; with the processes by which institutions develop and eventually evolve the specific and stable forms in which we know them. But customary cultural and moral relations are notoriously dependent on, and responsive to, political, economic, and, ultimately, those more elementary associations brought about by the sheer struggle for existence. And besides that, the more intimate and familial types of association grow up within an environment created by the freer, more individualistic, and secular association of a political and economic society.

II. INSTITUTIONS AND COLLECTIVE BEHAVIOR

Institutions have their setting in actual interests and affairs of ordinary life and sometimes arise quite suddenly in response to the

---

[5] Walter Heape *et al.*, *Emigration, Migration and Nomadism* (Cambridge: W. Heffer & Sons, Ltd., 1931), pp. 137-46; Charles Elton, *Animal Ecology* (New York: Macmillan Co., 1927), pp. 132-33.

pressure of some necessity—a flood, a famine, a war—anything which makes collective action urgent. This is, at any rate, the way in which fascist institutions have arisen in Italy and Germany. Labor organizations, for example, came into existence in order to carry on strikes and to direct the slow-burning revolution which is gradually transforming the capitalist system. Courts of arbitration have arisen in the same way in order to deal with the conflicts of capital and labor in situations where, because of the existence of a constitutional struggle, administrative law could not be effectively applied in dealing with the situation.

Not every social movement terminates in a new institution, but the necessity of carrying on programs initiated in some social emergency has been responsible for many if not most modern and recent institutions. Nor is it always possible to determine precisely the point at which a social movement merges into an institution. The ladies of the Y.W.C.A. used to say that theirs was not an institution but a movement. This was intended, perhaps, to distinguish it from the Y.M.C.A., which presumably had been a movement but had become an institution. Every social movement may, however, be described as a potential institution. And every institution may in turn be described as a movement that was once active and eruptive, like a volcano, but has since settled down to something like routine activity. It has, to change the metaphor, defined its aims, found its place and function in the social complex, achieved an organization, and, presumably, provided itself with a corps of functionaries to carry on its program. It becomes an institution finally when the community and the public it seeks to serve accept it, know what to expect of it, and adjust to it as a going concern. An institution may be regarded as finally established when the community and the public in which and for which it exists claim as a right the services to which they have become accustomed.

Other institutions arise more slowly and less obviously. Coming into existence under such circumstances, institutions are likely to be more deeply rooted in tradition and in the habits and human nature of the individuals of which the community is composed. In the natural course institutions may thus come to exist less as instruments for the performance of social functions than as interests of their functionaries or of one of the several classes of which the community is composed. In the latter case they are likely to impose themselves as a discipline and as external forms of control upon the generations that grow up under the influence of their tradition.

Much more might be said in regard to the manner in which social movements initiate and are eventually superseded by institutions. Social movements seem, in many instances, to be the source and origin not merely of new institutions but of new societies. But there are other aspects of collective behavior which, for the purposes of this paper, are more interesting and significant.

Sumner distinguishes between institutions which are (1) enacted and (2) institutions which are crescive—that is, institutions which grow up and take form in the course of the historic process and those which, in so far as they are the product of reflection and rational purpose, have the character of an artifact rather than of an organism. In the long run, however, every institution will tend to have the character of something that is at least indigenous to the situation and the society in which it exists. The distinction Sumner makes is obvious enough. We do set up institutions and expect them to go like machines. Society is always more or less a work of art. On the other hand, institutions are always, finally, the accumulated effects of tradition and custom; they are always in process of becoming what they were predestined to be, human nature being what it is, rather than what they are and were.

There is, as Sumner says, implicit in every institution a concept and a philosophy. In the efforts of men acting together to pursue a consistent course of action in a changing world this concept emerges and the philosophy which was implicit becomes explicit. It may take the form of a rationalization or a justification for the institution's existence—what might be described as the institution's *apologia pro vita sua*. Although there may be implicit in the practices of every institution an idea and a philosophy, it is only in a changing society where it becomes necessary to defend or redefine its functions that this philosophy is likely to achieve a formal and dogmatic statement; and even then the body of sentiment and ideas which support these principles may remain, like an iceberg, more or less completely submerged in the "collective unconscious," whatever that is. It is furthermore only in a political society, in which a public exists that permits discussion, rather than in a society organized on a familial and authoritative basis that rational principles tend to supersede tradition and custom as a basis of organization and control. Besides, mankind has never been as completely rational in either its behavior or its thinking as was once supposed. As Sumner remarks, "property, marriage, and religion are still almost entirely in the mores." [6]

It is, however, in the nature of political society that every class, caste, institution, or other functional unit should have its own dogma and its individual life-program. In a familial society, dogma and ideology may perhaps be said to exist potentially and in the egg. They are not so likely to be stated formally as a rule or principle of action.

One of the recent extensions of the realm of the social has been the inclusion in the field of sociological investigation of the subject of knowledge itself. "The principle thesis of a sociology of knowledge is," as Mannheim has stated it, "that there are modes of thought which cannot be adequately understood as long as their social origins are obscured." [7]

This means that, from the point of a sociology of collective behavior, the ideology of a society or of a social group is, like its customs and its folkways, an integral part of its social structure and that one can no longer proceed on the assumption that "the single individual thinks. Rather it is more correct to insist that he participates in thinking further what other men have thought before him." [8]

The ideology of a class, caste, or social group seems to perform the same role in the functioning of a collective unit that the individual's conception of himself performs in the function of his personality. As the individual's conception of himself projects his acts into the future and in that fashion serves to control and direct the course of his career, so in the case of a society its ideology may be said to direct, control, and give consistency, in the vicissitudes of a changing world, to its collective acts.

The psychiatrists seem to have been the first to direct attention to the importance of the individual's self-consciousness in the understanding of his behavior. They were, also, among the first to take account of the fact that the individual's conception of himself, as long as he is socially oriented and sane, is always a more or less accurate reflection of his status in one or more social groups.

In somewhat the same fashion sociologists, some of whom got their inspiration and took their point of departure from Karl Marx,

---

[6] William Graham Sumner, *Folkways* (New York: Ginn & Co., 1906), p. 54.
[7] Karl Mannheim, *Ideology and Utopia* (New York: Harcourt, Brace & Co., 1936), p. 2.
[8] *Ibid.*, p. 3.

have arrived at the conclusion that the ideologies, not merely of economic classes but of cultural groups generally, are a by-product of their collective acts. "It is not," as Mannheim puts it, "men in general who think, or even isolated individuals who do the thinking, but men in certain groups who have developed a particular style of thought in an endless series of responses to certain typical situations characterizing their common position." [9]

This extension of the field of sociological investigation to include the natural history of the ideas, ideologies, intellectual dogmas, and those unconscious understandings which make concert, collective action, and above all conversation and discussion, possible, has brought within the purview of systematic investigation those very elements, in personality and in society, namely, the conceptual and rational, which scholasticism had forever put beyond the sphere of an empirical science and the possibility of a naturalistic explanation.

The theory that the state is a legal construction and in that sense a logical artifact has remained the last stronghold of a sociology that conceives itself as a philosophy rather than as a natural or empirical science. As a matter of fact the sociology of knowledge might well serve as prolegomena to the study of what has sometimes been referred to, although in the language which Mannheim expressly repudiates, as the "group mind." [10] The rather ghostly conceptions, "group thinking," "group mind," including the "general will" have haunted the minds of writers on political science and sociology, whenever and wherever they have tried to conceive the intrinsic nature of the bond which holds men together in such manner as makes collective action possible.

Almost the first attempt to investigate and describe collective behavior was Gustave Le Bon's volume, *The Crowd: A Study of Popular Mind*.[11] The character of the crowd, or of the psychological crowd, as Le Bon described it, was that of a heterogeneous group which, under the influence of some contagious excitement, had achieved a momentary but relatively complete moral solidarity in which every individual was completely submerged and dominated by the mood and purpose of the group as a whole. He said:

---

[9] *Ibid.*, p. 3.

[10] *Ibid.*, p. 2.

[11] New York, 1900; see also Park and Burgess, *Introduction to the Science of Sociology* (Chicago: University of Chicago Press, 1924 ed.), p. 869.

The psychological crowd is a provisional being formed of heterogeneous elements, which for a moment are combined, exactly as the cells which constitute a living body form by their reunion a new being which displays characteristics very different from these possessed by each of the cells singly.[12]

But the solidarity by which a heterogeneous and casually assembled collection of individuals is transformed into a "new being" is, naturally, not anything physical. It is, to use Le Bon's term, "psychological." The crowd, when organized, behaves according to the "law of the mental unity of crowds," and it is just the consensus and moral solidarity thus achieved which Le Bon describes as the "mind of the crowd," which gives that *omnium-gatherum* the character of a social entity.

In contrast with the organized or psychological crowd is the crowd in dissolution, i.e., the crowd in a state of panic, a stampede. In such a stampede the excitement may be quite as contagious as it is in the organized crowd but it will not express itself in a collective act. On the contrary the crowd in a state of panic acts as if every individual were for himself and "devil take the hindmost."

Le Bon, more than any other writer, has been able to lend to his conception of the collective mind a sense of reality which is lacking in other descriptions of the same phenomenon. Mary Austin, who writes interestingly but somewhat mystically of the behavior of sheep and shepherds, speaks of the "flock mind." Elsewhere we hear of the "public mind" or the "medieval" or the "modern" mind where, in the context, we are not certain whether those terms refer to an individual type or to a collective unit.

However, none of these is the kind of social unit with which Mannheim is concerned in his studies of the sociology of knowledge. The collective mind which he has sought to investigate is not that of a crowd where there is complete unanimity but rather that of a public where there is diversity of sentiments and of opinion. Nevertheless there is in such a public an underlying and more or less unconscious unanimity of purpose and intent. Consensus, under the circumstances, takes a more complex form which in logic is described as a "universe of discourse." One purpose of Mannheim's studies seems to have been to bring into clear consciousness this underlying unity and identity of intent which exists, or may exist, within the obvious diversity of opinions and attitudes. Characteristic

---

[12] *Ibid.,* p. 889.

of a public or any group involved in conversation and discussion is what I may describe as the dialectical process. But the dialectical movement of thought, in the course of a discussion, tends to assume the character of a collective act.[13]

The group mind, so called, whatever else the implication attached to the term, is always the product of communication. But this communication takes different forms in the crowd and the public. In the case of the mob or the psychological crowd communication takes place, to be sure, but individual A is not able to distinguish his own attitude from that of B, and vice versa. As Mead puts it, "one form does not know that communication is taking place with the other." Le Bon seeks to express the same idea when he describes as one of the incidents of the formation of a crowd the "disappearance of conscious personality and the turning of feeling and thoughts in a definite direction." [14]

In the public, communication takes the form of a conversation; an interchange of attitudes or, as Mead describes it, a "communication of gestures." In this form of communication individual A becomes aware of his own attitude by taking the role of B. In this way A sees his own act from the point of view of B and each participates, from his own point of view, in the collective act. This, says Mead, "carries the process of cooperative activity farther than it can be carried in the herd as such, or in the insect society." [15]

III. PLANT COMMUNITIES AND ANIMAL SOCIETIES

In the meantime there has drawn up on the margins, if not quite within the framework of the social sciences, a body of organized knowledge that calls itself sometimes biological but more often sociological, but is, in any case, concerned with relations that are not ordinarily regarded as social; and it is concerned also with organisms, like plants and animals, which live together in forms of association that do not, in the sense that the term social applies to human beings, constitute them a society. Such, for example, are the plant associations, first observed and described by plant geographers, one of whom was the Danish ecologist, Eugenius Warming.

In 1895 Warming published a volume entitled *Plantesamfund*

---

[13] George H. Mead, *Mind, Self, and Society* (Chicago: University of Chicago Press, 1934), p. 7 n.

[14] Park and Burgess, *op. cit.*, p. 887.

[15] Mead, *op. cit.*, pp. 253-55.

(Plant Community) in which he described the different plant species living together within the limits of a habitat as "practicing" a
kind of natural economy and by so doing maintaining relations
which constituted them a natural community. It is this economy and
this community which is the special subject matter of the science of
ecology." [16] Ecology has been described as "an extension of economics to the whole world of life." [17] But it is at the same time, as
Charles Elton put it, not so much a new subject as a new name for
an old one. It is a kind of natural history.[18]

A vast literature has come into existence since Warming's first
attempt to describe and systematize what was known at that time
of the communal life of plants, and this literature has been succeeded
in turn by similar studies of plant and animal communities as well as
of insect and animal societies. Ecology is concerned with communities rather than societies, though it is not easy to distinguish between
them. Plant and animal sociology seems to include both forms of
association. A plant community is, however, an association of diverse
species. An animal society is more likely to be, like insect societies,
an association of familial or genetic origin.

The first ecological studies were, however, geographical, concerned quite as much with the migration and distribution of plants
and animals as with their dependence upon their physical habitats.
More recently, following a cue suggested by Darwin in his *Origin
of Species*, ecological studies have investigated not merely the interactions and interdependencies of the plants and of plants and animals, including man, living in the same habitat but they have studied
the biotic community itself in so far as it seemed to exhibit a unitary
or organismic character. This emphasis upon the communal organization of plants and animals has more and more disposed students
to describe the social and ecological relations of all living organisms

---

[16] Ecology is a term first used by Ernest Haeckel, the distinguished German
biologist, in 1878, and is derived from the Greek *oikos*, which means house
and is the root from which the word economics was coined.

[17] H. G. Wells, Julian S. Huxley, and G. P. Wells, *The Science of Life*,
Vol. III (New York: Doubleday, Doran & Co., 1931), Chap. V, p. 961.

[18] *Animal Ecology* (New York: Macmillan Co., 1927), p. 1; "Species that
form a community must either practise the same economy, making approximately the same demands on its environment [as regards nourishment, light,
moisture, etc.], or one species present must be dependent for its existence
upon another species, sometimes to such an extent that . . . symbiosis seems
to prevail between them" (Eugenius Warming, *Oecology of Plants* [Oxford,
1909], p. 12).

in the language of the social sciences, of economics, of sociology, and even of political science.

Recently, W. C. Allee published a volume [19] which he described as "A Study of General Sociology." It was, in fact, a sort of first book of animal sociology since it dealt with what happens to animals when they come together temporarily in large numbers, like bats in a cave or bees in a swarm. These associations were inevitably, under the circumstances, of the elementary and abstract sort which mere propinquity enforces. Such aggregations are, in fact, mere population units in which there is spatial integration, to be sure, but no indication of social solidarity.

This publication was followed by the translation from the German of an imposing volume by J. Braun-Blanquet,[20] in which the complexities of the interrelations and interactions of the plants and plant species that constitute a plant community—including the physical conditions under which this communal life is maintained—are systematically analyzed and described.

Ecology is, it seems, in the way of becoming a social, without ceasing to be a biological, science. It is still concerned with the physical conditions which make plant and animal life possible, but the life for which these conditions exist, is not that of the different species merely but of some sort of social entity or superorganism of which the species are integral parts.

The effect of this extension of the concept of society and the social to include every form of association short of parasitism in which organisms of the same or different species practice a natural economy seems to extend indefinitely the number and the variety of social relationships and of social entities with which a general sociology is concerned. "The whole field of interrelationships of organisms," says Allee, "must be taken as the content of a general sociology." [21] This conception of the social indicates a wide field for taxonomic explorations since it suggests that the realm of the social is coterminous with the active interaction of living organisms in what Darwin described as "the web of life." It is in this sense that Darwin's theory of the origin of the species may be regarded, as J. Arthur Thomson says, as an application of a sociological principle to the facts of natural history.

---

[19] *Animal Aggregations* (Chicago: University of Chicago Press, 1931).
[20] *Plant Sociology* (New York: McGraw-Hill Book Co., Inc., 1932).
[21] *Op. cit.,* p. 37.

Meanwhile the area within which a world-wide struggle for existence is operative is steadily expanding and, seeing that microbes travel by the same means as men, the dangers of disease and the dangers of war tend to grow *pari passu* with increased use of every form of transportation, including the most recent, the airplane. Thus the web of life which holds within its meshes all living organisms is visibly tightening, and there is in every part of the world obviously a growing interdependence of all living creatures; a vital interdependence that is more extensive and intimate today than at any other period in the course of the long historical process.

In spite of the extraordinary variety of associations which the studies of the plant and animal sociologists have revealed, all or most of the more general types seem to be represented in human society. In fact one thing that makes the study of plant and animal associations interesting is that plant and animal communities so frequently exhibit, in strangely different contexts, forms of associations that are fundamentally like those with which we are familiar in human society. Besides, they exhibit, singly and in isolation, types of association which in human society are overlayed by other later and more elaborate forms. For example, the plant community is an association in which the relations between individual species may be described as purely economic. The plant community, in other words, is not, as is the case of insect and animal societies, a genetic association in which the individual units are held together by natural and instinctive ties of family and the necessities of procreation and the protection of the young.

Plants cast down their seeds on the ground from whence they are borne away on wind, wave, or any other convenience which chance offers. Thus plants once established on the soil and in a habitat are obviously immobile, but the plant species are more easily and widely dispersed than animals. Plants of the same species, because they make the same demands upon the natural resources of the habitat, are likely to be dispersed by competition. For the same reason plants which make different demands upon the natural resources—i.e., light, moisture, and the chemical elements which they take from the soil and air—tend to become assiciated because, as each species finds its niche in the community, competition is diminished and the total production of the plant community, if one may speak of production in this connection, is increased.

Plant communities do not, of course, act collectively as animals do, but the associations they form, partly by a natural selection of species and partly by adaptation and accommodation of individuals —as in the case of the vine and the fig tree—do, by diminishing competition within and by resisting invasion from without, make more secure the life of the community and of the individuals of which it is composed.

The plant community is perhaps the only form of association in which competition is free and unrestricted, and even there competition is limited to some extent by the mere passive resistance offered by the association and co-ordination of different species of which the community is composed. This limitation of competition is, however, purely external and not the result, as in the case of animals and man, of either instinctive or intelligent inhibition.[22]

The needs of plants as of every other organism are twofold. There is the need to preserve the individual in his struggle to complete his own life-cycle and there is the need of preserving the continued existence of the species. Plants provide these two necessities, however, in ways that differ fundamentally from animals or at least from those animals that maintain a family and a social existence. Braun-Blanquet says:

> The principles of usefulness, of division of labor, of conscious support, of marshaling all resources for the accomplishment of a common purpose do not exist in the plant world. The struggle for existence rules here undisturbed. It regulates directly or indirectly all the unconscious expressions of the social life of plants. Herein lies the deep and fundamental difference between the vital relations of plant and those of animal communities.[23]

Insect societies, as contrasted with the freedom and anarchy of plant communities, are well-nigh perfect examples of an industrial regimentation and of a communism in which the individual is completely subordinated to the interests of the society. The explanation is that insect societies are merely large families in which the func-

---

[22] "Primitive man, just as much as civilized man, has his own strong inward and outward ties and inhibitions beyond which he cannot go (Thurnwald); and the behavior of an animal is determined in exactly the same way by the inner and outer restraints which are imposed upon it. Whosoever believes that sexual inhibitions do not exist for animals is on the wrong road altogether" (Friedrich Alverdes, *Social Life in the Animal World* [New York, 1927], pp. 12-13).

[23] *Op. cit.,* p. 5.

tions, not only of the sexes but of so-called castes, are fixed at birth in their physiological structure.[24]

This does not mean that there is in insect societies nothing that corresponds to the symbiotic forms of association characteristic of plant communities. On the contrary, social insects, notably the social ants, live in symbiotic relation with a number of other insects. In fact, as Wheeler remarks, "ants may be said to have domesticated a greater number of animals than we have and the same statement may prove to be true of their food plants which have been carefully studied." [25]

It is more difficult in the case of the social animals than of the social insects to define the difference between forms of association that are symbiotic and those which are social. Thus Alverdes [26] distinguishes between what he calls associations (mere collections) and societies. By associations he means those aggregations of animals that otherwise carry on a solitary existence, but do, at some period in their seasonal or life-cycle, come together in response to occasional and external causes. By societies, on the other hand, he means those more permanent groups, including insect societies, in which individuals come together in response to the needs and instinctive urges of the individual organisms. This means that the form which an animal society does take is the one it was predestined to assume by the nature of the inheritance of the individuals of which it was composed. "In short," says Alverdes, "no social instinct, no society."

There are two types of association, aside from those occasional

---

[24] . . . In striking contrast with men, ants have to be built for their jobs. They do not make tools; they grow them as parts of their bodies. . . . Each species of ant is thus built specially for its own particular kind of life and is quite unadaptable to any other. Even within the single community there is the same kind of specialized physical diversity. Only the males and females have wings; the neuters grow up wingless. The neuters have much bigger brains than the males or the queens; but, as they never have to fly, their eyes are smaller. . . . This physical diversity goes hand in hand with diversity of behaviour. The males do nothing but fertilize the queens when the time comes. The queens lay eggs eternally. The workers have the instinct of tending the young, the soldiers are impelled to bite and snap in defence of the colony. The workers of one kind of ant keep ant-cows, but never look at grain or make raids on other ants. Those of a second are only graminivorous, those of a third live by slave-labour. Thus the division of labour in an ant-community, unlike the division of labour in a human community, is based on marked, inborn individual differences of structure and instinctive behaviour between its members (Wells, Huxley, and Wells, *op. cit.*, IV, 1163-64).

[25] *Op. cit.*, p. 17.

[26] *Op. cit.*, pp. 14-16.

aggregations already referred to, which may have arisen in response to "instincts" rather than to external forces. These are the family and the herd or flock. In both cases the particular form which solidarity takes undoubtedly has an inherited and instinctive basis. What operates to modify this form of association and determine the collective activities of the individuals so associated is, among other things, the character of the communication of which the group is capable. Thus among the anthropoid apes, as among the birds, there seems to exist, as there frequently does between a man and his dog, a responsiveness, an understanding and intimacy not unlike that characteristic of personal relations among human beings.[27]

The extent to which animals of the herd or flock are responsive to the expressive behavior of other animals is most obvious on the occasions where some excitement, whipped up by the milling of the herd or flock, mounts to a point where it issues in a panic or stampede. The milling herd is in so many respects like the organized crowd, as Le Bon has conceived it, that one wonders that it does not, as in the case of a mob, express its excitement in a collective act. The mob is, in fact, the crowd that acts. But a stampede, because in this case the impulses and actions of the individuals involved are not co-ordinated, does not take the form of a collective act. There is no stampede "mind."

The herd does not act but it does, in the course of its milling about, perform something that might be called a dance. Mary Austin says:

It is doubtful if the herder is anything more to the flock than an incident of the range, except as a giver of salt, for the only cry they make to him is the salt cry. When the natural craving is at the point of urgency they circle about his camp or his cabin, leaving off feeding for that business; and nothing else offering, they will continue this headlong circling about a boulder or any object bulking large in their immediate neighborhood remotely resembling the appurtenances of man, as if they had learned nothing since they were free to find licks for themselves, except that salt comes by bestowal and in conjunction with the vaguely indeterminate lumps of matter that associate with man. . . . This one quavering bleat, (the salt cry) unmistakable to the sheepman even at a distance, is the only new note in the sheep's vocabulary, and the only one which passes with intention from himself to man. As for the call of distress

---

[27] Wolfgang Köhler, *The Mentality of Apes* (New York: Harcourt, Brace & Co., Inc., 1927); see Appendix, "Some Contributions to the Psychology of Chimpanzees," particularly pp. 282-311; see also Alverdes, *op. cit.*, "Mutual Understanding and Imitation," Chap. IX, pp. 164-78.

which a leader raised by hand may make to his master, it is not new, is not common to flock usage, and is swamped utterly in the obsession of the flock-mind.[28]

Why does this dance of the restless flock not, as Mary Austin's description suggests it might, assume the form of a ceremony? Why, in other words, does this collective excitement not take on the character of ritual or a symbolic act? The mass games described by Groos (*The Play of Animals*) and the sham, and sometimes very real, battles in which birds and other animals engage during the mating season, seem to be fundamentally expressive, merely. Groos calls them orgiastic in character.[29]

Mass behavior of that sort in animals is not unlike the same expressive and orgiastic behavior in human beings, since the crowd that dances rather than acts is at any rate a "psychological" if not an "organized" crowd. The behavior of animals under the influence of collective excitement is to such an extent like that of crowds everywhere that Alverdes, in his effort to indicate the character of the solidarity which is created by the rise in the herd of this contagious excitement, has recourse again to the conception of the "collective mind." This phrase cannot, however, be regarded as an explanation of the phenomena to which it refers. It may be, like the "instincts" to which Alverdes refers in his description of animal society, inexplicable. In that case "collective mind" is merely the name we give to a phenomenon that needs to be further investigated.

What are these phenomena? Alverdes says:

Among social species, courage and pugnacity grow in proportion to the number of individuals present; this is true of ants, bees, bumble bees, wasps, hornets, and others. In the case of the honey bee, a small and weak community often does not defend itself against enemies which it could easily repulse, whereas a strong community is always ready for attack, and expels every intruder. According to Forel, one and the same ant which is full of courage among its fellows will take to flight before a much weaker adversary as soon as it finds itself alone. State-building insects are overcome by profound depression if their nest disappears.[30]

What distinguishes the collective mind of the lower animals from that of the human crowd is the fact that the contagious excitements which arise in the herd do not, as in the case of the psychological

---

[28] *The Flock* (Boston: Houghton Mifflin & Co., 1906), pp. 127-29.
[29] Alverdes, *op. cit.*, pp. 144-51.
[30] *Ibid.*, p. 142.

crowd, issue in either collective action or in anything like ceremonial behavior. What is even more significant, these excitements do not finally take the form of institutions. It is the possession of institutions which distinguishes human from animal societies. Institutions, however, seem to be, finally, the product of the type of dialectical or rational communication which is the peculiar characteristic of human beings.

IV. SOCIALIZATION

This brief survey of the forms of association, the communal and social, in which individual organisms maintain some sort of collective existence, suggests that it is pertinent to repeat here in regard to socialization—the process by which associations are formed—what was said earlier, in somewhat different language, in regard to two types of association, or two aspects of society. Socialization and social organization seem at any rate to be brought about by the co-operation of two fundamental types of interaction. There is in every society a process or processes of individuation and a process or processes of integration. The effect of competition is to disperse existing aggregations of organisms and by so doing to bring about, as a result of adaptation to new environments, the creation of new races and species. But the existence within a habitat of diverse species and races makes possible a new association and a natural economy, based on genetic diversity rather than genetic identity.

In human societies a division of labor based upon a diversity of occupations and enforced by economic competition performs the function which, in the plant community or other biotic associations, is performed by symbiosis.

There is, however, or there presently emerges in both animal and human societies, the necessity for a more stable form of association than that which either biotic or economic competition and co-operation is sufficient to produce. Such a more stable form of association is likely to occur whenever the interaction of the competing organisms, by adaptation to the habitat or in any other fashion, achieves a relatively stable equilibrium. In such a situation, with the gradual rise in the animal species of a capacity for and means of communication—by which animals as well as human beings have been able to respond to the minds and intentions of other animals—a new and more intimate type of solidarity is made possible; a solidarity which enables societies to co-ordinate and direct the acts of their individual components in accordance with the interests and purposes of the society as a whole.

Thus a society may be said to arise upon the basis of a community. The distinction is that in the community, as in the case of the plant and animal community, the nexus which unites individuals of which the community is composed is some kind of symbiosis or some form of division of labor. A society, on the other hand, is constituted by a more intimate form of association based on communication, consensus, and custom.

The social organism, as Herbert Spencer conceived it, was based on the existence in society of a division of labor. It is in this sense, also, that F. E. Clements and others have described the plant community as an organism.[31] But the social organism thus conceived had, as Spencer points out, no sensorium. There was no central apparatus where the sensations and impulses of the individual units of which a society is composed could be sorted out, assimilated, and integrated, so that society could act consistently in response to them. Society and the superorganism have, to be sure, no sensorium, but individuals in society do communicate and somehow they do achieve that sort of consensus that Comte believed was the essential and fundamental trait of any society. This communication and the accumulated body of tradition on which it is based is what is sometimes referred to as the "collective mind."

Society, theoretically at least, begins as Allee pointed out, with a mere aggregation, i.e., a population unit. But even on this level of association there is interaction of some sort. On the economic level, as we know economic relations in human society, competition and the struggle for existence continue, but as social relations multiply this struggle is more and more restricted by understandings, by customs, by formal and contractual relations, and by law. All of these impose restrictions, in the interest of an evolving society and of the manifold social and collective units of which such a society is composed, upon the free competition of individuals in the original aggregate or population unit.

On the political level the freedom and competition of individuals is still further limited by the express recognition of the superior and sovereign interests and rights of the state or of the community as a whole, as against the adverse interests or claims of individuals or

---

[31] Braun-Blanquet, *op. cit.*, p. 21.

groups of individuals, living within or under the protection of the state or other political authority. The existence of such sovereignty as the state exercises, however, is dependent upon the existence of a solidarity within the state or other territorial and political unit, sufficient to maintain that authority and enforce its behests when they come into conflict with the interests and the purposes of individuals.

Eventually this competition of individuals is restricted and restrained on the personal and moral level of association by the claims which intimate associations with, and knowledge of, the needs, the attitudes, and the sentiments of others make upon us, particularly when these are re-enforced by tradition, customs, and the normal expectations of mankind. Every individual who is or will eventually be incorporated into any society, whether it be an alien coming from some other ethnic or cultural group or one born into the association and society of which he is a member, inevitably passes through such a process of socialization. The process of socialization as it takes place in the formation of any social group today reflects in a way the phylogenic processes by which existing types of association, or societies, and of institutions have come into existence in the course of the historic process.

Looked at in a historical perspective we observe that the progressive socialization of the world, that is, the incorporation of all the peoples of the earth in a world-wide economy, which has laid the foundation for the rising world-wide political and moral order—the great society—is but a repetition of the processes that take place wherever and whenever individuals come together to carry on a common life and to form the institutions—economic, political, or cultural—to make that common life effective.

But below the level of those forms of associations which we call social is the biotic community and the ecological organization in which man finds himself involved in competition and co-operation with all other living organisms. Thus we may represent human society as a kind of cone or triangle, of which the basis is the ecological organization of human beings living together in a territorial unit, region, or natural area. On this level the struggle for existence may go on, will go on, unobserved and relatively unrestricted.

If one is an alien he may live in the new society for a considerable time in a relationship which is essentially symbiotic, that is, a relationship in which he does not feel the pressure of the customs and expectations of the society by which he is surrounded. Or he may, if he is conscious of the social pressure, still experience it as something alien to him and continue to treat the people with whom he comes in contact as part of the flora and fauna, a situation in which their social pressures would impose upon him no moral claims which he felt bound to respect. But eventually the mere presence of an alien who is possessed by such a dispassionate and secular attitude toward the customs, conventions, and ideals of the society of which he has become, by the effect of propinquity and whether he chose to be or not, a constituent element, is certain to bring him, no matter how discrete his behavior, into conflict with those to whom their customs, if not sacred, are at least to such an extent accepted; that a too great detachment toward them is certain to be offensive if not a little shocking. Such an alien attitude, in any case, inevitably stimulates in the native a pervasive sense of malaise as if in the presence of something not quite understood and hence always a little to be feared.

This is not, of course, the only way so-called "culture conflicts" may arise. It is, perhaps, the most insidious form in which they are likely to appear. Conflict, which is merely conscious competition—that is, competition in a situation in which the competitor knows with whom and with what he is competing—creates, to be sure, a solidarity in the competing groups. Solidarity in the in-group, as Sumner has pointed out, is always more or less an effect of conflict with an out-group.

Conflict is, however, like competition, an individuating factor in society. It affects the individual not merely in his vocation and in his position in the economic order but affects him in his personal relations. It affects his status and very largely determines the conception which he forms of himself. It is in conflict situations that economic competition, the struggle for a livelihood, tends to become a struggle for political and social status.

However, conflict leads to understandings; understandings not merely implicit but explicit and formal. Conflict is the most elementary form of political behavior, and formal understandings, involving controversy and discussion, terminate in accommodations, in the formation of classes, and in formal and contractual relations of various sorts. Political conflict, when it does not lead to the formation of classes, does at least bring about class consciousness, and politics seem to be merely the classic and typical form in which the class struggle is carried on.

More intimate associations in the family and in the neighborhood as well as by occupation and class tend to develop more intimate personal understandings. Particularly is this the case within the limits of what Cooley calls the "primary group," i.e., the family, the neighborhood, and the village.

The process of socialization may be said to terminate in assimilation, which involves the more or less complete incorporation of the individual into the existing moral order as well as the more or less complete inhibition of competition. Under these circumstances conflict takes the form of rivalry, more or less generous.

The child born into a society may be said to go through the same process of socialization as the stranger who is finally adopted into a new society. The difference is that in the child's case the process begins with assimilation and ends with individuation and emancipation, i.e., emancipation from the traditions and claims of the family and primary group. The process of individuation ordinarily continues with his participation in an ever wider circle of political and economic association. The child's life begins, to be sure, without those human traits that we describe as personal. Most of the child's personality traits seem to be acquired in intimate associations with other human beings. But children are very rapidly and very completely incorporated into the societies in which birth or chance finds them. Only gradually do they achieve the independence and individuality we associate with maturity. One is assimilated into the little world of the family, but he achieves independence and individuality in the larger, freer world of men and affairs.

One begins life as an individual organism involved in a struggle with other organisms for mere existence. It is this elementary form of association that we describe as ecological. One becomes involved later in personal and moral, eventually economic and occupational, and ultimately political, associations; in short, with all the forms of association we call social. In this way society and the person, or, the socialized individual, came into existence as a result of essentially the same social processes and as a result of the same cycle or succession of events.

INDEX OF NAMES

A

Abbott, Edith, 76
Addams, Jane, 75
Adler, Alfred, 54-55
Adler, Herman M., 82
Allee, W. C., 252, 259
Alverdes, Friedrich, 254, 257
Anderson, Nels, 60, 78, 93, 98, 189
Aristotle, 49
Austin, Mary, 256, 257

B

Bagehot, Walter, 27, 141, 226-7
Baillie, J. R., 115
Barrows, H. H., 154, 155
Bergson, H., 172
Besant, Walter, 21, 34-35
Bland-Sutton, J., 186
Boas, F., 15
Booth, Charles, 76-77
Braun-Blanquet, J., 252, 254, 259
Breckinridge, Sophonisba, 76
Bridgman, P. W., 121
Bryce, James, 41, 45
Burgess, E. W., 165, 167, 173, 186, 190, 207

C

Carr-Saunders, A. M., 183
Cavan, Ruth Shonle, 197

Child, C. M., 140, 161
Clements, F. E., 227, 259
Comte, Auguste, 54, 180, 259
Cooley, C. H., 32, 203, 262
Cruickshank, J. G., 102

D

Darwin, Charles, 145, 146, 227, 228, 241, 251
Dewey, John, 173, 200
Dixon, R. B., 138
Durkheim, Emile, 166, 182

E

Elton, Charles, 147, 149, 150, 244, 251

F

Faris, E. F., 107
Febvre, L., 166
Freud, Sigmund, 50
Friedlander, Ludwig, 233

G

Gee, Wilson, 178
Gosnell, H. F., 86
Gras, N. S. B., 83, 231
Grierson, P. J. H., 243

H

Haeckel, E., 147
Haig, R. M., 193
Harrison, S. M., 78
Hawley, Amos H., 7
Hayner, N. S., 189
Heape, W., 244
Hobbes, A., 228
Hobson, E. W., 198
Huxley, Julian, 151, 154, 251, 255

J

James, William, 60, 111
Johnson, C. O., 86
Johnson, C. S., 206
Johnson, James W., 19

K

Kenngott, G. F., 224
Kohler, Wolfgang, 256

L

Le Bon, Gustave, 248, 249
Levasseur, Emile, 185
Levy-Bruhl, L., 103, 108, 110
Lewis, Sinclair, 58-59
Lippmann, W., 135
Lind, A. W., 233
Loeb, Jacques, 38
Lowie, R., 15

M

MacGill, Helen G., 190
Magnus, Albertus, 111
Malinowski, B., 202
Malthus, R., 183
Mannheim, Karl, 247, 248, 249
Marx, Karl, 247
McCormick, R. C., 225
McKenzie, R. D., 6, 134, 189
Mead, George H., 250
Merriam, C. E., 85, 86
Meyer, Edward, 129
Mowrer, E. R., 197

O

Ober, F. A., 110
Ogburn, W. F., 169
Ogden, C. K., 202
Oppenheimer, F., 131

P

Palmer, Vivian M., 201
Park, R. E., 122, 186, 242, 248
Pearl, Raymond, 70
Price, M. T., 205, 206

R

Ratzel, F., 131
Reuter, E. B., 224
Richards, I, A., 202
Rickert, H., 20, 178
Robinson, J. H., 128
Ross, E. A., 182
Rountree, B. S., 76

S

Salisbury, E. J., 148
Shaw, C. R., 206
Simmel, G., 81, 155, 156
Smith, Adam, 23
Sombart, W., 238
Sorokin, P., 187, 188
Spencer, Herbert, 91, 118, 148, 180, 259
Spengler, Oswald, 14, 15, 129, 130
Sumner, W. G., 43, 58, 71-2, 86, 161, 246, 247

T

Tarde, G., 178, 201
Teggart, F., 120, 178, 187, 227
Thomas, W. I., 28, 36, 52-53, 59, 69, 85, 106, 181, 205, 208
Thompson, Edgar T., 225
Thomson, J. A., 145, 146, 147, 156, 227, 229, 252

Thorndike, E. L., 118, 123, 124, 125, 126
Thorndyke, Lynn, 103, 107
Thrasher, F., 63, 96, 206

v

Vance, Rupert B., 224
Vogt, Von Ogden, 88

w

Waitz, T., 187
Wallas, G., 57, 137
Warming, E., 165, 250, 251
Weatherly, U. G., 109

Wells, G. P., 151, 154
Wells, H. G., 151, 154, 251, 255
Wheeler, W. M., 156, 242, 255
White, L. D., 86
Whitehead, A. N., 179, 199
Wilcox, W. F., 183
Wirth, Louis, 78, 99
Wissler, C., 138
Wooddy, C. H., 86
Woods, R. A., 18, 75

z

Znaniecki, F., 106, 205, 208
Zorbaugh, H. W., 78, 88

SUBJECT INDEX

A

Accommodation, 69
Adaptation
    of plants and animals, 146
Administrative agency, 125
Africa
    North Africa, 130
    succession in South Africa, 225-226
Area; *see also* Natural area
    anthropological approaches to study of, 15
        downtown area, 171
    of dominance, 164
    of greatest mobility, 171
    of transition, 89
    second immigrant settlement, 170
Asiatics, 110
Assimilation, 36, 99, 169
    in Hawaii, 237
    of immigrants, 169
Association
    basis of human, 94
    forms of, 242-243, 258
    human, distinguished from plant and animal, 122
    political level, 259
    personal and moral level of, 260
    type of, 253
Athens, 108, 134
Attitudes
    sentiment, 26, 38

B

Balance
    biotic, 154
        changes affecting, 149
    of nature, 148-151 (*see also* Web of life)
Banks, 135
Barbados, 113
Behavior
    human, 20
    instincts, 174
    naive, of individual, 204
Bell Telephone Company, 16
Biological
    economics, 153-155
Biotic Community, 260
    competition in, 119
    cooperation in, 119
Boers, 150, 226
Bohemia, 89, 168
Bombay, 133
Brazil, 135
Bureau of Municipal Research, 44

C

Caribbean, 102
Caste, 24, 243
    and class, 131
Change; *see also* Social change
    catastrophic, 120

in industrial organization and population, 32
rapidity of, in present period, 59
Charleston, S.C., 124
Chicago, 16, 137, 166, 193
  elections in, 42
  gangs in, 96
  (Lower North Side, 88)
  studies of, 78-80
    housing, 76
    neighborhood, 64-65
  urban community, 101
China, 187
  Nanking, 132
  Peking, 132
  Shanghai, 133, 134
Chinatown, 21, 134, 170
Chinese, 98
Cicero, Illinois, 124
Christianity, 129
  and dominance, 162-163
Church
  in city, 85
  Roman Catholic, 111
City; *see also* Great city
  and civilization, Chapter 11
  and the gang, 98
  and habits and customs of people, 16
  and human relations, 31
  and human nature, 16, 51, 73-75
  and individual types, 47
  and the state, 132
  as artificial construction, 15
  as center of intellectual life, 167
  as kind of social organism, 5
  as meeting place of strangers, 188
  as melting pot, 84, 140-141
  as moral order, 16
  as natural environment of free and civilized man, 23, 133
  as natural phenomenon, Chapter 10
  as news centers and money centers, 136
  as organism, 100
  as political and moral order, 121

as product of natural forces, 167
as social laboratory, 73-87
as state of mind, 13
as workshop of civilization, 133
business areas, 17
church in, 33-34, 85
colonies and segregated areas in, 20-22
conceptualizations of, 118
crimes in, 34, 36
early, 132
ecological organization, 14
economic organization, 14
family in, 33-34
free cities of Germany, 22-23
growth of, 17, 100, 167, 168
imperial, 132
individual in, study of, 81-82
industrial area, 17
life as distinguished from village life, 16
local organization of, 15
modern, 22, 120
moral order of, 16
organization of and population size, 17
pattern of organization of city and civilization, 136-137
personality problems in, 81-82
plan, 15, 16-18
political system in, 90
population, 17, 18
political power, 132
schools in, 33-34
size and dominance, 136
social studies of, 75-78
types of association, 120
Civilization, 49, 73-75, 77, 84, 128
  ancient, 22, 133
  and the rise of new cities, 129-130
  automobile as force in, 59
  beginning of, 129-130
  cities' contribution to, 140
  cyclical process, 129
  effect of newspaper and motion picture on, 60
  Egyptian, 129-130

migration, 129
modern and ancient, 133-134
modern and its economic base, 134-136
of great port cities, 134
racial and cultural traits of, 132-133
Class, social, 20, 25
Collective action (Behavior), 31
forms of, 243-244
financial panics, 30
nature of, 37-38
Collective psychology, 30
Colonies
immigrant, 35, 170
immigrant and racial in city, 20-22
Commerce, 22, 134-135
Communal efficiency, measurement of, 68-72
Communication, 135, 244
and transportation, effect on social control, 59
as social-psychological process, 122
function of, 119-120
gestures, 250
individual, 174
self-consciousness and, 176
society and, 174
world dominance and, 236
Community, 14, 88, 165, 166, 181; *see also* Urban community
and common life, 181
and emergence of formal organizations, 58
and the individual, 168, 181
and moral codes, 58
and moral order, 168-169
and primary relations, 56-57
and social institutions, 58
as Great Society, 57
as independent cultural unit, 80
as mosaic of minor communities, 196
as population aggregate, 182
as spatial and geological, 181
as unit of investigation, 187

as visible object, 182
biotic, 154
characteristics of, 148
conception of, 120
contrasted with society, 180-182
council, 90
cultural, 153
defined and characterized, 56-57, 66-68
descript, defined, 88
development, climax phase of, 153
differential interests of people in, 64-65
effect of migration on, 60
gang in, 62-63
growth of, 169, 170
human, 158, 241
immigrant, 69
local, 65, 166
non-descript, 88-89
numerical classification of, 183
organization, and romantic temper, 64-72
plant, 250-251, 253-254, 258
population movement as pulse of, 189
structure of, 196-197
unstable equilibrium, 241
world, 242
Competition, 150, 151-153, 154, 184, 228, 229, 244
and dominance, 161
and occupational organization, 67
and success, 23-24
function of, 119
in the exchanges, 29
limits to, 67, 158
Competitive-cooperation, 146, 147
Concept, 109
Conceptual knowledge vs. Perceptual knowledge, 109
Conflict, 153, 204
and competition, 261
and race-consciousness, 72
cultural, 261
of individuals in society, 57-58

Concentration, 28, 130, 136
Concentric circles, 171
Consensus, 175, 228
Contact, indices of, 188
Control; *see* Social control
Cooperation, 121
Crime
 effect of punishment on, 52-3
 rates of Mexicans and Japanese
  in U.S., 71-72
Criminal, 21
 tribes of India, 243
Criminality
 among the second generation, 36
Crisis
 and its control, 30
 and the courts, 34-39
 and the exchanges, 30
 defined, 35-36
 financial, 30
Crowd
 and public, 29-30
 psychological, 249, 257-258
Cultural; *see also* Culture
 and moral relations, 244
 and political organization, 67-68
 centers, 138
 groups, 99
 lag, 169
 order, 121-122
 process, 116-117
 tradition, 104
  criticisms of, 108
Culture, 24; *see also* Cultural
 cosmopolitian, 236-237
 fusion of, 111
 great cultures as city born, 14
 modern vs. folk, 108
Custom, cake of, 141

D

Definition of the situation, 181
Delinquency; *see also* Juvenile delinquency
 and the migrant, 60
 as group problem, 62
Demographer, 241
Diffusion, 141

Disorganization; *see* Social disorganization
Distance, social, 166, 175
Division of labor, 22, 24, 119, 141,
  154, 156, 166
 as product of competition, 67
 and human societies, 258
 development in modern era, 68
 differentiation of occupations,
  119
 effect of, 24-25
 growth of in city, 59
 rise of new professions, 17
Dominance, 151-153
 area of, 151-152, 163
 communication system as basis
  of, 236
 function of, 162
 in human society, 162
 in plant community, 151
 in the social world, 140
 levels of, 163-164
 newspaper as index of, 213
 origin and natural history of
  concept, 159-164
 of cities, 138-139
 of New York, 139
 struggles for world dominance,
  235

E

Ecological
 pattern, determined by dominance, 152
 organization, 176
 in a community, 66-67
 primary factors in, 14
Ecology, 165, 252
 and community, 251
 and economics, 154-155
 animal, dominance in, 160-161
 human, 5, 155, 158; *see also* "Human Ecology"
 and human society, 240-244
 approach to society, 230-231
 defined, 13, 14
 versus human geography, 165
 plant and animal, 119

Economic
  order, 121
  organization, 107
  relations, 121
Economics, biological, 153-155
Economy
  history of, 83-84
  money, 23
  nomadic to sedentary life, 130
Elements, nature of, 173
Enclaves, in metropolitan regions,
    221-221
Environment
  biological vs. social, 53-54
  delinquent's need for favorable
    environment, 62
  man's attachment to locality, 91-
    92
  natural vs. city, 74-75
  of lower animals and humans, 52
  physical, man's vs. animals' de-
    pendence upon, 156
  social, 54, 55-56
    in city, 82
Equibrium, 27, 119
  social, changes in, 229-230
  stable, 186
Europe
  dominance of, 234, 235
  expansion of, 231-232, 234-235
  segregation in older cities, 21-22
European
  cities, 20
  population, 110
    expansion of, 224
Event
  as datum, 179
Evolution, 145
Expansion, 163
  population, 13; *see also* European
    population

F

Family
  and development of human traits,
    56
  and the person, 55-58
  as environment for children, 56

changes in, 84-85
  city's effect on, 84-85
  disorganization, 197
  home in urban area, 63
  marriage, 50
Fashion, 139
  in Obeah, 112-115
Folkways and mores, 58
Food chain, 146
Frame of reference
  city as, 81
    study of urban community,
      196-199
Freedom
  levels of man's freedom, 229
Fusion
  of cultures, 111

G

Gang, 206
  and local community, 62-63
  as a form of human association,
    97
  as vocational school for ward
    politicians, 63
  habitat of, 96-98
  in Chicago, 61, 63
  influence on character of mem-
    bers, 63
Geography, human, 174
  physical, 17
    and urban plan, 17
Ghetto, Chapter 8, 20, 78-79, 168,
    170
  as "natural area" of city, 100
  as segregated racial and cultural
    group, 99-100
  historical, 100
  Jewish, 98
  origin of, 99
Gold Coast, 21, 88, 89
Government
  problems of city, 41-42
Gradient
  land value, 191-192
Great city, 134, 166, 184; *see also*
    City

as mosaic of segregated peoples, 99
as melting-pot of races and cultures, 46-47
population of, 47
unstable equilibrium of, 31
social changes in, 188
Greeks, 129
Greenwich village, 21, 168
Group
　mind, 250
　primary, 262

H

Habit
　and gangs, 97
Habitat; *see* Environment
Harlem, 19
Hawaii
　as melting-pot of race and cultures, 237
　and natural history of world economy, Chapter 18
　evolution in economy of, 237-238
History, 199-202
Historical process, 17
Hobo
　mind of, 91-95
　poetry by, 94-95
Hobohemia, 60-61
Hollywood, 140
Homeless man
　area of, in city, 60-61
"Human Ecology," 145-158; *see also* Ecology, human
Human nature, 20, 81, 97
　and city, 73-75, 86-87
　and vice, 39
Human relationship
　elementary form of, 32-33

I

Ideology
　of society, 247
Immigrant and immigration
　accommodation in America, 69, 70

immigrant communities, 70
letters to family, 56
succession in residences, 223
Index (Indices)
　mobility as, of social phenomena, 172
　of contacts, 188
　of low and high grade communities, 125-126
Industrial
　competition, 22
　organization and the moral order, 22-25
Institutions, 61, 161-162, 201-202
　and the mores, 247
　concept of, 246
　enacted and crescive, 246
　in cities, 83-87
　kinds of, 86
　origin of, 245-246
　social settlements as, 75-76
Invasion, 148-149
Island communities
　and racial situation, 110
Isolation, 34, 99
　and island communities, 109-110
　and cultural and mental stagnation, 187
　moral and cultural consequences of, 99, 100

J

Japan
　Osaka, 133
　Yokohama, 133
Japanese
　in U.S., 71-72
Jews, 72, 98, 100
　and Diaspora, 100
　as city-folk, 28
Juvenile court, 82
Juvenile delinquency, 57-58, 82-83, 172, 206-207
　and community organization, 52-63
　control of, 62-63
　emergence of, in community, 58

family and neighborhood of, 207
sources of, 62

L

Labor, 94
  agitator, 30
  organization, 245
Land values, 167
  and area of dominance, 151-152
  map of Chicago, 194
Life-history, 80-81, 202-209
  and the study of family, 208
  immigrant biographies, 204
Little Sicilies, 21, 88, 89, 170
Local
  association, 24
  boss, 18
  communities in the metropolis, Chapter 5
  improvement society, 18
Locomotion
  and mentality, 92 ff.
London, 76, 133, 134, 137, 162
  East, 21-22

M

Magic, 103
  and art, 107
  and human activities, 106, 107
  and medicine, 106
  and reform, 106
  and science, 103, 106, 107
  as a form of thought, 105-108
  as index of cultural level, 109
  mentality, and city life, Chapter 9
Malaya, 135
  rubber plantations in, 135
Market, 130-131
Market place, 22, 28, 84, 141
Mass behavior, 169
  in animal societies, 257
  milling herd, 256
Measurement
  of intellectual life of a community, 166-167
  of social values, 122-126
Mentality, 103-104

and city life, 108-110
and mobility of hobo, 91-95
of primitive people, 103-104, 107
of modern men, basis of, 108
Mexicans
  in U.S., 71
Metropolitan
  City, 100
  economy, 137
  regions, 136
    enclaves in, 221-222
    newspaper circulation and, 210-222
    newspaper circulation as index of, 218-222
Metropolis
  attraction of, 47-48
Migration, 17, 148, 200; *see also* Mobility
  and movement of population, 187
  disturbing influence of, 60, 63
  of Negro, 149
Minorities
  ethnic and linguistic, 243
  militant, 37
Mobility, 120, 172, 175, 187
  and changes in status, 188
  and crisis, 30
  and isolation, 27-28
  and land values, 168, 187-196
  and news, 25-29
  and social change, 172-173
  and social contact, 175
  measurement of, 189
  of population, 27
  vertical and horizontal, 188
Modern life
  characteristics of, 107-108
Money, 22, 26
Moral order
  and industrial organization, 22-25
  and social order, 74-75
  and social ritual, 35
Moral region, 49-50
Mores
  and folkways, 58
  changes in, 40

Movement
of capital, 137
conditions affecting, 150
religious, 40
revival, 30

N

Natural areas, 14, 18, 78, 79, 100,
151, 170, 172, 196, 198, 199;
see also Areas, Chinatown,
Ghetto, Little Sicily
and cultural areas, 201
Natural history, 252
of cities, 122
of ideas, 248
of institution, 244
of world economy, Hawaii, 233-
239
Negro, 98, 124, 126
in U.S., 72
migration of, 60, 149
in the West Indies, 110, 116
changing mentality of, 113-114
Neighborhood
as a locality, 17
as a social unit, 18
as a social and political organization, 18
effects of city life on, 19, 20
efforts at reconstruction of, 19
sentiment, 17, 22
changes in, 19
News
and mobility of social groups,
25-29
as distinguished from mere information, 29
Newspaper, 15
and its function, 45-46
as a commodity, 211-212
as factor in civilization, 60
circulation
and metropolitan regions, 210-
222
limiting factors in, 211 ff.
in Europe and America, 211

metropolitan and local, 201, 212-
213
New York, 17, 35, 76, 133, 137, 139,
162, 167
Niche, 147, 154

O

Obeah, 102
as Negro magic, 102, 110-112
fashion in, 113
man, 111
Occupation; *see also* Niche; Specialization
organization of community, 67
suburbs, 21
Organization; *see also* Community;
Society
newspaper circulation as index
of, 217-218
social, 228-229

P

Paris, 140, 162
Person
and status, 179-180
and private experiences, 175
self conception, 176-177
self-consciousness, 54-55, 175
solitary, 97
Personality; *see also* Person
and culture, 203-204
and self-consciousness, 54, 55
problems in city, 81-82
types, 208
Planning
effect of, on ecological organization, 66-67
Plant; *see also* Community; Ecology; Society
community
dominance in, 160
species of, 165
Plantation
succession in, 225
Playground, 20, 61, 62-63

Polish peasant
culture of, 205
family life, 55-56
Political
authority, 132
boss, 30
and machine, 42
and party politics, 42-43
process in cities, 37, 85-86
system based on local community, 65
Politician
professional, 41
Politics, 77
party, and publicity, 41-44
Population, 183; *see also* Expansion; Locomotion; Migra-
tion; Mobility
anomalies, 186
characteristics of, in city, 80
density of, 182
and cultural development, 226
enumeration of, 183
expansion of European, 231-232
gradient of, by age and sex, 185
growth of, 183
movement, 199
conditions affecting, 150
organization and distribution of,
16
pressure, 148, 153-154
selection of, 172
segregated, 20
pyramid, 182-187
and social metabolism, 184
as a device of social exploration, 186
Position, 166, 175
changes in, 189
Press, 45; *see also* Newspaper
agent, 44
Prejudice
and sentiment, 26
and social distance, 26
racial, 20
Primary group; *see also* Group
defined, 32
relations, 56-57

Professional
people, 24
disinterest of, in local community, 65
Progress, 74
effect of, on social order, 60
Public
and secondary relationship, 42
opinion, 37, 88, 205
and social control, 45, 57
Pyramid, *see* Population, pyramid;
Social order

R

Race
consciousness, 72
relations
in Chicago, 206
on Pacific Coast, 69
riots, 169-170
Racial
antagonism, 20
communities (*see also* Natural
areas), 22
differences, 132
groups, 184
Region; *see* Metropolitan region
Rent
map of, 192
Residential; *see also* Area
areas, 190
quarters, 17
suburb, 125
Rome, 134, 138-139
Rooming-house areas, 89, 171, 190
Russell Sage Foundation, 16-17, 44,
76, 77, 167

S

St. Louis, 113
Salvation Army, 30
San Francisco, 133
Satellite cities, 215, 216
Science, 105-106
and history, 178
business of, 175

empirical, 103
experiments in, 103
method of, 178
social, 179
Segregation, 79-80
and moral distance, 47
and social contagion, 50-51
and temperament, 49
basis of, 170
in older cities of Europe, 21-22
of urban population, 47, 186
of vocational classes, 34
Sentiments
and interests, 26
and prejudice, 26
Shanghai, 137
Singapore, 133
Slum
area of immigrants' first settlement, 98, 168
gangs in, 63, 96, 98
in city, 17, 61, 89, 168, 171
life in, 127
Social change, 148-149, 169, 174,
229-230; *see also* Change, social
and social disorganization, 58-
61
and succession, 226-227
organizations to cope with, 61
population migration and, 187
Social control, 75, 156
advertising and, 44-46
and the city, 59
changes in, 35, 39
gossip, 46
informal and formal, 58-59
in Japanese immigrant groups,
71
in primary group, 33
in secondary group, 32-46
publicity as a form of, 44
Social disorganization, 83, 130
and individualization, 58
and social change, 58-61
Social metabolism, 183-184
Social morphology, 182; *see also*
Social structure

Social movement
and social institutions, 245-246
Social order
four levels in pyramid of, 157
Social organism, 259
Social organization, 25, 29, 92-93,
174; *see also* Organization
and institutions, 33-34
basis of, 156
Social problems, 74, 81, 186, 201
Social settlements, 19
Social structure, 166
determinants of, 156
Social survey, 44-45, 75 ff.
Pittsburgh survey, 44, 77
Socialization, 258-262
and assimilation, 262
Society, 53, 96, 97, 147, 166, 181,
199, 227, 259
and communication, 173, 259
and human ecology, 240-244
and individual, 52, 53, 57, 174,
181, 202-203
and moral order, 177, 181
and persons, 179-180
and symbiosis, 155-158
animal, 250
ant, 38
as collective action, 241-242
as consensus, 180
as contrasted with community,
180-182
as division of labor, 180
as forms of association—symbiotic vs. social, 255
as moving equilibrium, 59, 235
as natural product, 58
characteristics of, 240-241
Community and Chapter, 15
composed of groups, 54
ecological view of, 150-151
functions of, 157-158
Great, 57, 137
human, 117
insect, 254
levels of, 157, 228
morphological aspect of, 166
nature of, 93-94

organized on familial basis, 246
political, 247
primitive, 43
solidarity of, 181
stable, 81
symbiotic, 148
two aspects of, 180, 240
Sociology, 179
  and anthropology, 200-201
  animal, 252
  as empirical science, 61
  general, 252
  of knowledge, 247-249
  urban, 98
Solidarity
  personal forms of, 119-120
  social, 26
Specialization; *see* Division of La-
    bor
State
  origin of, 130-131
Statistics, 179
  and social studies, 125
Status, 24
  and social distance, 176-177
  determinants of, 47
  struggle for, 176
Stock exchange, 28, 107
  and the mob, 29-32
Struggle for existence, 146, 149, 241
Suburb, 79
  garden, 20
  residential, 65
  types of, 137
Succession, 151-153, 223-232
  and frontiers, 222-223
  and social change, 226-227
  defined, 152-153, 224-225
  in Hawaii, 238-239
  in South Africa, 225-226
  of boll weevil, 149
Suicide, 197
Symbiosis, 80, 227, 228; *see also*
    Community
  and socialization, 240-262
  and society, 155-158
  defined, 242
  forms of, 242

T

Tammany Hall, 42-43
Technology, 120-121
  effects of technologic devices,
    121
Temperament
  and social contagion, 50-51
  and the urban environment, 46-
    51
Territorial
  order, 120-121
  organization of society, 118
Trade, 22
  area
    and circulation of newspapers,
      212-218
    outer limits of, 217-218
    silent, 243
Traffic, liquor, 39-41
  commercialized vice and, 39-41
Transient
  dwellers in cities, 189
Transportation
  effect of, on social control, 59
Travel; *see also* Migration; Mobil-
    ity
  Roman interest in, 233-234

U

Urban community, 78-81, 118-119;
    see also City; Community
  as a spatial pattern and a moral
    order, Chapter 14
  as a unit of investigation, 187
  limit of, 119
  structure of, 196, 197
Urban neighborhood, 18-20, 49; *see*
    also Neighborhood

V

Vice districts, 21
  as a "moral region," 49
Village
  in America, 58-59

Vocation
  effect of, 24
Vocational
  classes and types, 23-25
  training, 67

w

War
  function of, 228
Washington, D.C., 66-67

Web of life, 145-148, 227-228, 253;
    see also Balance, of nature
West Indies, 109, 111, 112, 114, 116
  Dominica, 112
  Hindus in Trinidad and Deme-
    rara, British Guinea, 110
  Montserrat, 112
Wichita, Kansas, 124
Wishes
  fundamental wishes of man, 69
  of society, 106